LOUISVILLE
in 1854

LOUISVILLE PANORAMA

LOUISVILLE
PANORAMA

A Visual History of Louisville

Compiled, Written, and Designed by R. C. Riebel

PUBLISHED TO COMMEMORATE THE *100th Anniversary*
OF LIBERTY NATIONAL BANK AND TRUST COMPANY
LOUISVILLE, KENTUCKY · 1954

Merle E. Robertson PRESIDENT
AND CHAIRMAN OF THE BOARD

FOREWORD

The Liberty National Bank and Trust Company is the only financial institution in the history of Louisville that has attained the age of ONE HUNDRED YEARS

A financial firm must be sound in its structure, progressive in its policies, and fortunate in its leadership to survive the economic and political vicissitudes of *any* century, much less the wars, disasters, and alternating periods of inflation and depression that have characterized the past ten decades.

"Louisville's Oldest Financial Institution" was originally chartered by the Kentucky Legislature on March 9, 1854, as an insurance company with certain banking privileges. Early in its history the banking division outgrew the insurance department. In 1935 when Liberty became a National bank it sold its remaining interest in its insurance company affiliate.

Certainly we deem it a privilege to have arrived at the threshold of our *second century* of service to the people of Louisville and of the Commonwealth; to have enjoyed a natural and continuing growth through the years; and to have achieved our present position without benefit of merger or consolidation.

The directors and officers currently responsible for the bank's management, today pause to pay tribute to their predecessors, who perhaps join them in spirit to celebrate the Hundredth Birthday, and the completion of "A Century of Liberty".

On this occasion, the bank is especially mindful of the multitude of men and women who in a real sense have been and *are* the bank—the five generations of Liberty customers.

It recognizes with special regard and gratitude the "old" customers—the individuals and firms that have dealt with this bank continuously for twenty-five, fifty—yes, even seventy-five years and more.

We hope that this "picture-story" history of Louisville, this panorama of the years, will prove interesting to our friends; that it will make Louisvillians (native or adopted) proud of their brave pioneer heritage; and that the chronology and the large collection of early photographs may be of some permanent historic value.

It is well, on occasions, to look back—for the inspiration we shall always find in the lives of the founders of our nation; but it is not good to *dwell* on the past. America has been great because Americans are forward-looking. Tomorrow is always more important than yesterday. Thus we look upon our "first hundred years" as a *preparation* for the century ahead.

And therefore we dedicate this book to the YOUNG PEOPLE of our city, in whose hands will rest the destiny of the brave new Louisville of Tomorrow!

Louisville, March 9, 1954.

GEORGE ROGERS CLARK
BY MATTHEW H. JOUETT
Loaned by the Filson Club, Louisville

GENERAL GEORGE ROGERS CLARK, FOUNDER OF LOUISVILLE, AND ONE OF THE GREAT AMERICANS OF ALL TIME

THE DIGNITY, character, and ability of a great leader are revealed in this magnificent portrait by Kentucky's historic painter, Matthew H. Jouett, the original of which hangs in The Filson Club of Louisville. A striking resemblance may be discerned between General Clark and his Commander-in-chief George Washington, to whom he ranks second in achievement as a military leader in the American Revolution.

Sycamore under which an iron hatchel was found in 1808

LA SALLE Historians agree that Robert Cavalier de La Salle passed the Falls of the Ohio in either 1669 or 1670. In view of this, our city might appropriately have been named for him. But it WAS named for another famous Frenchman who lived a century later, Louis XVI— the monarch who was popular here because of the aid he had extended the colonies in the American Revolution. The origin of the name explains why we say *Louie*ville rather than Louisville.

THE HATCHET This is exhibit "A" —an actual photograph of the hatchet which SOMEONE buried under the very old sycamore pictured at the left. The present whereabouts of the instrument could not be ascertained, but the photograph is authenticated by The Filson Club. Historically this weapon should take its place with the hatchet that young Washington used to chop down his father's cherry tree; and the tomahawk that almost killed Capt. John Smith!

THE SYCAMORE This is obviously an early drawing, possibly made in 1808 after the tree had been felled; not likely before, and therefore not likely to be an accurate picture of the actual tree. Wouldn't stand up in court!

SCENE OF THE CRIME The Falls of the Ohio probably looked very much like this in 1669 when La Salle visited here, except no cabins and no corn on Corn Island; the smoke, indicating Indian camps on the Indiana side, could have been present in 1669 or 1778.

The bird's-eye view of the first settlement here denotes a good deal of skill on the part of the early artist. A more important example of these "air-views" of the past is the view of Louisville in 1854 re-produced on the front end-papers of this book, the large original lithograph of which hangs in Liberty National's directors' room.

Who buried the HATCHET under the sycamore tree?

Story from R. T. Durrett's Centenary of Louisville published by The Filson Club, 1893.

IN THE YEAR 1808, while digging the foundation of the great flour mill of the Tarascons in that part of Louisville known as Shippingport, it became necessary to remove a large sycamore tree, the trunk of which was six feet in diameter, and the roots of which penetrated the earth for forty feet around. Under the center of the trunk of this tree was found an iron hatchet, which was so guarded by the base and roots that no human hand could have placed it there after the tree grew. It must have occupied the spot where it was found when the tree began to grow. The hatchet was made by bending a flat bar of iron around a cylinder until the two ends met, and then welding them together and hammering them to a cutting edge, leaving a round hole at the bend for a handle. The annulations of this tree were two hundred in number, thus showing it to be two hundred years old according to the then mode of computation.

Here was a find which proved to be a never-ending puzzle to the early scientists of the Falls of the Ohio. The annulations so fixed the date *earlier* than any white man or user of iron was known to have been at the falls. One thought that Moscoso, the successor of DeSoto, in his wanderings up the Mississippi and Missouri Rivers, might have entered the Ohio and left the hatchet there in 1542; another, that it might have come from the Spaniards who settled St. Augustine in 1565; another, that the Spaniards who went up the Ohio in 1669 in search of silver might have left it where it was found; and another, that Marquette, when he discovered the Upper Mississippi in 1673, or La Salle, when he sailed down to its mouth in 1682, might have given the hatchet to an Indian, who left it at the Falls But from these reasonable conjectures their learning and imagination soon led these savants into the wildest theories and conjectures.

One thought that the Northmen whom the Sagas of Sturleson made discoverers of America in the eleventh century, had brought the hatchet to this country; another that Prince Madoc, who left a principality in Wales in the twelfth century for a home in the western wilderness, might have brought it here. One of these learned ethnologists finally went so far as to advance the theory of the Egyptian priests, as related by Plato, that the autochthons of our race brought it here before the Island of Atlantis, lying between Europe and America, went down in the ocean and cut off all further communication between the continents!

Story concluded on page 14

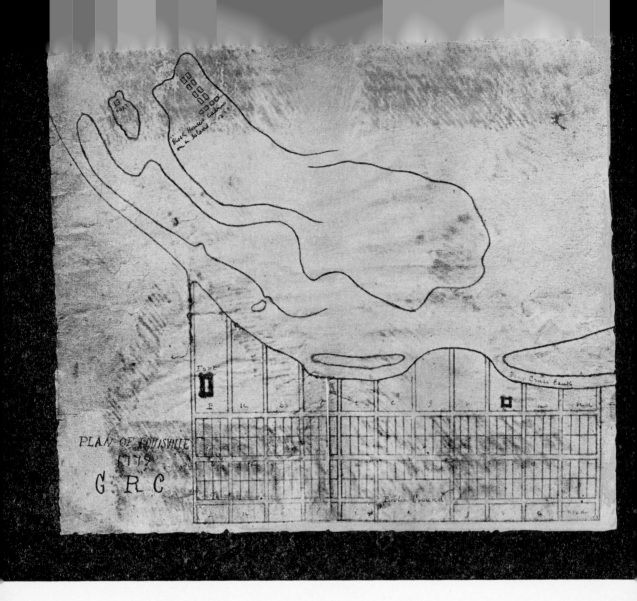

G. R. C.'S OWN MAP OF LOUISVILLE

THIS FIRST PLAN of the town of Louisville, apparently drawn by George Rogers Clark himself, is dated 1779, and was probably made by him on his return to this settlement after the successful campaign against the British and Indians at Kaskaskia and Vincennes. Clark's ability as a military leader and a strategist was shown in the capture of Kaskaskia on July 4, 1778, and in the surrender of Vincennes by the British General Hamilton on February 25, 1779. Some of Clark's ability as a city planner is indicated in this sketch, which dedicates a large area for "Public Ground."

Note the large Fort, sometimes referred to as "Station-on-Shore", at 12th Street, and the smaller one protecting the mouth of Bear Grass Creek. The block houses and cabins on Corn Island are also shown, as well as a small "fort" on the tiny island in the "harbor" of Corn Island.

SINCE there was no artist or photographer to depict the actual landing of George Rogers Clark on Corn Island May 27, 1778, we reprint the re-enactment of this momentous event, which took place on the 175th anniversary of the landing, May 27, 1953. J. Paul Keith Jr., is Clark; A. L. Mirus is Chief Grey Eagle. Touchout the skyline, the bridge, and the loud speaker, and you have the real thing, except there's no Corn Island—it washed away many years ago.

10

Immigration of Daniel Boone and Party into Kentucky thru Cumberland Gap
A FAMOUS PAINTING BY GEORGE CALEB BINGHAM (1851)

WHILE ANY HISTORY of Louisville will naturally sing the praises of the brave men and women who came down the Ohio River in crude rafts to settle here, we must not forget the pioneers like Daniel Boone, who did it the *hard* way—overland, through the tangled wilderness. James McBride, John Findley, Simon Kenton and many others came thru the mountains, and settled at Logan's Station, Harrodsburg, Boonsborough, Lexington and other parts of the Western Country.

McMurtrie, the first historian of Louisville, writes as follows of these hardy adventurers:

"The first person who visited Kentucky of whom we have any account, was James McBride, who traveled through it, in 1754.*

"In 1767, John Findley, an Indian trader, on his return to North Carolina depicted the fertility of its soil in such glowing colours, to Colonel Daniel Boon (correct spelling as of that day), as induced the latter, in 1769, accompanied by said Findley and others, to venture thither. Disastrous was the result of their expedition: with the exception of Boon, who remained a solitary inhabitant of the woods, until 1771, when he returned, they were all plundered, dispersed, and killed by the Indians.

"In 1779, Boon, whose daring soul was undismayed at the fate that had befallen his companions, and reckless of the hardships he himself had suffered, (hardships which many a "gayer crest" would scarcely have ventured to encounter) with all his family, and forty men from Powell's Valley, again braved the terrors of the wilderness, penetrated to the banks of the Kentucky River, and erected thereon some cabins, naming the place Boonsborough."

We naturally note the interesting coincidence that this year (1954) is the 200th anniversary of McBride's visit, as well as the 100th anniversary of Louisville's oldest financial institution. Ed.

THE STORY OF CATO AND THE FIRST CHRISTMAS

This is Cato Watts, slave of Captain John Donne, one of the original settlers on Corn Island. Cato was the only negro in the small community, and apparently he was the only musician—or at any rate, he could play the fiddle. It is supposed that he was very much in demand to play the Virginia reel, Highland fling, and Irish jig—for dancing was one of the few amusements possible in that primitive settlement.

As Christmas approached and the "Fort-on Shore" neared completion, a big Christmas party and dance was planned as a "house-warming". Cato, of course, being the only fiddler in the settlement, was expected to put on a big show—but alas, he had worn out all his fiddle strings!

Just in the nick of time, according to the old story, a Frenchman (named Jean *Nickle,* incidentally) happened along. He was going down the river and stopped to get some repairs made to his boat. Louisvillians, being hospitable even then, asked him to spend Christmas and come to the housewarming. When they apologized for no music for the dance, Monsieur Nickle said that it just happened that he had brought his fiddle down the river with him.

He was of course asked to play, and responded with some light French airs, which no doubt sounded rather "sissy" to the settlers who were used to the loud-and-fast hoe-downs.

Then some one called on Cato to borrow the Frenchman's fiddle and play some real Kentucky music, *country style.* Monsieur reneged on lending Cato his violin, but he gladly gave him a set of strings, and the dance began in earnest!

It's heart-warming to think of this little band of pioneers, a spark of life and light burning in the dark primeval wilderness, celebrating their first Christmas with gusto and with good humor.

. . . .

It is the historian's sad duty to add a lugubrious footnote to this happy story. Cato, who was the property of John Donne, was hanged 3 years later for the murder of his master, though he claimed it was an accident. He therefore has the dubious honor of being the first man in Louisville to be tried and hanged. The gibbet was the limb of a large oak tree which stood opposite the jail, then on Jefferson Street.

THE FORT ON CORN ISLAND ☞

The corn was for camouflage, they said; but there have been other explanations. Gen. Clark himself liked his "corn-squeezins."

THIS ACT OF THE VIRGINIA LEGISLATURE INCORPORATED LOUISVILLE

Hatchet Story Continued—

Col. Durrett goes on to explain:

This hatchet, however, really furnished no occasion for such strained conjectures and wild speculations. If the sycamore under which it was found was two hundred years old, as indicated by its annulations, it must have begun to grow about the time that Jamestown in Virginia and Quebec in Canada were founded. It would have been no unreasonable act for an Indian or white man to have brought this hatchet from the English on the James, or from the French on the St. Lawrence, to the Falls of the Ohio in 1608, just two hundred years before it was discovered by removing the tree that grew over it. The known habit of the sycamore, however, to make more than one annulation in years particularly favorable to growth

suggests that two hundred annulations do not necessarily mean that many years. If we allow about fifty per cent of the life of the tree to have been during years exceptionally favorable to its growth, and assign double annulations to these favorable years, we shall have this tree to have made its two hundred annulations in about one hundred and thirty-nine years, and to have sprung from its seed and to have begun its growth about the year 1669 or 1670, when La Salle, the great French explorer, is believed to have been at the Falls of the Ohio.

So Col. Durrett concludes that "The hatchet is a souvenir of the first white man who ever saw the Falls of the Ohio. It is a memento of Robert Cavalier de La Salle, the discoverer of the site of the city of Louisville."

HISTORICAL DOCUMENTS OF LOUISVILLE

This is the original hand-written charter 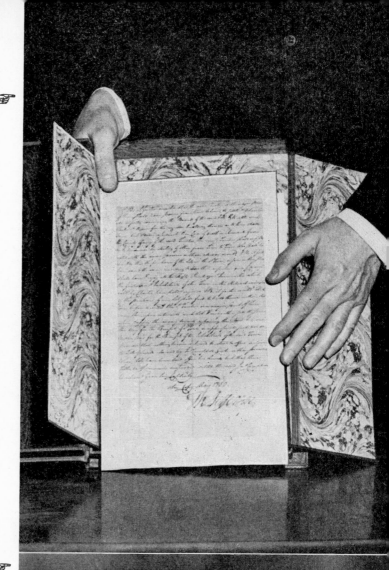 of the City of Louisville, signed by Thomas Jefferson, then governor of Virginia, in May 1780. For many years it was lost; then it reappeared among the papers of General Bennett H. Young when they were sold at public auction in Louisville some years ago. The purchaser had no idea that this unique document was in the collection when he bought it, probably paying only a nominal amount for the lot. Later W. K. Stewart, local bookdealer, saw the charter in a New York book store priced at $3,000!

Eventually he purchased it and offered it for sale to several local collectors. The Courier-Journal and Louisville Times bought it, and Barry Bingham, editor of The Courier-Journal and president of the newspaper companies, presented it to the city on December 10, 1951. Later Mayor Farnsley presented it to the Library of the University of Louisville for permanent care and display.

MINUTES OF FIRST MEETING OF THE TRUSTEES OF THE TOWN OF LOUISVILLE
(exact transcript)

Falls of Ohio April 24th, 1779.

William Harrod, Richard Chenoweth, Edward Badger, James Patton, Henry French, Marsham Brashear, and Simeon Moore, Trustees chosen by the intended citizens of the Town of Louisville at the Falls of Ohio met the 17th day of April 1779 and came to the following Rules, to wit—

That a number of Lots not exceeding 200 for the present be laid off to contain half of an acre each 35 yard by 70 where the Ground will admit of it with some publick Lots and Streets

That each adventurer draw for only one Lot by equal chance.

That every such person be obliged to clear of the under-growth and begin to cultivate part thereof by the 10th of June and build there on a good covered house 16 feet by 20 by the 25th of December.

That no person sell his Lot unless to some person without one but that it be given up to the Trustees to dispose of to some new adventurer on pain of forfeiture thereof.

Marsham Brashears, Sec'y.

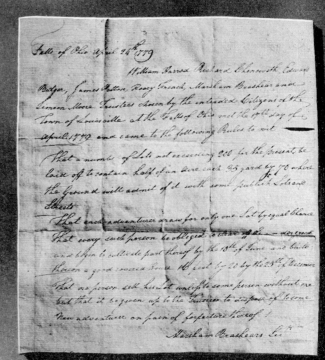

15

DR. JOHN CONNALLY

JOHN CAMPBELL

These Men Once Owned All of Louisville!

THIS MAN owned *all* of Louisville in 1773, or rather all the ground it stands on. His name was Dr. John Connolly or Connally and he received the grant of 2,000 acres at the Falls of the Ohio from Virginia Governor Dunmore, for his services to the British Crown. Connolly was a Pennsylvanian of good education, and was surgeon's mate in the British navy during the French and Indian Wars.

After the land grant, or "grab" as it has been called, because it was contrary to the British King's wishes (and consequently really illegal) Connolly sold half of his acreage to his friend John Campbell who joined him in a project to lay out a town at what they rightly believed to be an ideal location.

A survey was made by Capt. Thomas Bullitt, but before the actual plans for founding the city could be carried out, the Revolutionary War started and Connolly joined the British side. He was arrested and imprisoned and made to forfeit his title to his property here.

THIS MAN once owned *half* of Louisville—and sold it for $4,091, plus an I. O. U. for $753. He was John Campbell, the man who bought half of John Connolly's grant. After Connolly lost title to his 1000 acres, the Legislature of Virginia was petitioned by the settlers at the Falls to charter a town at this location. The Charter was granted May 1st 1780, but reserved to Campbell his title to the 1000 acres he had previously purchased from Connolly.

Several years later Campbell came to town and demanded payment for the land, which in the meantime had been divided into lots by the town's trustees, and had been purchased in small plots by various individuals. Campbell's demands, which had the legal backing of the legislature, almost wrecked the young town.

All the public lots remaining, except the Court House Square and the Cemetery, had to be sold to satisfy Campbell, and this is why the fine town planning of the founders *floundered*, so to speak.

THE "FIRST FAMILIES" OF LOUISVILLE

OF THE FIRST SETTLERS of Louisville, we are sure of only five names, which survive from the earliest records: James Patton, Richard Chenowith, William Faith, John Tewell and John McManness. However, after many years of research including conversations with men who were children of the original settlers, Col. Durrett came to the conclusion that the following is a reasonably accurate list of the "first families" of Louisville:

¶ James Patton, his wife Mary, and their three daughters, Martha, Peggy, and Mary. ¶ Richard Chenowith, his wife Hannah, and their four children, Mildred, Jane, James, and Thomas. ¶ John McManness, his wife Mary, and their three sons, John, George, and James. ¶ John Tewell, his wife Mary, and their three children, Ann, Winnie, and Jessie. ¶ William Faith, his wife Elizabeth, and their son John. ¶ Jacob Reager, his wife Elizabeth, and their three children, Sarah, Mariah, and Henry. ¶ Edward Worthington, his wife Mary, his son Charles, and his two sisters, Mary (Mrs. James Graham) and Elizabeth (Mrs. Jacob Reager). ¶ James Graham and his wife Mary. ¶ John Donne, his wife Martha, and their son John. ¶ Isaac Kimbley and his wife Mary. ¶ Joseph Hunter and his children, Joseph, David, James, Martha (Mrs. John Donne), and Ann. ¶ Neal Dougherty, ¶ Samuel Perkins, ¶ John Sinclair, and ¶ Robert Travis.

Louisville's First Banker?

According to Col. Reuben T. Durrett, in his *Centenary of Louisville*, "A crude kind of banking was conducted in Louisville in early times by a man named John Sanders. In the spring flood of 1780 a large flatboat was floated to the lot on the northeast corner of Main and Third Streets. Sanders made the boat fast to a tree, and when the water subsided it rested on dry land. Sanders then put a roof on the boat, and prepared it with doors and windows for a kind of warehouse which he called his "keep". Here he would receive the skins of fur-bearing animals from the pioneers, and issue receipts for them, (which we would call "certificates of deposit").

"These certificates circulated as a kind of currency, and really did the work of modern bank-notes. As the skins would accumulate the stock was depleted by traders, who readily bought them, or they were sent to the markets of the East or South as opportunity offered. When the skins for which a certificate had been issued were sold, the certificate was called in and paid off. The skins of the beavers were the favorites, and these animals were abundant in the neighborhood of the Falls for many years. The remains of their work in enlarging some ponds and diminishing others, and in making dams across Beargrass and other creeks, are still visible in the neighborhood of Louisville (1880). A beaver skin was the unit of value in those early times, just as a silver dollar is now. A horse, a cow, or any thing for sale was worth so much in *beaver skins*, and so understood by everybody."

1780 LOUISVILLE'S FIRST BANK SITE

Cornerstone of old building ☞ **at Third and Main indicates location of Sander's "Keep"**

THE FIRST FORT ON THE MAINLAND

The fort of the early settlers consisted of cabins, blockhouses, and stockades. A range of cabins commonly formed one side at least of a fort. Divisions, or partitions of logs, separated the cabins from each other. The walls on the outside were ten or twelve feet high. A few of these cabins had puncheon floors, (split logs laid with level side up) the greater part were of tamped earth.

The blockhouses were built at the angles of the fort. They projected about two feet beyond the outer walls of the cabins and stockades. Often the upper stories were about eighteen inches every way larger in dimension than the under one, leaving an opening at the commencement of the second story to prevent the enemy from making a lodgment under the walls. A large folding gate, made of thick slabs nearest the spring closed the fort. The stockades, bastions, cabins and blockhouse walls were furnished with port holes at proper heights and distances. The amazing thing is that all were built without the aid of a single nail or spike of iron; for such things were not to be had in the wilderness.

STONE MARKS SPOT

THIS mass of concrete and stone at 12th and Rowan marks the location of the "Fort-on-Shore", the first settlement on Louisville's mainland. This was formerly a memorial fountain containing a bronze plaque, and was erected in 1912 by the Kentucky Society of the Sons of the American Revolution. Vandals have since destroyed the fountain and carried away the plaque. The ruin is here contemplated by the owner of a nearby factory. This Fort was built in 1778-79 by Richard Chenoweth, a carpenter from Berkeley County, Virginia, in compliance with instructions from General George Rogers Clark. For four years it was occupied by American soldiers of the Revolutionary war.

HAVE YOU EVER STOOD AT SEVENTH AND MAIN AND VISUALIZED THIS?

Judging by the lay of the land today this quite impressive, almost medieval-style Fort was situated where the Seventh Street Railroad Station now stands. One would think it would have been located on the higher ground at the level of present Main Street, but obviously the moat would have been impossible much above river level.

The bronze plaque to the right is ☞ a tablet of a larger monument of rugged stone erected in 1912 to commemorate the first important Louisville settlement on the mainland.

TO COMMEMORATE
THE ESTABLISHMENT
OF THE TOWN OF
LOVISVILLE 1780.
ON THIS SITE STOOD FORT NELSON
BVILT 1782 VNDER THE DIRECTION
OF GEORGE ROGERS CLARK AFTER
THE EXPEDITION WHICH GAVE TO THE
COVNTRY THE GREAT NORTHWEST.

THE COLONIAL DAMES OF AMERICA
IN THE STATE ⊕ KENTVCKY 1912.

19

"D. BOONE KILLED A BAR" HERE IN 1781

DANIEL BOONE, the greatest and most famous of all the early American explorers and backwoodsmen, did not participate in the founding of Louisville or figure in its early history. However, if the carving found on this beech tree in 1850 is authentic, old Dan'l was here in 1781 and has left this memento of his hunting ability. The section of the tree bearing the inscription is preserved in a sealed glass case at The Filson Club, but the tree was much older when it was cut down than shown in this photograph, and the lettering is partially obscured.

The name in the early days was generally spelled Boon. The final "e" visible above is perhaps an illusion caused by markings in the bark.

CHRONOLOGY OF LOUISVILLE

BEFORE 1669 Col. Wood, an Englishman, explored Kentucky as far as the Meschacebe (corrupted to Mississippi) River and discovered several branches of this and the Ohio River.

1669 The great French explorer, La Salle, passed the site of Louisville in 1669 while on his westward journey to the Pacific. He was the first white man to set eyes on the Kentucky wilderness and the first to see the falls.

A party of 23 Spaniards came up the Mississippi and Ohio past Pittsburg.

1769 Daniel Boone forged his way through Cumberland Gap.

1773 Capt. Thomas Bullitt led the first exploring party into Jefferson County. Founded first temporary settlement at Louisville at mouth of Beargrass Creek, which at that time emptied into the Ohio River at point between present 2nd and 3rd Streets. Expedition was a surveying trip for William and Mary College of Virginia.

1778 May 27 ... George Rogers Clark landed on Corn Island and erected a fort. In his party were 11 married couples, 26 children, 4 bachelors and 1 negro slave.

Settlers celebrated their first Christmas in Louisville this year.

July ... A stockade designed by Richard Chenoweth was begun on the mainland, where 12th and River Streets are today. Early Louisville on the mainland stretched from First to 12th Street.

1779 Seven different stations had risen on Beargrass Creek.

William Bard (or Beard) made first map.

April 24 ... First meeting of the Trustees of Louisville.

"The Hard Winter", bitter cold, great hardships endured by man and beast.

1780 300 families immigrated to Louisville during this year.

May 1 ... Act for Establishing the Town of Louisville, at the Falls of the Ohio, passes Assembly of Virginia.

Louisville was named for Louis XVI because of the aid given the American colonies by France during the Revolution. The name was made official by the Incorporation of the city.

Louisville's first trading post and "bank", Sander's Keep was begun at what is now the north east corner of 3rd and Main Streets. (See p.17)

150 state militia soldiers were stationed at the falls, later they joined George Rogers Clark's forces.

Louisville was first laid out by William Pope.

1781 Early law ... George Rogers Clark was involved in one of the earliest suits. He had confiscated a keg of whiskey from Eli Cleveland for his troops. Cleveland pressed charges.

Fort Nelson was completed. It replaced the 12th Street fort. It was bounded by 6th, 7th, Main and River Streets, and was surrounded by an 8 foot moat and a high wall of pointed, sharpened logs.

February 7 ... Louisville was organized as a village at the first meeting of Trustees after incorporation. The following men were present Marsham Brashear, John Floyd, William Pope, George Slaughter, John Todd, Jr., and Stephen Trigg. Sale of lots, construction of a canal and erection of a grist mill were discussed. (See p.15)

January 22 ... Col. George Rogers Clark was made Brigadier General of the Virginia Militia by Governor Thomas Jefferson in recognition of his many outstanding campaigns and victories.

1782 The first commercial trip was begun from Louisville to New Orleans by the two French traders, Tardiveau and Honore. This trip began the great river trade.

Indian raids in Western Kentucky with severe retaliation by Col. Floyd.

During this year, Michael Humble became Louisville's first gunsmith.

1783 Daniel Broadhead opened Louisville's first general store on the north side of Main between Fifth and Sixth Streets. He was the first to move out of the protective neighborhood of Louisville's forts.

Evan Williams makes first whiskey, possibly first in Kentucky.

Col. John Campbell erected a tobacco warehouse at Shippingport.

The people of Louisville celebrated the news of the Revolutionary War's Treaty of Paris.

Chronology continued on page 27

WE the Subscribers, inhabitants of Kentucke, and well acquainted with the country from its first settlement, at the request of the author of this book, and map, have carefully revised them, and recommend them to the public, as exceeding good performances, containing as accurate a description of our country as we think can possibly be given; much preferable to any in our knowledge extant; and think it will be of great utility to the publick. Witness our hands this 12th day of May, Anno Domini 1784,

DANIEL BOON,
LEVI TODD,
JAMES HARROD.

Benj. Bourne
1705

THE
DISCOVERY, PURCHASE
AND
SETTLEMENT,
OF
KENTUCKE.

THE first white man we have certain accounts of, who discovered this province, was one James M'Bride, who, in company with some others, in the year 1754, passing down the Ohio in Canoes, landed at the mouth of Kentucke river, and there marked a tree, with the first letters of his name, and the date, which remain to this day. These men reconnoitred the country, and returned home with the pleasing news of their discovery of the best tract of land in North-America, and probably in the world.

THIS BOOK COMPLETE WITH MAP IS WORTH $5,000 OR MORE

JOHN FILSON was Kentucky's first historian; the first edition of his book KENTUCKE, published at Wilmington in 1784, is one of the rarest, most important, and most *expensive* items of Americana. The first edition of the famous map of "Kentucke" was engraved and printed the same year. Its description of the attractions and opportunities of Kentucky brought many new settlers to this State.

Born in 1747, Filson was in the Colonial Army, taught school, and was a surveyor. In 1785 he was in the fur business in Louisville; in October 1788 at the age of only 41 he was killed by Indians. It is fitting that Louisville's Filson Club (founded 1884) should be named for John Filson.

THERE WERE ONLY 8 BUILDINGS IN LOUISVILLE WHEN THIS MAP WAS MADE

A SECTION of Filson's "Map of Kentucke", an original of which hangs in the president's office at Liberty National. The earliest edition of this map today would probably bring a higher price at auction than any other map in the world!

It is much more valuable than the book, and it is surprisingly accurate considering that it was drawn not from surveys, but simply from observation. A close study of this section of the map will reveal many interesting facts about the early history of this territory.

THE SIMPLE TOOLS OF AN EMPIRE BUILDER

☞ The long Kentucky flintlock, the hatchet, watch, compass, hunting knife, powder horn, pistol and sword—all belonged to George Rogers Clark, and may be seen in the museum of The Filson Club.

The large log house on the hill is the home which Clark built in 1803 in Clarksville, just across the river from Louisville. Clark laid out his new town with great care and enthusiam, hoping that it would some day be one of the most attractive cities in the country, but it failed to grow—and another dream of Clark's was shattered.

CLARK WOULD HAVE APPROVED OF THIS MEMORIAL ☞

It was particularly appropriate that Louisville's newest Municipal bridge should on January 17, 1949, be re-named by State Highway Commissioner Garrett L. Withers as *The George Rogers Clark Memorial Bridge,* since it forms the closest connection between the two towns Clark founded—Louisville and Clarksville. Clark would indeed be gratified if he could return to see both of "his towns" today.

The view on the opposite page showing the bridge and downtown Louisville from the Indiana side, was taken at dusk by Lin Caufield. The illuminated tower of Liberty National Bank can be discerned to the right of the Louisville end of the bridge.

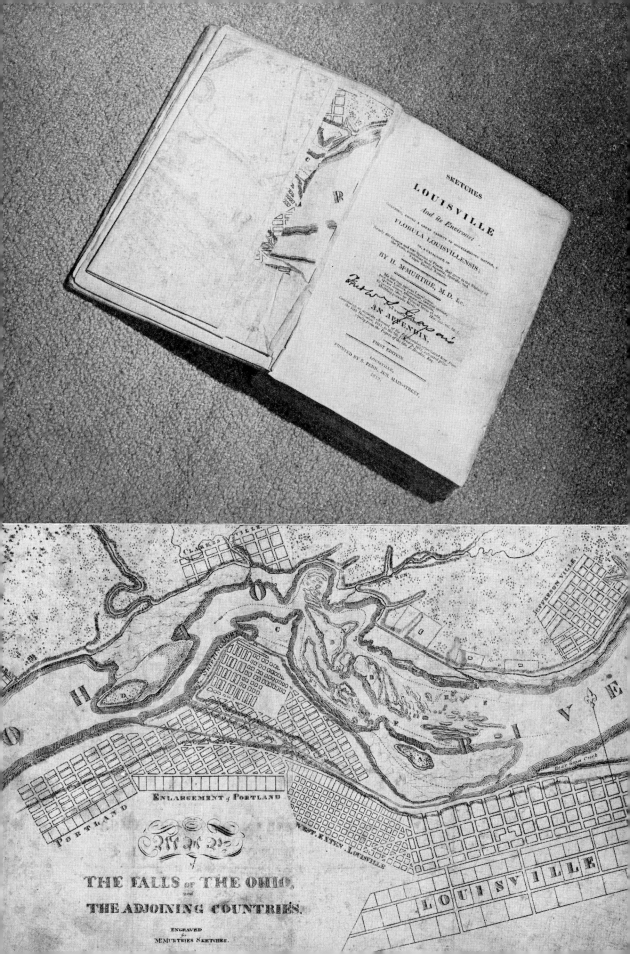

FIRST HISTORY OF LOUISVILLE

This is the source book for much of the very early history of Louisville. The first edition (1819) was printed in Louisville, and is dedicated to President James Monroe.

McMurtrie gets enthusiastic at times on the attractions of this section; as for instance when he describes the Ohio River as "by far the noblest river in the universe"; but he is generally more matter-of-fact. A large part of the book is devoted to geological descriptions and natural history. McMurtrie pointed out that the two great faults of the town were the lack of alleys and of public squares. He was the first to urge beautification of the water front, a project which has not yet materialized (135 years later). A most interesting feature of the book is the day-by-day account of the long series of earthquakes which shook Louisville and a great part of the western hemisphere during 1811 and 1812. There were only 8 shocks of first magnitude, but the recorded quakes reached a total of 1,874!

FIRST PUBLISHED MAP

This map which accompanies McMurtrie's Book is well drawn and gives a perfect picture of the whole community including Clarksville and Jeffersonville. The difference in the size of the blocks in Louisville proper and in the "Western Extension" of Louisville may be explained by the fact that alleys in the latter running in both directions, break up the normal "block" into four sections. Another interesting feature is the short block between Jefferson and Green (Liberty) which still exists. McMurtrie explains that this entire strip (180 feet wide) from Preston to 12th had originally been dedicated to public use as a "common"; he maintains that the trustees had no authority to sell the strip to individuals, as they had none-the-less done. However, when we learn on page 116 that lots in 1817 were bringing $300 a foot, we may have more sympathy with the action of the trustees! Certainly this was Louisville's first real estate boom.

Chronology continued—

Louisville's first batch of 'corn likker' was made at 4th and Water Streets.

Horse races were held on Main Street.

1784 The first courthouse completed—a log house 16 x 20 feet, one story high with puncheon floor and board roof. Erected by George Wilson at a cost of $309.79.

Louisville contained 63 clapboard finished houses, 37 partly finished, and 22 raised but not covered houses, and over 100 log cabins.

Daniel Boone transacted the first banking business when he deposited 6 beaver skins with John Sanders who carried on a crude sort of exchange.

"Know all men by these presents, that Daniel Boone has deposited six beaver skins in my keep in good order and of the worth of six shillings each skin, and I have took from them six shillings for the keep of them, and when they be sold I will pay the balance of 30 shillings for the whole lot to any person who presents this certificate and delivers it up to me at my Keep."

Louisville, Falls of Ohio,   May 20, 1784
John Sanders

Samuel Beale began to build a fine brick house from a Thomas Jefferson plan—one of three erected in Kentucky that sprang from the fertile mind of Jefferson. Called "Old Spring Station" on site of original fort "Spring Station", it is located near present Cannon's Lane and Lexington Road.

1785 Because goods had to be transported around the falls, Shippingport begun and incorporated this year.

Conventions met twice to take action in relation to the formation of a new state.

Col. Richard Taylor settled in Louisville. His son Zachary became president of the United States and is buried in Zachary Taylor Cemetery on Brownsboro Road.

1786 General Clark left Louisville with 1000 men for Vincennes. Virginia passed a law allowing Kentucky independence.

1787 Horse racing was held at Oakland Track. Grey Eagle *vs.* Wagner. The contests were run in four mile heats, best 2 out of 3. Louisville tradition of horse racing goes back to this date and even before.

The court house burned and important early records were lost.

The first Kentucky newspaper, the Kentucky Gazette, was seen at rare intervals during the

Chronology continued on page 29

JOHN C. BUCKLIN

FIRST MAYOR OF LOUISVILLE

1828-1833

**A RARE EARLY PRINT (1873):
"NEW CITY HALL AT LOUISVILLE"**

If this is the architect's drawing, only ha
of the building has been completed!

"Evening Showers," an etching by Kent Hagerman made for Liberty National Bank & Trust Co.

Chronology continued—

summer and autumn. It was published by John Bradford in Lexington.

1788 A new stone courthouse was erected. Louisville's second courthouse was 40 feet square, two stories high, with spire and belfry.

1789 First brick house was built in Louisville by a Mr. Kaye, ancestor of Frederick A. Kaye, (Mayor 1838-45) upon the "square" where the courthouse now stands (Market Street side). The second brick house was built by a Mr. Eastin on the north side of Main below Fifth Street.

1790 A rude log structure at 12th & Main was used by all the faiths as a *house of worship—* first church in city.
First census: Jefferson County—4,565; Louisville—300.

1791 Volunteers from "the Ohio Rapids settlement" served in the *Virginia militia* under George Rogers Clark.

1792 June 1 . . . Kentucky formally admitted to the Union.

1793 Major John Harrison opened a tavern at 6th & Main; first hotel in city.

1795 First postoffice opened—Mr. Michael Lacassagne, postmaster; office in his handsome residence at 5th and Main.

Hayfield built (first section) at end of present Tyler Lane; by David L. Ward.

1797 First tax assessment levied on city's property owners in July—on horses, slaves, billiard tables, tavern licenses, retail stores, carriage wheels, town lots, etc.; total was $106.

The young Duke of Orleans, afterwards Louis Philippe, the "Citizen King" of France, accompanied by two younger brothers, the Ducs de Montpensier, and Beaujois, all virtually exiled by the terrors of the Revolution, visited Kentucky, and included Louisville in their tour. They also visited Gen. Washington at Mount Vernon. Forty years afterwards when the Duke became King he sent Bishop Flaget at Bardstown a beautiful clock for his cathedral.

1798 Kentucky donated 6000 acres and authorized lottery to endow Jefferson Seminary in Louisville; marks start of public school system here. First fire company formed.

Chronology continued on page 32

TWO BIG DAYS IN COURTHOUSE SQUARE

ABOVE: Public celebration of Washington's birthday, February 22, 1861—the very day a plot was discovered assassinate President-Elect Lincoln in Baltimore, enroute to Washington.

BELOW: September 22, 1952—Candidate Dwight Eisenhower, top hero of World War II, speaks to the peop

HOW FIRM A FOUNDATION

It is appropriate that this bronze statue of Thomas Jefferson atop a replica of the Liberty Bell should be the center of attraction in our Civic Center and also that it should stand on the Street named in his honor. But perhaps it is a bit ironical that the man who wrote the *Declaration of Independence* should perpetually face the County Jail where a man forfeits his freedom and independence, temporarily at least. This handsome statue modeled by Sir Moses Ezekiel was presented to the city in 1901 by Louisville industrialist Isaac W. Bernheim. It cost $60,000. A tradition of long standing in Louisville is the public reading of the Declaration of Independence every year on the Fourth of July at this place: in memory of Jefferson, in honor of Independence Day, and in rededication to the American principles of democracy.

CLAY IN MARBLE

Visitors to the Court House must be impressed with the calm, benign figure of Henry Clay, which greets them in the rotunda—the man who is second only to Abraham Lincoln as Kentucky's greatest statesman—Congressman, Speaker of the House, Senator, three times candidate for the Presidency, and "The Great Pacificator."

The statue cost $15,000, raised by public subscription. It was made—TWICE in fact—by Kentucky's most famous sculptor, Joel T. Hart; the Sereverra marble original sank in a vessel bringing it to America; Hart modeled it again, and came here from Florence, Italy, for the unveiling May 30, 1867.

31

1799 Louisville was named by the United States Government as a "port of entry."

Good progress on Bardstown and Lexington Roads; beginning of Kentucky's highway system.

1800 Louisville's first bank, the unincorporated "Louisville Bank" began operating (absorbed in 1812 by Branch Bank of Kentucky). City trustees act to level streets and cut down weeds.

June 16 . . . First ocean-going sailship comes to Louisville; up from the Mississippi with cargo of 720 barrels of flour.

1801 Bridge at foot of Second Street completed across Beargrass Creek. Cost $420.00. At that time creek ran parallel to Ohio river to a point between 3rd and 4th.

January 18 . . . First Newspaper published in Louisville—the "Farmer's Library", by Samual Vail; press from Vermont; paper from Georgetown. "It is only known from an enactment of the Assembly requiring certain laws to be published in its columns. Similar mention is also made during the next year of a paper called the "Louisville Gazette". Whether it succeeded the Farmer's Library or was a contemporary is not known. In any event it speaks well for the intelligence and progress of the place that in two successive years, two public journals could be hopefully started."

1802 "Louisville Gazette", second paper was started.

Louis Tarascon built and operated first water-power project, a large mill at Shippingport, used until the Canal was built.

1803 Masonic lodge (chartered 1802) moves from Middletown to Louisville; 1st Fraternal order in this area. Abraham Lodge of Free and Accepted Masons.

1804 Ohio Canal Co. incorporated to build a canal around the falls on December 19th.

1805 Aaron Burr visited Louisville.

1806 1st. stone building, erected by Captain James Patten, between Main and River and 6th and 9th.

Grayson House, 432 S. 6th, oldest home standing in Louisville completed; built by John Gwathmey.

Brick laid in Flemish bond, shipped down Ohio on flatboats, outer walls 17" thick, inner walls 13" thick. Bambergers, who owned house till recently, said it was completed in 1806;

R. T. Durrett said 1810; anyway it is the oldest house in downtown Louisville.

1807 $913.50 collected in Louisville taxes.

John and Louis Tarascon open flour mill on river at what is now foot of 26th.

April 8 . . . six inches of snow fell.

1808 1st theater built, "only a barn", called "City Theater", north side Jefferson bet. 3rd. and 4th; destroyed by fire in 1843.

John J. Audubon, celebrated naturalist, came to Louisville.

Iron hatchet found beneath a 200 year old sycamore tree, while digging for the foundations of the great Tarascon flourmill in Shippingport. Warehouse erected by Elisha Applegate who was first white child born in Jefferson County; pioneer tobacco dealer in Louisville.

1809 January 19 . . . duel between Henry Clay and Humphrey Marshall, who wrote second history of Kentucky. Clay challenged Marshall. They crossed river from Shippingport in boats; Clay was slightly wounded.

April 20 . . . First circus came to Louisville; principal attraction a great elephant.

1810 Police Department begun; John Ferguson and Edward Dowler named public watchmen, at $250.00 per year; (Ferguson replied that it was "poor watching he did" when someone commented that $250. was poor salary).

County courthouse begun; fronted on 6th Street where City Hall now stands. "It was composed of a main building, fronted by a lofty portico of Ionic architecture, supported by four columns and surmounted by a cupola terminating in a spire"; torn down in 1836—one pillar actually severed by whittlers.

Population: 1,397.

1811 First steamboat to Louisville—the "Orleans" built by Robert Fulton—came from Pittsburgh—arrived at midnight and threw town into panic. Captain was Nicholas J. Roosevelt of New York. (ancestor of Franklin D. and Teddy.)

"The annus mirabilis".

Earthquakes rocked Louisville; from December 16, 1811 to March 15, 1812 there were 1,874 shocks; first shock lasted 3½ minutes. These quakes were maliciously described as the cause of church building in Louisville. "Good citizens of Louisville in their paroxysms of piety subscribed large sums of money for a house of worship, but when the earthquake ceased, the money was used to build a theater"—"Gazette" of Bedford, Pa.

Chronology continued on next page

Courthouse finished; "handsomest structure of its kind in the western country; built after plan of John Gwathmey.

Year of the Comet.

Year of Battle of Tippecanoe; Louisville hero—Col. George Rogers Clark Floyd.

First church built exclusively for one sect; built by Catholics at 10th and Main; brick, of Gothic design.

1812 City mustered company of light dragoons and battalion of infantry; served under Jackson at Battle of New Orleans.

Official names for streets given for first time; South Street (Chestnut); Rudd Street (Market); Green and Hachney (Liberty); Dunkirk Road (Prather; later Broadway).

First Methodist church; old Methodist Episcopal, side Market, between 7th and 8th.

John Skidmore established first iron foundry.

First regular bank; branch of the Bank of Kentucky; absorbed the Louisville Bank, capital $75,000; $25,000 added making capital of $100,000.00; situated N. side of Main, near corner of 5th. Thomas Prather, president, and John Bustard, cashier.

1813 First paved street—Main, 3rd to 6th.

1814 First regular trip of the "Enterprise", from New Orleans.

First paper mill established by Messrs. Jacob and Hikes.

Town of Portland laid out by Alexander Ralston.

Bad sanitary condition, stagnant pools causing fever, arousing citizens.

1815 February 2 . . . News of victory at Battle New Orleans received.

March 24 . . . Day of thanksgiving and celebration.

Stale tobacco inspection started.

Flood in spring, devastating the Ohio Valley.

Captain Shreve arrived in Shippingport from New Orleans in 25 days, a new record.

Louisville had: 24 mercantile stores, 1 book store, 1 leather store, 1 auction store, 1 clothing store, 1 theater, 5 medicine shops, 2 coachmakers, 1 gunsmith, 1 silversmith, 2 printing offices, 1 soap factory, 6 blacksmiths, 1 nail factory, 1 Methodist and 1 Catholic Church, 2 taverns ("second to none in the country"), etc.

1816 First distillery "Hope Distillery", started by a New England company with $100,000; 100 acres at foot of Main Street; then perhaps largest in world; first to substitute machinery for hand methods. Failed and later buildings were destroyed by fire.

First Presbyterian Church—4th between Market and Jefferson.

Ohio Methodist Conference met in Louisville. Company formed to undertake the building of a steamboat.

Branch bank of the Bank of the United States, established in Louisville.

First insurance company, Louisville Insurance Co., incorporated.

Louisville Theater reconstructed and refitted on grand scale.

Jefferson Seminary opened.

1817 Smallpox epidemic.

David Byers established first drug store in Louisville, "opposite Washington Hall" (corner Second and Main). In 1818 became Byers & Butler. Apparently Peter-Neat-Richardson traced its origin to this store.

First steam engine built in Louisville by Prentice and Bakewell.

Marine Hospital begun February 5; Thomas Prather and Cuthbert Bullitt donated the land.

Branch of Bank of United States opened on NE corner of 5th and Main; Judge Stephen Ormsby, president.

1818 Public Advertiser, a daily newspaper, first of this kind in city started by Shadrach Penn.

Samuel Drake remodeled 1808 theater, north side Jefferson, between 3rd and 4th—capacity 800. (Destroyed by fire, 1943.)

First steamboat to be built here was completed —"The Exchange".

Rafinesque visited Louisville; later taught at Transylvania in Lexington. First year thermometrical observation made; 22° below zero that winter.

Masonic lodge, chartered in September, named Clark's Lodge No. 51.

February 13 . . . George Rogers Clark died at Locust Grove, the home of his sister on Blankenbaker Lane; buried in family cemetery, later removed to Cave Hill.

1819 First book produced in Louisville; Dr. H. McMurtrie's "Sketches of Louisville and its Environs", from Shadrach Penn's press at the Public Advertiser, established 1818. This is the first history of Louisville. Quotes: "not yet 4000 population; 670 dwelling houses (most brick); 3 banks; 2 hotels, 2 distilleries . . . preferred lots $300 per front foot".

Population of Louisville still behind Lexington.

June 23 . . . President James Monroe and Gen. Andrew Jackson visited Louisville. Great public dinner at Washington Hall (near 2nd and Main), then city's finest hotel.

First map of falls.

Continued on page 35

Gideon Shryock

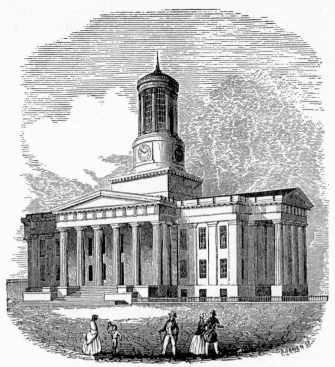

JEFFERSON COUNTY COURT HOUSE, LOUISVILLE.
Tower and side porticos were never built.

Master Builder of Early Louisville

Kentucky's greatest architect of public buildings was Gideon Shryock, the man principally responsible for a return to the classic style. Shryock completed the handsome Capitol at Frankfort (now called the *Old* Capitol) in 1830, but two of his greatest works are the Jefferson County Court House, (1859) and the Old Bank of Louisville building at 320 W. Main Street, (1838) now the home of the Louisville Credit Men's Association. Shryock, a devout Baptist, lived in Louisville for 45 years; he died here at the age of 78, June 19, 1880, and is buried in Cave Hill Cemetery.

Another great architect of the period was Henry Whitestone, (fitting name for an architect whose principal work was in stone). His masterpiece was the last Galt House. The Ford Mansion at Second and Broadway, (now the Y.W.C.A.) and the Montford Home on Broadway (recently razed) were designed by him.

The old Bank of Louisville building, now the home of the Louisville Credit Men's Association.

1820 First Fire Department organized; several hand engines purchased. (Louisville had been the scene of frequent fires.)

William Nock opened the second drug store in Louisville on NE corner of 2nd and Market; later moved to SW corner and name changed to Nock and Snyder.

1821 George Keats, brother of the great English poet, opened lumber business here.

A committee drafted regulations for the government of the watchmen who were also to be lamp lighters; 4 watchmen hired.

Rev. M. Hosten became 1st. resident Catholic priest.

Louisville & Cincinnati Packet Co. organized.

1822 "The fever year":

Yellow fever 'terrible epidemic'—almost every house a hospital; hundreds died—very existence of town threatened. Up to this time the growth of Louisville had been continuous but slow . . . the great obstacle had been reputation for healthfulness; stagnant ponds and unsanitary condition, the two principal ponds: "Long Pond" between 6th and Market to 16th; "Grayson's Pond", Center, opposite Grayson to 8th.

First musical organization: The Saint Cecilia Society.

Only date found in connection with adventurous life of Mike Fink: "Found his favorite occupation gone and departed for the far Northwest". Mike was most notorious and dangerous of the "river men".

1823 First hospital (called "Marine Hospital" because it was built to accommodate the river men) finished, on Chestnut between Floyd and Preston; 150 beds; (later moved to West End).

Ponds drained; lottery raised $40,000 to drain them; result: very low death rate from cholera in following years!

John P. Morton & Company, book store, William Worseley and James Collins, Jr. formed a partnership.

1824 Stage coach line established from Maysville, 60 miles above Cincinnati, through Lexington and Frankfort; 2 days either way; Louisville to Washington, 6 days.

Powder mill built on Corn Island.

1825 Portland Canal Co., chartered. Louisville Cement Company traces origin to this project.

Marquis de Lafayette visited Louisville May 8—great celebration.

DISTINGUISHED VISITOR

On May 8th, 1825, the Marquis de Lafayette, friend of Washington and of America, visited Louisville. His reception here, as everywhere else, was enthusiastic in the extreme. The Trustees of the city gave John Rowan, the chairman of the committee of arrangements for the reception, a considerable sum of money, to be expended in such manner as the committee might direct for this purpose. The meeting of Lafayette with some of the old officers of the revolution, who lived in Louisville, particularly that with Col. Anderson, is said to have been extremely affecting. The whole city turned out to receive this distinguished patriot; processions were formed, arches erected, bevies of young girls strewed his pathway with flowers, and the whole town was a scene of festivity and rejoicing.

Horse races at foot of 16th Street.

First Episcopalian Church erected on 2nd between Liberty and Walnut; present Christ Church Cathedral still contains parts of original structure.

Area from Water Street to river's edge and from 2nd to 7th paved as a wharf—Trustees bought from John Rowan and agreed to give heirs half of receipts of this wharf.

De Witt Clinton promoter of steam navigation and builder of Erie Canal, broke ground for the Louisville Canal.

"The Focus", a new weekly, started. Edited by Dr. Buchanan; John P. Morton printer (Became daily in 1831.) merged with Louisville Journal under name of Journal and Focus.

Hospital (on Chestnut) transferred from jurisdiction of state to city.

1827 Population: 7,063.

Cassedy & Raney, importers of china and glass, established; later to become Bayless Bros. & Co.

Sallie Ward born (famous belle).

Ice bridge across Ohio.

Steam locomotive built by T. H. Barlow of Lexington displayed on circular tract at Woodland Gardens at head of Market Street.

Steamer "Lexington" reached Louisville from New Orleans in eight days, twenty-one hours.

1828 February 13 . . . LOUISVILLE WAS INCORPORATED AND BECAME A CITY.

Portland had declined to become a part of the new municipality, but Shippingport by consent of her people was included.

March 4 . . . J. C. Bucklin was elected mayor under the new charter.

Ordinance was passed to counteract the increasing rat population.

First Baptist Church, 5th and Liberty, used jointly with Free Masons.

Celebration of 50th anniversary of town.

Lemon and Son, Jewelers established: (now oldest retail firm in Louisville.)

1829 First public school "free to all white children between the ages of 6 and 14," was opened in the upper story of the Old Baptist Church (5th and Liberty).

Lewis Pottery Co., founded.

First city schoolhouse: erection begun SW corner 5th and Walnut.

"Uncus" first steamboat to be "squeezed" through unfinished canal, December 21.

First Bank robbery, September 18, $25,000 from Commonwealth Bank; reward $2,500.— Thief never caught.

1830 Louisville Journal established by Prentice and Baxton.

Louisville Cement Co., founded.

First actual public school in Louisville completed (5th and Walnut); 700-800 pupils; opened in September.

Joseph Potter made first piano in Louisville.

Surveying of Lexington and Ohio Railroad began (2nd steam railroad constructed in United States.)

Population over 10,000; property valuation $4,316,432; slaves comprise 24% of population (was only 19.5% in 1860).

Powder mill on Corn Island exploded.

First institution for care of poor, aged and in-firmed established; combination **poo**rhouse and workhouse; 8th and Chestnut.

L. & N. R. R. chartered January 27, 1830, by the Lexington and Ohio, later absorbed by L. & N.

1831 Canal began operations; cost over $1,000,000; tolls for 1831: $12,750; 406 steamers and 421 flat and keel boats passed through in 1831.

Beginning trickle of livestock into present site of stockyards.

First rail laid on Lexington and Ohio Railroad October 23, (Lexington to Louisville).

Louisville Lyceum began (lasted only a few years).

May 21 . . . Drake's Theater burned down.

Presentation Academy founded in basement of the Church of St. Louis, where the Cathedral is now.

Wm. Kendrick's Sons founded when William Kendrick, then 20 years old started a jewelry store.

1832 First great flood 51 feet above lower water mark. City suffered greatly.

Louisville Hotel built, first large one in the city.

First Louisville Directory was published by R. T. Otis; 198 pages; contains first authentic map of city. Louisville had: 1 steam woolen factory, 1 cotton factory, 2 foundries, 1 steam planning mill, 2 white lead factories, 4 rope walks, 1 steam grist mill, 16 brickyards, 3 breweries, 2 lotteries, etc., etc.

St. Vincent Orphan's Asylum founded.

Pearson, the mortician, established business. Now L. D. Pearson & Son, Funeral Directors.

1833 Cholera all over state and area—Louisville alone spared.

The Medical College was established here about this time.

Louisville Museum founded; lasted but short time; J. R. Lambdin in charge.

Vogt Bros. Mfg. Co. founded.

Great fire at wharf. "Sentinel", "Delphine" and "Rambler" totally destroyed.

Shipment at Louisville of 102 slaves from Kentucky down river to New Orleans and to freedom in Liberia.

August 23 . . . Prentice and Trotter exchange shots.

Bradas & Gheens open candy business; (now oldest candy factory in United States).

Grainger & Company established 1833 under name of Phoenix Foundry & Machine Shop.

1834 "Year of Disaster and Gloom"; prices fell, business slumped, long established houses closed.

Continued on page 42

Early woodcut view of Louisville from Indiana side—Type of steamboat indicates year about 1820

☆ "THE BEAUTIFUL OHIO" ☆

LOUISVILLE'S first historian, speaks of the Ohio as "by far the noblest river in the universe"; and for those who love the Ohio—*and flowery prose*—we quote further: "Its wooded islands still charm the eye with their symmetry and the swan-like grace with which they sit upon its bosom and reflect their forms in the clear waters of a summer's day. Its long reaches of lake-like repose, its wooded hills, its terraced banks are still here, as when the Indian canoe glided over the surface or the buffalo and deer drank at its brink. The cultivated slopes, the peaceful homes embowered in orchards, the cities with their teeming life which line its shores, the steamers which plow its waters, the railroads which thread along its banks, and the majestic bridges which span it only heighten the grandeur which nature gave it.

"There has been much change by the handiwork of man, but the Falls remain unchanged, and all the lovers of the beautiful should rejoice to know that the utilitarian spirit has, after a century of speculation and study, decided that its waters shall not be diverted from their channel for man's selfish use, but shall, now and forever, go on their way sparkling in the sunlight, dancing in the rapids, and leaping over the falls, as has been their wont forever."

JOHN FITCH, INVENTOR OF THE STEAMBOAT
This Kentuckian from Bardstown made the greatest contribution to river transportation, but died broke—unrewarded, unhonored.

MIKE FINK

Most notorious river boatman of Louisville's early days.

BEN Cassedy, our Louisville historian of 100 years ago, stated that "among the most celebrated of the Ohio River boatmen every reader of western history will at once remember MIKE FINK, the *hero* of his class." (They were making heroes of criminal types even then!)

Mike Fink was born in or near Pittsburgh. In his earlier life he acted in the capacity of an Indian spy and while in the exercise of this calling, the free, wild and adventurous life of the boatmen attracted his youthful fancy, and off he was to try his fortunes on the broad Ohio. He had learned to mimic all the tones of the boatman's horn, and he longed to go to New Orleans where he heard that the people spoke French and wore their Sunday clothes every day. He went, and from an humble pupil in his profession soon became a glorious master.

When the river was too low to be navigable, Mike spent his time in the practice of rifle-shooting, then so eminently useful and desirable an accomplishment; and in this, as in all his serious undertakings, he soon surpassed his compeers. His capacity as a drinker was enormous; he could drink a gallon of whiskey in twenty-four hours without its effect being perceptible in his language or demeanor. (The latter were generally bad anyway.)

Mike Fink's person is described as: weight, about 180 pounds; height, about five feet, nine inches; broad round face, pleasant features, brown skin, tanned by sun and rain; very expressive blue eyes, inclining to grey; broad white teeth; and square brawny form, well proportioned. Every muscle of the arms, thighs and legs, was fully developed, indicating the greatest strength and activity.

Of his character, "Modest Mike" used to say, "I can out-run, out-hop, out-jump, throw down, drag out and lick any man in the country. I'm a Salt River roarer; I love the wimmin and I'm chock full of fight." In all his ticks, as Mike called them, he never displayed any very accurate respect of the laws either of propriety or property. One example will suffice to show how "tough" this guy Mike Fink really was.

The friendship of Mike and a man by the name of Carpenter was unbounded. Carpenter was equally as good a shot as Mike, and it had been their custom to place a tin cup of whisky on each other's head by turns and shoot it off at the distance of seventy yards. This feat they had often performed and always successfully. One day Mike Fink and Carpenter had a fierce quarrel caused probably by rivalry in the favors of a certain squaw.

After the quarrel, and when spring had returned, they re-visited the fort and over a cup of whisky they talked over their difficulty and rendered their vows of amity, which were to be ratified by the usual trial of shooting at the cup. They "skyed a copper" for the first shot and Mike won it. Carpenter, who knew Mike thoroughly, declared he was going to be killed, but scorned to refuse the test. He prepared himself for the worst. He bequeathed his gun, pistols, wages, etc, to Talbot in case he should be killed.

They went to the field, and while Mike loaded his rifle and prepared for the shot, Carpenter filled a tin cup to the brim, and without moving a feature, placed it on his own head. At this target Mike leveled his piece. After fixing his aim, however, he took down his gun, and laughingly cried, "Hold your noodle steady, Carpenter, and don't spill the whisky, for I shall want some presently." Then raising his rifle again, he pulled the trigger, and in an instant Carpenter fell and expired without a groan.

The ball had penetrated the center of his forehead about an inch and a half above the eyes. Mike cooly set down his rifle and blew the smoke out of it, keeping his eye fixed on the prostrate body of his quondam friend. "Carpenter", said he, "you have spilt the whisky!" He was told that he had killed Carpenter. "It is all an accident", said he. "I took as fair a bead on the black spot on the cup as ever I took on a squirrel's eye. How could it happen?" And he fell to cursing powder, gun, bullet and himself.

In the wild country where they then were, the hand of justice could not reach Mike and he went unmolested. But Talbot had determined to avenge Carpenter and one day, when Mike in a drunken fit of boasting, swore in Talbot's presence that he had killed Carpenter intentionally and that he was glad of it, Talbot drew out one of the pistols which had been left him by the murdered man and shot Mike through the heart. In less than four months after this Talbot was drowned attempting to swim the Titan River, and with him perished "the last of the boatmen."

BRIDGE OVER BEARGRASS CREEK, LOUISVILLE.

The Jackson Street Bridge over Beargrass Creek.

Big business apparently was already encroaching on this "peninsula park" referred to above, as can be seen in the old woodcut. The location and size of this Beargrass Creek bed and the position of the creek can be seen on the 1832 map reprinted on the next page. The creek, of course, has eventually been filled up. But, anent the very substantial stone bridge in our illustration, let us quote again from McMurtrie who writes about *another* bridge—possibly the predecessor of this one:

"A bridge was thrown over this creek near its mouth during the last summer (1818), but owing to the miserable mode of forming the abutments, they in a few weeks gave way, and the superstructure was consequently precipitated into the water. This is a lesson to those whose business it is to superintend such matters, not to be so economical, and for the future instead of employing a carpenter or stone cutter, to have the advice and assistance of a professional engineer, in all public works of this nature. Where the creek crosses the main turnpike road leading to Lexington about two miles from the town is another one, constructed of stone that is neat and durable."

BEARGRASS CREEK
As described in McMurtrie's "Sketches"

"BEARGRASS, which gives its name to the fertile and wealthy settlement through which it passes, is a considerable mill stream, affording a plentiful supply of water, eight or ten months in the year. It rises by eight different springs 10 miles east of Louisville, that unite and form the main body of the creek within two miles of that place. This like the preceding one, sometimes disappears, pursuing a secret course for a quarter of a mile together, subsequently emerging with a considerable force. On its banks are several grist mills and one for paper. It enters the Ohio, (to which for the last half mile it runs nearly parallel) opposite Louisville, leaving between it and the river, an elevated slip of land, covered with large trees, that affords a delightful and shady promenade to the citizens during the heats of summer."

Flat boat of the era of Mike Fink. Note tent, for sleeping quarters, and open fire on deck.

Large load of pipe going down the Ohio — typical shipment today of American Barge Lines.

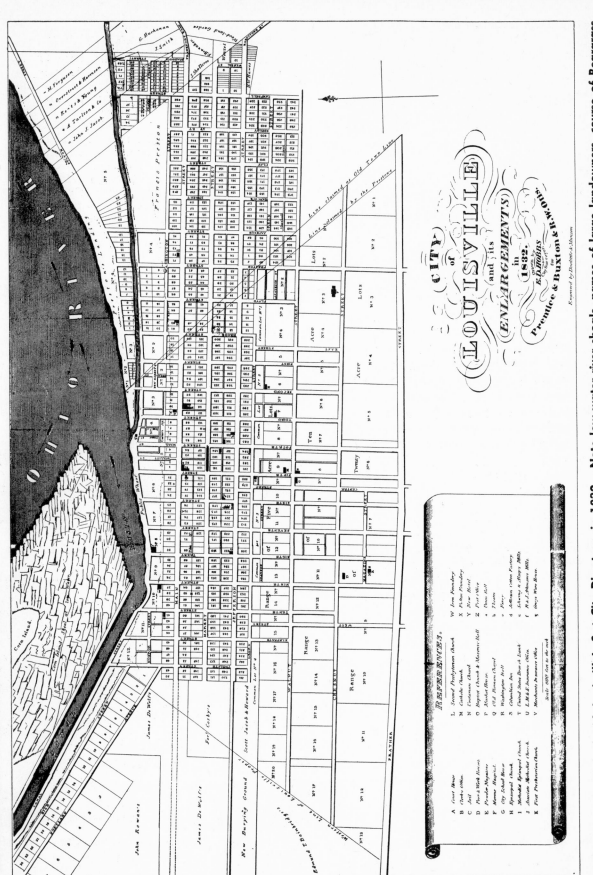

This map was published with Louisville's first City Directory, in 1832.   Note low-water river shoals, names of large landowners, course of Beargrass.

The beauty of the falls before river controls of various kinds were installed is shown in this photograph taken some years ago. Harnessing this power was a dream of the Tarascons which came true a century later. However steady year-round power is not feasible.

To Right—The Coast Guard—or as it ☞ was called in the 90's—the "U. S. Life Saving Station" is the only inland station of its kind in the country. Established because of the dangers of the falls, it has been indispensable in times of flood and war and in all times of disaster.

When transportation was mainly by river there were a number of Mail Lines which carried freight, passengers, and the U. S. mail. To the right is one of the posters of the Louisville-St. Louis Line. Another important Line was Louisville-Evansville.

Louisville and Saint Louis U. S. Mail Line
FOR SAINT LOUIS
FROM LOUISVILLE!
THE NEW AND SPLENDID LIGHT DRAUGHT PASSENGER STEAMER

HIGHFLYER!
T. T. WRIGHT, Master,
Will leave LOUISVILLE on the inst. at o'clock M.
Passengers by Mail Boats will connect.

Louisville Hotel finished in 1833, in operation; built on general plan of Tremont House at Boston; Louisville's first large hotel.

Bourbon Stock Yards begun.

"Woodbourne" built by Starks Fielding; included in estate was Big Rock.

1835 Population: 1830–10,336; 1835–19,967.

Court House (the 4th) begun; called "Guthrie's Folly" after Mayor Guthrie who was a strong supporter of the movement to move the seat of state government from Frankfort to Louisville, and consequently planned the Court House on a much larger scale than was necessary for the city government of that day. After the walls were up and roofed, it was covered in and the windows boarded up and left incomplete for 20 years (for lack of funds).

June 17 . . . Jefferson Davis, later to be president of the Confederacy, and Sarah Knox Taylor, daughter of Zachary Taylor, are married in Louisville "in the east parlor of the rectory", by the Rev. Christopher Ashe, rector of Christ Church. Taylor had objected to the marriage, "because Jefferson was an army man." The newlyweds immediately take a river packet for a honeymoon at Hurricane Plantation in Mississippi. Mrs. Davis dies of malaria in less than 3 months.

Original Galt House built at 2nd and Main—it was small, only 60 rooms; opened by Major John Joyes; Aris Throckmorton, proprietor. It was built to prevent further shift of business westward to the Louisville Hotel—burned in 1865.

Mechanic's Institute, a savings organization was incorporated.

Walker's famous exchange established, on Fifth Street.

1836 Chestnut Street Hospital remodeled and renamed the Louisville City Hospital.

City police court established.

September 7 . . . Cornerstone of bridge laid at foot of 12th Street. Because of lack of proper financing took 34 years to complete.

1837 Nation wide monetary panic; Louisville's first severe depression.

May 19 . . . "Banks of Louisville and of Kentucky suspended species payment by a resolution of the citizens so authorizing them. Financial convulsion was left . . . House after house sank beneath the waves of austerity. Progress of Louisville didn't stop: "The banks in the meantime were conducted with prudence and ability and forbore to press their debtors severely. They cautiously and gradually lessened their circulation and increased their species, until after a suspension of more than a year they ventured to resume specie payment." Casseday.

Portland annexed. First major extension of the city limits.

Louisville Medical Institute began; teachers from Transylvania in Lexington; first medical school in the west; original enrollment was 80.

First notable balloon ascension at Louisville— traveled over 100 miles around the city.

Daniel Webster, the great American Statesman and orator visited city.

1838 The Louisville Gas Company was incorporated by the Legislature in 1838 under the name of the Louisville Gas and Water Company, The Company also had a banking privilege, but this was surrendered on March 6, 1854.

"Galt House Tragedy" occurred. Two brothers from Mississippi and a companion from Richmond Va., attacked by a dozen or so men of which they killed two and wounded two, themselves being wounded and mobbed; the three were acquitted at their trial in Harrodsburg.

Medical Institute erected, SW corner 8th and Chestnut (still standing, 1954).

"Literary News Letter" started.

Local section, from Louisville to Portland, of Lexington and Ohio Railroad completed (later abandoned to become city's initial street-car line).

Statistics show one liquor selling store for every 70 men, women and children!

River lowest ever recorded to that date.

1839 Gas was first supplied to the main and service pipes on Christmas day; gas works in the western country, 5th in the United States.

Kentucky & Louisville Mutual Insurance Co., chartered.

Famous Louisville Legion (First Regiment of Kentucky State Guard), organized. Saw action in Mexican war at Monterey and Buena Vista.

First iron steamer passed falls.

September 30 . . . Famous Grey Eagle *vs.* Wagner horserace; purse $14,000; 4 mile race; Wagner won first heat; beat Grey Eagle by only 10 inches on the second heat; time 7 min., 44 seconds.

1840 Great Fire of Louisville "originated in John Hawkins' Chair Factory on Third between Main and Market and burned south within one door of the Post Office, then at corner of Market and Third; and north as far as Main. It then took a westwardly direction down Main Street, destroying all the houses within two doors of the Bank of Louisville. The flames then crossed the street and coming back, on their course destroyed nine large stores and

Continued on page 46

☞ The famous *City of Louisville* side-wheeler. The fastest and most graceful of all the steamers remembered by present-day river enthusiasts. Built at Jeffersonville in 1894, she left Louisville on Thursday, April 19, 1894 at 3 P.M. going up-stream, against the current, to Cincinnati in 9 hours and 42 minutes, a record which has never been equalled. Two years later she set the down-stream record of 5 hours and 58 minutes. She was as fabulous on the Ohio River as the *Robert E. Lee* was on the Mississippi. She sank in an ice gorge at Cincinnati on January 30, 1918—along with her sister-ship *City of Cincinnati*.

A Gallery of Famous
OLD STEAM BOATS
of the Ohio River

FROM THE COLLECTION OF
ASHBY MILLICAN

☞ The magnificent *J. M. White* was the 276th boat built by the Howard Shipyards at Jeffersonville, and was their crowning effort. This was the supreme triumph in side-wheel cotton-boat architecture and was considered the most elegant boat on inland waters.

The modern term "state-room" originated with this boat, it is said. It is an interesting story, but a rather long one—which Ashby Millican, first vice president of Liberty National will be glad to relate "at the drop of a hat". One of Mr. Millican's hobbies is "river steamboats" and we are indebted to him for these pictures. His more modern hobby is Aviation as evidenced by his twelve years on the Louisville & Jefferson County Air Board.

Continued→

The favorite excursion steamer of 50 years ago—*The Sunshine*—built at Jeffersonville. Made hundreds of trips to Fern Grove, a delightful spot in the river near Charlestown, later known as Rose Island. At one time Fern Grove had a large summer hotel; for years it was a favorite spot for all-day church picnics. Remember Lovers' Lane and the Devil's Backbone? Wonderful view of the river.

Steamer "Tell City" built in 1889 at Jeffersonville, Ind. Traveled regularly between Louisville and Tell City. Sank April 6th, 1917—same day U.S. declared war on Germany. Was a favorite subject of top-notch muralist Dean Cornwell, the famous Louisville artist, who started his career at age 13 drawing pictures of her. She resembles the stern-wheel steamer painted in 1952 by Cornwell for the Early Times Distilling Company entitled, "Kentucky River Boat".

A picture of the famous Howard Shipyard at Jeffersonville, Indiana. Among the steamboats is the well-known ferry boat *W. C. Hite* (first from left) which plied between Louisville and Jeffersonville. Among the other boats are the excursion boat *Sunshine* of Fern Grove fame and the *Morning Star*.

City of Cincinnati built at the Howard Shipyards in Jeffersonville in 1899. One of the two famous Mail Boat steamers operating daily between Louisville and Cincinnati; sank in an ice gorge at Cincinnati in 1918 along with her faster sister-ship, City of Louisville. Many present day Louisvillians will remember the famous "Meet-the-Boat" trips when these two boats met at Carrollton, Kentucky every Sunday afternoon and exchanged passengers. She "tied up" regularly at the wharf at Second and River, and her bell was often "drowned-out" by the bell in the Liberty National clock tower at Second & Market which had been ringing every hour since its installation in 1887.

Another well known side-wheeler, The America, which was built at Jeffersonville, Ind., by the Howards in 1918, and operated out of Louisville until she burned September 8, 1930. Was a regular Louisville-Cincinnati packet before being altered as a full-time excursion boat.

The last of the steam boat races! Photographed by the late Judge Arthur E. Hopkins in August of 1928, when great crowds lined the Kentucky and Indiana shores to see the two big side-wheelers, America and Cincinnati stage a race from Louisville to Fern Grove, Indiana. The Cincinnati won. Judge Hopkins' fine river collection of oil paintings and photographs was bequeathed to The Filson Club where they may be seen by anyone interested.

other buildings". Loss over $300,000; more than 30 buildings were destroyed.

Professor E. W. Gunter conducted concert composed of all musicians in Louisville; later became Mozart Society, sang Haydn's "Creation" at St. Paul's Church. Lights went off instead of *on* at the words, "let there be light" (were new gas lights).

Louisville College chartered.

Louisville has five daily newspapers.

Wm. B. Belknap started in business in 1840. Later to be known as the Belknap Hardware & Manufacturing Company.

1841 Bishop Flaget removes Roman Catholic espiscopal see from Bardstown to Louisville. New Orleans to Louisville by steamboat; 5 days, 14 hrs; with 22 stops.

Geo. Keats died.

1842 Charles Dickens arrived; described city and Jim Porter, the Kentucky giant as "a lighthouse among lampposts."

State Institute for Education of the Blind established by legislature; $10,000 appropriated; located on Sixth between Walnut and Jefferson. School started by Dr. T. S. Bell and Hon. Wm. Bullock with five pupils; later moved to Prather House on Green between Third and Fourth; in 1843 moved to new home built by state at Broadway to Jacob between First and Second. First school was destroyed by fire in 1850.

Peter and Robinson, wholesale drugs, established.

1843 Louisville Democrat Newspaper founded.

Thirty-five steamboats built here.

Few slight earthquakes felt.

1844 Louisville Courier started this year by Mr. Walter N. Haldeman.

Jockey Club headed by Col. Samuel Churchill active in Louisville; races held at Oakland Course near what is now 7th and Magnolia.

October 25 . . . Steamboat "Lucy Walker" explodes; 80 dead.

Louisville has 162 wholesale and retail stores.

1845 Benjamin Franklin Avery started a plow factory in Louisville at Preston and Main. Later became known as B. F. Avery & Sons.

Strassel Co., interior decorators, established.

February 10 . . . Control of canal passed to Federal Government. Over 1900 boats through canal this year.

J. Bacon opened store on Market between Jackson and Preston.

Property valuation almost $15 million.

1846 Mexican War: within four days Louisville Legion leaves; cited for "obedience, patience, discipline, and calm courage in battle."

February 7 . . . University of Louisville, incorporated by General Assembly; Louisville Medical Institute became Medical Department of University of Louisville.

Liederkranz Society formed, as a quartet originally.

Louisville and Frankfort Railroad Co., Incorporated, replacing Lexington and Ohio.

"New Theater" opened, SE corner Fourth and Liberty; lasted about thirty years; later called Louisville Theater; great actors of the day appeared here.

Durkee, Heath & Company, established what was later called the "New York Store", now Stewart's Dry Goods Company on Market Street, (1862 to Fourth where Sutcliffe's is now, then to Fourth and Jefferson, and then to present location.)

Banvard's Marvel Picture of the Mississippi Valley, three feet wide and a mile long painted on bolts of canvas, each piece hundreds of feet long, a moving panorama; took two hours to see.

Louisville has 162 mercantile establishments.

Steamboat "Peytona" launched.

1847 July 25 . . . Cave Hill Cemetery dedicated with impressive ceremonies; once called "Cave Farm".

First telegraph line, O'Reilly's Lines, established with offices at 3rd and Market, to become part of Western Union.

U.S. Marine Hospital completed and opened.

First telegraph—O'Reilly Lines, Pittsburg to Louisville; office corner Third and Market.

Law Department of University of Louisville organized and building erected.

1848 Tobacco trade showed great improvement.

Property valued in excess of $18 million.

1849 (Gold Rush in California).

Stitzel-Weller Distillery founded.

Cholera again; June—60 died; July—120 died.

Louisville Anzeiger, first German language newspaper started. First day of March, by Geo. P. Doern and Otto Scheefer.

Cornerstone of Catholic Cathedral laid with due ceremony August 15.

General Zachary Taylor, hero of Mexican War, president elect, visits his home and Louisville.

Macready plays Hamlet, Richelieu and Macbeth here.

The Bradstreet Company was founded by J. M. Bradstreet, furnishing information concerning

Continued on page 55

Administration Building, University of Louisville—an etching by William K. Hagerman

THE UNIVERSITY OF LOUISVILLE

A History of the Oldest Municipal University in America

When we consider the elemental nature of the settlement of Louisville, the crudeness of its homes and way of life, the location of the little village in the heart of a primeval forest with hostile Indians on all sides, and many weeks or months from any city of importance, or seat of learning, it is remarkable that within 18 years of the chartering of the town plans were being made for the establishment of a college.

The University of Louisville traces its origin back to 1798, when the Legislature gave Jefferson County 6,000 acres to establish a seminary, and the trustees of the proposed seminary were authorized to raise $5,000 by public auction for the establishment of said seminary. Thus, Louisville's first municipal educational institution was endowed, although a site for the building was not secured until 15 years later when a lot of 2½ acres was purchased on the west side of Eighth Street between Walnut and Green. The school, called Jefferson Seminary, opened at last in 1816 with between 40 and 50 students. Mann Butler was the first principal at $600 a year, not a bad salary for those times. Butler is therefore known as Louisville's first educator, as well as the author of a very valuable *OUTLINE of the Origin and Settlement of Louisville* which was published as part of Louisville's first City Directory in 1832.

It was in 1837 that the city council of Louisville, composed of James Guthrie (he was active in *everything*), Simeon Buckner, G. E. Pendergrast, William H. Field, Joseph Metcalfe, James A. Rogers, James Rudd, Daniel Smith, and Charles M. Thruston, approved the establishment of a city college or university which today, as the University of Louisville, is the oldest municipal university in America.

Medical Department of the University of Louisville, 1846. Destroyed by fire December 31, 1856—but rebuilt and still standing.

Frederick A. Kaye was mayor when the cornerstone of the Medical building was laid February 22, 1838, by the Ancient Order of Masons. It was the fourth medical school west of the Alleghenies.

A "block" of the town, between 8th and 9th and Chestnut and Magazine Streets, was given, and $50,000 appropriated for a building. The first professors were Dr. Charles Caldwell, Dr. J. E. Cooke, and Dr. L. P. Yandell, all of whom had taught at Transylvania University in Lexington, and Dr. Henry Miller. They held, respectively, the chairs of Institutes of Medicine, Theory and Practice, Chemistry, and Obstetrics. Dr. Yandell also filled the chair of Materia Medica.

After a period of controversy and discussion regarding the establishment of a college of Science, Literature and Liberal Arts to be added to the College of Medicine to form a more complete University.

The University of Louisville was chartered in 1846, absorbing the then defunct College of Louisville. The building for the Academic Department was completed in 1848, but no plans had been made to finance its operation. The trustees' plan to raise $100,000 by a "drive" soliciting 200 scholarships at $500 each, failed with only 16 pledges.

The Law Department, organized in 1846, was doing better (apparently there was more demand for legal knowledge than general culture) and when the Academic Department failed to materialize, moved into its building, and remained until 1851. The School Board of Louisville finally agreed to take over the Academic Department of the University, and it opened April 7, 1856 with an enrollment of 42 students. The college succeeded under School Board administration and in 1859 agitation started to sever its connection with the U. of L. on February 28, 1860.

This school became Male High School with a college rating, by an act of the legislature. It had the independent right to grant degrees of B.A., B.S.S., and M.A., and retained this status until 1913 when it became a high school in the regular sense. By the Act of 1860 the University of Louisville unfortunately lost all revenue from taxes, a situation which continued for more than 50 years. Strangely, and wrongly, (although legally) Male High continued to use the academic building of the university until 1898, when it moved to the building on First Street

Academic Department of the University; Building is still standing at 9th and Chestnut.

between Walnut and Chestnut where the modern Ahrens Trade School is now located.

The Medical College was a success from the start. During the second year enrollment increased to 120, and almost doubled the next year. Of the 24 medical schools in the country at that time it ranked *third*. The school became a leader in adopting new techniques of teaching. It was the first medical school west of the Alleghenies to establish a clinical amphitheater where large numbers of students could watch operations by the leading surgeons of the day. The Institute became the Medical Department of the U. of L. on May 6, 1846, and in the more than 100 years that have followed it has become one of the finest medical schools in the world and has produced more than its share of the world's leading surgeons and doctors. The School of Medicine, as it is now called, has occupied the large stone building at the corner of First and Chestnut since 1909 (built as the Louisville Medical College in 1893) and is a part of Louisville's rapidly growing Medical Center. The School of Dentistry is in the same neighborhood at Brook and Broadway.

On the 18th of May, 1846 when the U. of L. trustees took over the Medical Institute, they resolved to establish a Law Department as well. On August 6, 1846 the establishment of the Law Department was announced, located in the three northeast rooms in the basement of the Court House, previously occupied by the Law Library Company. Since then the Law School has been moved around more than any other department of the University.

At the beginning of the Twentieth Century the University of Louisville consisted of only two schools—Medicine and Law—operating independently but under the same board of trustees. The Academic Department was finally established in the fall of 1907 in the old Silas Miller mansion at 119 West Broadway, built by the retired steam boat captain many years before. Besides the main building, a stable and another building in the rear were utilized. One hundred and four students registered for the first semester, and according to the pretentious catalogue 70 courses in 18 different departments were offered; of course, not all of them were given.

In 1925—almost a century after the first suggestion for an engineer school—the Speed Scientific School was established, now a major department.

The very fancy Commencement Program of the University of Louisville Medical Department, Class of '92. Note that the ceremonies were held in the afternoon—at Macauley's.

The old Louisville Medical College on Second Street—no connection with the U. of L.

A drawing of The School of Reform Grounds, circa 1900—now Belknap Campus, U. of L.

In 1924 the property of the Reform School on the east side of Third Street south of the Confederate monument was acquired as the new campus for the University, at a cost of about $250,000. It was at first called simply *University Campus,* but in 1927 the name was changed to *Belknap Campus* in honor of William R. Belknap, whose family had been a big benefactor of the University.

There were twelve large buildings and a number of frame cottages on the property—all of them old. The old buildings were altered and improved for their new purposes, and most of them are still in use. A handsome administration building of classical design was completed in 1928.

A completely new plant is rapidly emerging from a master-plan. Large splendid new buildings have already been dedicated for the Speed Scientific School and the School of Law. The recent acquisition of Parkway Field for eventual use by the University indicates the far-sighted plans of its present trustees. The Little Theater, in its quaint frame Playhouse on the campus, and the School of music in the magnificient Norton Mansion miles away in Cherokee Park, are departments of the University, and dominant influences in the cultural life of Louisville today. U. of L. teams, particularly in basketball have distinguished themselves and spread the fame of America's oldest municipal university. Under the leadership of men like ex-mayors Farnsley and Wyatt and President Davidson, the University, like Louisville itself, seems to be smoothly but powerfully moving into high gear.

"The first *150 years* were the hardest!"

Old U. of L. Academic Department on Broadway

Night view of the new Speed Scientific School of the University of Louisville

BENEFACTORS OF THE UNIVERSITY

In the 117 years that the University of Louisville has served Louisville many individuals have made contributions to its growth and development. Among the more important benefactors have been Mr. and Mrs. Allen R. Hite, Mrs .J. B. Speed, Justice Louis Denbitz Brandeis, Morris B. Belknap, Dr. Preston Pope Satterwhite and Judge Lafon Allen.

The Allen R. Hite Art Institute, which is under the direction of the U. of L. Board of Trustees, represents an endowment of more than one million dollars, which is more than half of the total of all the University's endowments. As a municipal university U. of L. operates primarily on taxes and tuitions.

Mrs. Speed built and endowed the J. B. Speed Memorial Museum to house her art collections, though today it is used primarily for the showing of loan exhibits. The Speed Museum, while it is on the campus, is not administratively connected with the University.

Justice Brandeis of the Supreme Court, (who incidentally changed his middle name from David to *Denbitz* in honor of a remarkable friend whom he greatly admired), was for many years a friend and benefactor of the U. of L., making many thoughtful contributions in various departments and activities. Upon his death he bequeathed all of his private papers and documents to the University.

Mr. Belknap donated the large and important collection of books which forms the nucleus of the University Library, located in the Administration Building, and also provided funds to furnish the library completely.

Dr. Preston Pope Satterwhite, descendant of several famous Louisville families was a native Louisvillian who lived in New York most of his life, but he never forgot Louisville. A man of great wealth and erudition and an ardent art collector, he gave a great part of his collection to the Speed Art Museum, including a magnificient Elizabethan panelled room, which has been set up permanently and furnished with rare antique furniture of the period. A new Satterwhite wing of the Museum is now under construction. Dr. Satterwhite is perhaps equally famous in Louisville for the beautiful memorial where he and his wife are buried in Cave Hill Cemetery.

Planned by him with the assistance of leading sculptors and landscape artists, it may well be the most beautiful (and costly) private memorial of its kind in America or the world.

Judge Allen, another friend and booster of the U. of L., gave it his private collection of early views and prints of Louisville, items of interest and value to all future historians.

One of the handsomest gifts made to the University of Louisville was Gardencourt, the delightfully landscaped 14-acre Norton estate in Cherokee Park. The large Georgian-style mansion with its great courts and gardens was given to the University of Louisville School of Music in 1947 by the heirs of Miss Mattie A. Norton.

The Southern Baptist Theological Seminary

When the Southern Baptist Convention was constituted in 1845 there was no theological seminary within its territory. Education for the ministry was at that time provided by the Baptist colleges, and by private study in the homes and under the direction of individual ministers. A few ambitious men studied in institutions in the North. There was a growing sentiment for a general theological seminary for the Convention.

James P. Boyce, of South Carolina, had graduated at Brown University, and upon yielding to a conviction of a call to the ministry, had studied in Princeton Theological Seminary. As Professor in the Theological Department of Furman University he manifested unusual ability and insight.

Taking up advocacy of a general theological institution, Boyce delivered a notable inaugural address before the University in 1856. In 1859, with a faculty made up of James P. Boyce, John A. Broadus, Basil Manly, Jr., and William Williams, the Theological Department of Furman University was merged with the new Seminary.

Beginning auspiciously and developing with fine promise, the young institution was soon embarrassed by the Civil War. By the end of the session in 1862 it was found necessary to suspend operations. At the close of the War, although it seemed almost impossible to resume operations because of the loss of resources and of the widespread destitution, the indomitable courage of the members of the Faculty caused them to reopen the Seminary October 1, 1865.

To raise any adequate endowment seemed hopeless while the Seminary was located in the most impoverished section of the South, and it was decided that the insititution might be moved into some other region where more prosperous conditions prevailed.

Certain Baptists of Kentucky lent encouragement to that end, and the Seminary was moved to Louisville in 1877. Its support remained uncertain and its future precarious until 1880, when, in an hour of desperate need, the Hon. Joseph E. Brown, of Georgia, made a gift of $50,000 which preserved the life of the school.

It was many years before sufficient funds were procured to establish the Seminary in its own grounds and buildings. It pursued its work in rented buildings in different locations until it was able to occupy its own property at Fifth Street and Broadway in 1888. Here four buildings were erected which housed the institution until the spring of 1926.

Early in the present century it became increasingly evident that it would be wise for the Seminary to seek a more quiet site with larger campus facilities. Movements in this direction were halted by World War I. In 1921 a tract of fifty-one acres was purchased on Lexington Road, to which some nineteen acres have subsequently been added. The building of the new home was projected on a vigorous plan.

The cornerstone of the first building was laid in November, 1924.

The removal to the new site, known as "The Beeches," was effected March 26 and 27, 1926.

Southern Seminary is one of the largest theological seminaries in the world, and its campus is one of the most beautiful. Dr. Duke K. McCall, a brilliant young educator, preacher, and administrator is president.

Louisville Presbyterian Theological Seminary

The Louisville Presbyterian Seminary ranks high among the theological institutions of America, as its magnificent buildings rank high among the handsome edifices of Louisville

There are seven stone units in the traditional Gothic style, forming three sides of a quadrangle. Haldeman Hall, a dormitory, is a memorial to Walter N. Haldeman, a former owner and publisher of The Courier-Journal. It was he who originally secured the fine Barrett home at First and Broadway for the use of the Seminary. Other prominent families are memorialized in the various buildings.

The Seminary traces its origin back more than 100 years to the organization of the Danville Seminary in 1853. The consolidation with the Louisville Seminary (founded 1893) took place in 1901.

Among the Seminary's prominent leaders have been Dr. C. R. Hemphill, Dr. John M. Vander Meulen, Dr. John Rood Cunningham, and today's president, Dr. Frank Hill Caldwell. Incidentally, Dr. Caldwell on February 4, 1954, announced the purchase by the Seminary of 31 acres near Seneca Park as a future campus, necessitated by the proximity of the proposed North-South Expressway, which will make expansion impossible at First and Broadway.

Top—The open quadrangle of impressive Gothic Buildings of Louisville Presbyterian Seminary, 1st & Broadway.

Right—The original Norton Hall of Southern Baptist Seminary, at 4th & Broadway till 1926.

Below—Aerial view of the beautiful campus of Southern Seminary on Lexington Road.

ZACHARY TAYLOR, 1784-1850
Twelfth President of the United States

SOLDIER, HERO, PRESIDENT—

AND CITIZEN OF LOUISVILLE

"ROUGH AND READY" he was called, and he was a strong and rugged character, a truly great American—a hero and the son of a hero. His father helped General Washington to win the Battle of Trenton.

Zachary was born on a farm in Orange County, Virginia, November 4, 1784. When only a year old he was carried on horseback by his mother from Virginia to his new home in Kentucky, near Louisville. The future President grew up in a log cabin on a farm where life was primitive and a constant struggle. Like many other frontier boys he grew up strong, courageous, used to hardships, with great physical and moral stamina. It is said that as a lad, Zachary swam the Ohio River from the Kentucky to the Indiana shore when the river was full of floating ice. Taylor was described by a contemporary as "a perfect specimen of the Kentuckian." Louisville may well be proud of this man, for it was here that he spent the formative years of his life—from infancy to sturdy manhood.

It is true that he later ventured far from his boyhood home to distinguish himself as a soldier, a plantation owner, and finally as the Chief Executive of his country. Zachary Taylor fought in Illinois, sloughed through the Florida Everglades, successfully defended Fort Harrison in Indian Territory, fought in the Black Hawk and Seminole Wars and commanded the Army of Occupation on the Mexican Border (1845-46). The hostilities his army engaged in precipitated the War with Mexico, April 23, 1846. He won a victory at Palo Alto, May 8th; and another the next day at Resaca de la Palma, winning also a promotion to Major General.

Ignoring President Polk's order to fight a defensive war, he advanced into Mexico and captured Monterrey on September 23, 1846. Even though compelled to send many of his best troops to re-inforce Gen. Winfield Scott, he continued the invasion of Mexico and decisively defeated Santa Anna at Buena Vista on February 23, 1847.

"Old Rough and Ready" was now a National hero, and the next year (1848) he became the Whig candidate for president. He defeated his Democratic opponent, Lewis Cass. He was president only until July 9, 1850, when he died suddenly at the age of 56 in the midst of the struggle over the Compromise of 1850. His remains were brought back to Kentucky and placed in the family vault on the burial grounds adjacent to the Taylor home—now the Zachary Taylor National Cemetery—a beautiful and honored spot on the Brownsboro Road in Louisville.

Zachary Taylor spent at least half of his life in and around Louisville. Five of his children were born here, including his son Richard Taylor, who distinguished himself in the Civil War. Louisville will always revere the memory of this great man—the only native son to date to become President of the United States.

The Zachary Taylor Homestead on Blankenbaker Lane

The only President of the United States buried in Louisville; Monument and tomb of Zachary Taylor.

Chronology continued

mercantile persons and firms. (Now Dun and Bradstreet.)

1850 Cholera again; in eight days 113 died.
Beginning of Ballard & Ballard flour mills.
Louisville Axe & Tool Co., founded.
February 11 . . . Rt. Rev. Benedict Joseph Flaget dies; succeeded by Most Rev. Martin John Spalding.
April 4, 8:05 P.M. . . . Earthquake, no damage.
September 29 . . . Blind School fire, building destroyed.
March 5 . . . L. & N. incorporated, Leven L. Shreve first president.

R. G. Dun & Company established in 1850, as a standard authority on mercantile credit now Dun and Bradstreet.
June 29 . . . Colored woman gave birth to seven children (4 boys, 3 girls) fully and well formed but were still-born.
Jenny Lind, musical sensation of her time gave concert here; streets packed with people. She stayed at home of Mr. L. L. Shreve (where Armory now stands). Concert at old Mozart Hall at Fourth and Jefferson. Jenny Lind, "Swedish Nightingale", seats sold at auction; first for $175.; many over $100.

Continued on page 58

He gave us the Dickens back in 1842!

EDITORS' NOTE: *The celebrated English novelist Charles Dickens on his tour of America in 1842 visited Louisville. His description of the town as published soon after in his* American Notes *angered the citizens of Louisville, many of whom boycotted his books because of this write-up. At least he praised the Galt House!*

One hundred and twelve years later—it should be safe to reprint Dicken's notes; and since he is generally considered the greatest English novelist, we are reprinting the excerpt on Louisville in full. Nice to get such a famous author—for free! (Copy-right expired.)

CHARLES DICKENS, 1812-1870

CHARLES DICKENS: ON LOUISVILLE

There was nothing very interesting in the scenery of this day's journey which brought us at midnight to Louisville. We slept at the Galt House; a splendid hotel; and were as handsomely lodged as though we had been in Paris, rather than hundreds of miles beyond the Alleghanies.

The city presenting no objects of sufficient interest to detain us on our way, we resolved to proceed next day by another steamboat, the Fulton and to join it about noon, at a suburb called Portland, where it would be delayed some time in passing through a canal.

The interval, after breakfast, we devoted to riding through the town, which is regular and cheerful; the streets being laid out at right angles and planted with young trees. The buildings are smoky and blackened from the use of bituminous coal, but an Englishman is well used to that appearance, and indisposed to quarrel with it. There did not appear to be much business stirring; and some unfinished buildings and improvement seemed to intimate that the city had been overbuilt in the ardor of "going ahead", and was suffering under the reaction consequent upon such feverish forcing of its powers.

On our way to Portland, we passed a "Magistrate's office", which amused me, as looking far more like a dame-school than any police establishment; for this awful institution was nothing but a little lazy, good-for-nothing front parlor, open to the street; wherein two or three figures (I presume the magistrate and his myrmidons) were basking in the sunshine, the very effigies of languor and repose. It was a perfect picture of Justice retired from business for want of customers; her sword and scales sold off; napping comfortably with her legs upon the table.

Here, as elsewhere in these parts, the road was perfectly alive with pigs of all ages; lying about in every direction, fast asleep; or grunting along in quest of hidden dainties. I had always a sneaking kindness for these odd animals, and found a constant source of amusement when all others failed, in watching their proceedings. As we were riding along this morning I observed a little incident between two youthful pigs, which was so very human as to be inexpressibly comical and grotesque at the time, though I dare say, in telling, it is tame enough. One young gentleman (a very delicate porker with several straws sticking about his nose, be-

Kentucky Giant Jim Porter on his hackney-coach

View of Main Street looking east from Third, about the time Dickens visited here. Note the Galt House at Second Street, Belknap's on corner of Third, Bank of Kentucky (with columns) in between, tandem mule-team in street.

tokening recent investigations in a dunghill) was walking deliberately on, profoundly thinking, when suddenly his brother who was lying in a miry hole unseen by him, rose up immediately before his startled eyes, ghostly with damp mud. Never was pig's whole mass of blood so turned. He started back at least three feet, gazed for a moment and then shot off as hard as he could go; his excessively little tail vibrating with speed and terror like a distracted pendulum. But before he had gone very far, he began to reason with himself as to the nature of this frightful appearance; and as he reasoned, he relaxed his speed by gradual degrees; until at last he stopped, and faced about. There was his brother, with the mud upon him glazing in the sun, yet staring out of the very same hole, perfectly amazed at his proceedings. He was no sooner assured of this—and he assured himself so carefully that one may almost say he shaded his eyes with his hand to see the better—than he came back at a round trot, pounced upon him, and summarily took off a piece of his tail; as a caution to him to be careful what he was about for the future, and never to play tricks with his family any more.

We found the steamboat in the canal, waiting for the slow process of getting through the lock, and went on board, where we shortly afterwards had a new kind of visitor in the person of a certain Kentucky Giant whose name is Porter, and who is of the moderate height of seven feet eight inches, in his stockings.

There never was a race of people who so completely gave the lie to history as these giants, or whom all the chroniclers have so cruelly libelled. Instead of roaring and ravaging about the world, constantly catering for their cannibal larders, and perpetually going to market in an unlawful manner, they are the meekest people in any man's acquaintance: rather inclining to milk and vegetable diet, and bearing anything for a quiet life. So decidedly are amiability and mildness their characteristics that I confess I look upon that youth who distinguished himself by the slaughter of these inoffensive persons, as a false hearted brigand, who pretending to philanthropic motives, was secretly influenced only by the wealth stored up within their castles, and the hope of plunder. And I lean the more to this opinion from finding that even the historian of those exploits, with all his partiality for his hero, is fain to admit that the slaughtered monsters in question were of a very innocent and simple turn; extremely guileless and ready of belief; lending a credulous ear to the most improbable tales; suffering themselves to be easily entrapped into pits; and even (as in the case of the Welsh Giant) with an excess of the hospitable politeness of a landlord, ripping themselves open, rather than hint at the possibility of their guests

The Filson Club has this portrait of Jim Porter as well as one of his boots and cast of his hand.

being versed in the vagabond arts of sleight-of-hand, and hocus-pocus.

The Kentucky Giant was but another illustration of the truth of this position. He had a weakness in the region of the knees, and a trustfulness in his long face, which appealed even to five feet-nine for encouragement and support. He was only twenty-five years old, he said, and had grown recently, for it had been found necessary to make an addition to the legs of his inexpressibles. At fifteen he was a short boy, and in those days his English father and his Irish mother had rather snubbed him, as being too small of stature to sustain the credit of the family. He added that his health had not been good, though it was better now; but short people are not wanting who whisper that he drinks too hard.

I understand he drives a hackney-coach, though how he does it, unless he stands on the footboard behind, and lies along the roof upon his chest, with his chin in the box, it would be difficult to comprehend. He brought his gun with him, as a curiosity. Christened "The Little Rifle", and displayed outside a shop-window, it would make the fortune of any retail business in Holborn. When he had shown himself and talked a little while he withdrew with his pocket-instrument, and went bobbing down the cabin among men of six feet high and upwards, like a lighthouse walking among lamp-posts. Within a few minutes afterwards, we were out of the canal, and in the Ohio River again.

Chronology continued—

Geher & Son, established July 5, 1850, by Anthony Geher, retail stove house.
1851 Direct railroad line from Lexington finished.
First steam locomotive put in service on Louisville & Frankfort Railroad.
New city charter went into effect March 24; Sinking Fund created.
Government Building erected at Third and Green; cost $246,640; most imposing and ornamental public edifice; later home of the Courier Journal and Louisville Times.
1852 Mr. Ben Cassedy publishes his History of Louisville.
Bamberger, Bloom & Co. established. Dry goods—largest in world in jeans.
American Printing House for blind started—moved into present site on Frankfort Avenue.
German Protestant Orphans Home established.
Deaths of Clay and Webster observed here.
First telegraphic communication between Louisville and New Orleans.
Cathedral of Assumption dedicated; at that time was "grandest example of Gothic architecture in the U.S."
1853 First Kentucky Fair, in area which is now Crescent Hill; lasted five days—ended with Grand Calvacade at Galt House.
Edward H. Marcus Paint Company founded.
Professor Wm. H. G. Butler, school principal, killed by Matthew F. Ward, after the former disciplined Ward's younger brother; great public indignation—the big crime story of the era.
Henry H. Timberlake established Insurance Agency, now Timberlake & Trueheart.
"A. L. Shotwell" came from New Orleans in four days nine hours 29 minutes; "Eclipse" one minute behind.

Continued on page 72

Compare this recent picture of Main Street east of Third with the one taken a hundred years ago shown on page 57.

Oxen were still used to draw carts when this sketch of the waterfront was made. Note the long line of steamboat smoke stacks of boats docked.

This photographic view made some years later indicates less activity on the wharf. The railroads were probably cutting in.

The Port of Louisville Terminal, on the Ohio River at the foot of Preston Street, is now the busy hub of river transportation.

View of the Locks in the 80's while under construction or enlargement. Part of the Old Settlement of Shippingport* can be seen in background.

The Locks today—handling a greater volume of river traffic than ever. This is a fascinating operation under U.S. Government control. Visitors are welcome and it is easily accessible.

*SHIPPINGPORT, under the enterprise of its thrifty French settlers, at one time transacted a much larger amount of business than did Louisville. The existence of great natural water-power marked it as a place to be developed for manufactures. In 1815 the Tarascons began the erection, at a cost of over $150,000, of an enormous flour mill. The building of stone and brick, with massive foundations and six stories, reached to a height of 102 feet. It had a capacity of 500 barrels of flour per day. Its imported machinery was the most perfect that could then be designed. The building itself was of the most advanced architecture of the period, and was so constructed that wagons could be driven under an arch and weigh and discharge grain at the rate of 75 bushels in ten minutes. The Tarascons experimented with the most improved machinery with the purpose of erecting cotton, fulling, and weaving-mills, but their modern ideas were too advanced for their times, and resulted in failure.

Main Street in the 1850's—when the original Louisville Hotel was one of the city's handsomest buildings.

★ 1854 ★

We hope the reader will not think that we are giving undue prominence to this year—but, after all, it was the year of our beginning . . .

☆ LOUISVILLE IN 1854 ☆

JAMES S. SPEED
Mayor of Louisville in 1854

OUR CITY one hundred years ago, according to a contemporary writer was, "strictly a *river town* where business was principally measured by its boat traffic." She was in the middle of the decade 1850-1860 which was the period of her greatest development in river trade and travel. While the era of the railroad was "just around the bend," so to speak, the steamboat was still the great carrier of produce and of prosperity for Louisville. The year was almost the apex of the Golden Era of the passenger packet, but the L & N had already been established, and Louisville was destined to become the hub of a great new transportation system.

Strategically located on a great waterway at the "Gateway to the South", Louisville was indeed the mistress of the commerce of the South. Her great need was for a bridge (or, as they thought then, a tunnel) to connect the North with the South. Such a bridge or tunnel would have proved invaluable later in the prosecution of the War Between the States, to say nothing of the commercial advantages to the city in the ante-bellum era.

Louisville one hundred years ago was a town of about 50,000 souls, with a total tax assess-ment valuation of $32,281,354.00 (the *whole city* valued at less than *one-third* of today's deposits in Louisville's oldest financial institution!). Of course, prices were lower and the dollar was therefore worth more. James S. Speed was mayor. According to Ben Casseday's History (1852), beef ranged from 6 to 8 cents a pound, pork was 5 cents, potatoes 25 to 40 cents a bushel, eggs 4 to 8 cents a dozen, butter 15 to 20 cents a pound; they priced spring chickens by the *dozen*—75 cents to $1.50.

There were five immense Market Houses located in five different places on Market Street in the center of the street. While few persons alive today remember even the last of these markets, the places where they stood are easily discernible because Market Street is considerably wider in those blocks.

Market Street was the principal shopping street, exclusively retail. Fourth Street (later called Fourth Avenue) was entirely residential south of Jefferson—a street of neat, well-kept, aristocratic homes. Main Street was the wholesale street—actually one of the most important commercial streets in America at that time. Broadway (also called Prather) was the "outskirts" and the widest and most beautiful street in the city, which in 1855 exended south to Kentucky Street. The eastern limits of the city were Cave Hill; in the west, Portland; on the north, of course, the river—the only boundary which has remained stationary, more or less! The worst feature of the Louisville of a hundred years ago was MUD—and the series of ponds and quagmires in the very streets. (A street-paving Mayor like Charlie Farnsley was the crying need of the day!) People had to go blocks out of their way, even on horseback and in carriages, to avoid lakes and ponds and impassable streets of mud. In rainy weather it was indescribable.

During the days of slavery there were two slave markets in the blocks between Second and Brook Streets and Main and Jefferson. Signs of these terrible institutions are still visible today (1954). The alley just north of the Falls City Top and Buggy Company, on the east side of the street, was a mart where the unfortunate slaves were auctioned off; and adjacent to it is the old building where the slaves were kept before the sales. The heavy iron grating can still be seen in one of the windows.

The other slave market was on the east side of First Street, south of Market, now a parking lot for one of Louisville's oldest shoe dealers, Frank Cleve. Here divisions of the original "slave pen" where the negroes were incarcerated before the sales are still visible on the wall. There was another old Slave block at Fifth and Green (now Liberty). It is well that there are few reminders of the inhuman traffic in human lives—in the State that gave Abraham Lincoln to the world.

During 1854 there were a few individuals who realized that Corn Island, the original site of Louisville, ought to be preserved for posterity, but it was already showing signs of being washed away. Every year more trees were being cut down and none replanted, and as the roots died the river encroached more and more on the island. R. T. Durrett was then a member of the city council, and having a great interest in Louisville's historical landmarks, he urged the mayor and councilmen to have willows planted along the edge of the island or to have projecting walls erected to stop the erosion. But apparently the other city fathers did not see the wisdom of spending money for this purpose; hence the original site of Louisville has gone down the river; like the fabled continent of Atlantis, it has sunk beneath the waves.

Another radical change in the city's river front took place in 1854, when the "cut-off" was made opposite Towhead Island, causing Beargrass Creek to flow into the river at that point (since called "The Point") rather than at its original mouth between Third and Fourth Street. The cut-off creek bottom was filled, eliminating a series of bridges—also a beautiful park-like area—and providing additional new space for commercial purposes.

It has been suggested by various individuals and civic organizations in recent years that the beautification of Louisville's river front would be a great asset to the city, particularly the bridge and river approaches. This is a good project for some dreamer, who combines vision with energy, determination and singleness of purpose. The City government last year (1953) made a good start several miles up the River Road by creating a new and attractive riverside park, with plenty of parking space for river lovers—and incidentally, just lovers . . .

☆ THE NATION IN 1854 ☆

ONE of the most important and sensational diplomatic-commercial ventures in American history culminated on March 8, 1854, when Commodore Matthew C. Perry established friendly relations with the Japanese government at a conference held near present day Yokohama, after Japan had been almost completely isolated from the Western world for more than 200 years. At this meeting, held just one day before the German Insurance Company of Louisville received its charter (*commercial!*), Commodore Perry presented the Japanese authorities with gifts from America which showed the mechanical and commercial progress of this country—a fully equipped miniature railroad, a steamboat, a telegraph line, and other items representing the arts of Western civilization.

This conference resulted in a treaty of peace, friendship and commerce on March 31, 1854, which opened the Japanese ports of Shimoda and Hakodate to U.S. trade (a friendship which ended most abruptly on December 7th, 1941 at Pearl Harbor, when we learned to our sorrow that the lessons in "western progress" which Japan had received from us since that day in March 8, 1854, when Commodore Perry "opened their eyes"—had been learned very well indeed!).

Nationally, the biggest political event of 1854 was, of course, the founding of the Republican Party, which was the result of the dissatisfaction of various groups of politicians who were united on a common ground of opposition to the extension of slavery into new states and territories of the union. There was a coalition meeting on February 28, 1854 at Ripon, Wisconsin, of Anti-slavery Democrats, Whigs and Free-Soilers who believed that a new party should be formed with this single platform. The name "Republican" was recommended at this meeting. On July 6, the name was officially adopted at a State meeting of Michigan delegates held at Jackson. Similar meetings were held in other states and before the end of the year the new "Republican Party" had become organized throughout the North.

On October 16, 1854, Abraham Lincoln entered the national political limelight with his famous "Peoria Speech". Before this time he was known only in Illinois as a lawyer and politician. This speech, which had previously been delivered in Springfield, Illinois, on October 4, was Lincoln's first public denunciation of slavery. He made it very clear, however, that he had "no prejudice against the Southern people"; he readily acknowledged the constitutional rights of the South; and was careful to point out that he favored *gradual* emancipation of the slaves.

Another political development of 1854 which was a blot on the American escutcheon, was the growth of the "Know-Nothing" Party, an anti-Catholic and anti-immigrant movement which had started in the 1840's, revived in 1852, and grew to be a threatening political force in 1854. The official name was the "American" Party, but its popular name was the "Know-Nothing" Party because when its members had their secret meetings the password was "I don't know".

Their platform denied foreigners and Roman Catholics public office, and required a 21 year residence for foreign born persons to qualify for citizenship. The Know-Nothing Party was responsible for atrocities all over the country, such as the Bloody Monday of August 6, 1855, in Louisville, described elsewhere in this history.

Other national events of 1854 were: the passage of the Kansas-Nebraska Act (May 30); the organization of the Massachusetts Emigrant Aid Society (April 26); the Canadian Reciprocity Treaty (June 5); the Ostend Manifesto (October 18) which almost resulted in war with Spain. An event of tremendous importance for better inter-national communication took place May 6, 1854, when Cyrus W. Field organized an American company to raise funds to lay a *submarine cable across the Atlantic Ocean*—a titanic job which was eventually accomplished after numerous set-backs and disappointments.

The first Y.M.C.A. in the United States was established June 7, 1854, in Buffalo, N.Y.; the cornerstone of the first railroad bridge across the Mississippi River was laid between Rock Island and Davenport, Iowa, September 1, 1854.

By 1854, the Gold Rush was well over, but settlers, adventurers, and speculators were pouring across the Mississippi into the West, most of which was still virgin territory. By this time all of the prairie lands east of the Mississippi had been occupied or were in the hands of speculators. Franklin Pierce was president of the United States. The census of 1850 showed that the United States had a population of 23 million. The movement for equal rights for women was getting started. There was a great temperance movement across the entire country; Timothy Shay Arthur wrote "Ten Nights in a Bar Room" in 1854; and that great American classic "Walden", written by the naturalist-philosopher Henry David Thoreau, was also published in 1854. Art was at a low ebb in this year and decade; architectural style and the style of women's (and men's) clothes was atrocious; the first paper collar was patented; the Pennsylvania Rock Oil Company was incorporated in 1854; the first street cleaning machine was employed in Philadelphia; gambling, including State and municipally sponsored lotteries, was rampant every where; the bath at best was a weekly event in most American homes!

These are the highlights (and some of the low-spots) of the year 1854. The nation as it looks from here—100 years later!

OHIO RIVER RAILROAD BRIDGE, LOUISVILLE.

☆ THE WORLD IN 1854 ☆

ON MARCH 12, 1854, a treaty of alliance between England, France and Turkey was signed; on March 28, Great Britian and France declared war on Russia.

The Russo-Turkish war which began in 1853, grew out of a dispute regarding holy places in Palestine. In January 1854, the allied fleets entered the Black Sea; allied armies disembarked at Varma May 29; the Danube was blockaded June 1; in July and August the allied armies and navies suffered severely from cholera. September 14 the Allies land in the Crimea, and on October 17 the Siege of Sevastopol commences; on November 6, Miss Florence Nightingale and nurses arrive at Scutari. (Hostilities ended February 29, 1856, and a treaty of Peace concluded the Crimean War in Paris, March 30, 1856.)

In Rome, Italy, on December 8, 1854, the Pope proclaimed the "Immaculate Conception of the Virgin" as a dogma of the Roman Catholic Church.

In September 1854, Livingston left Loanda on his famous trip through the wilds of Africa. (He discovered Victoria Falls, November 17, 1855.)

There was internal war as usual in China in 1854, and in August and November rebels besieged Canton without success.

Japan, after signing a treaty with the U.S.A. on March 31, signed a similar treaty with great Britain on October 14, 1854. In India the great Ganges Canal opened on April 8th; on the Hawaiian Islands King Kamehameha III died. In Canada, January 27 marked the opening of the Great Western Railroad; on February 1, the Parliament House in Quebec burned.

In this hemisphere to the South in 1854, the independence of the Isthmus of Panama was declared by the provincial legislature; in San Salvador, on April 16, an earthquake destroyed the city; there were 200 dead, 4 millions lost. The Capital was removed to Cojutepeque. In Brazil, the first railroad was opened April 30, 1854; Peru experienced a year of revolt and battle, and all slaves were freed. Slavery was also abolished in Venezuela—on March 24, 1854.

This quick summary of world happenings in 1854 proves again what Nicholas Breton, a quaint old English writer of the 17th Century observed: "A mad world, my masters!"

rly Louisville—reproduced from original steel engraving belonging to Liberty National Bank & Trust Co.

Old Woodcut View of Louisville about 1854—from the Indiana side.

☆ CITY CHRONOLOGY OF 1854 ☆

THIS WAS the "Ante-Bellum" era, when the questions of slavery and of "Southern rights" were the burning issues of the day. In 1850 Henry Clay made a valiant effort to settle the differences between the North and the South, and submitted a series of compromise resolutions to Congress. His 8-point program was supported by Daniel Webster, and several of the measures were adopted, but there was a strong undercurrent of dissatisfaction and the movement for secession continued to grow stronger.

In 1852, Harriet Beecher Stowe's Uncle Tom's Cabin was published, a sentimental novel based on factual evidence and directed against the injustice of slavery and of the Fugitive Slave Act. This book, one of the leading "best sellers" of all time, did much to arouse the North (and even some people in the South) against slavery.

In 1854, when Liberty National Bank and Trust Company had its origin in the chartering of the German Insurance Company, Franklin Pierce (Democrat) of New Hampshire was President; William R. King of Alabama was Vice President; Jefferson Davis was Secretary of War; and Louisville's own James Guthrie was Secretary of the Treasury.

Now for the local happenings of 1854, just one hundred years ago, gleaned from the newspapers of that year.

January 6 . . . *Uncle Tom's Cabin* as a play was performed in Louisville, starring Harry Lehr.

January 6 . . . There was discussion in the legislature regarding a proposal that the seat of State Government be removed to Louisville.

January 9 . . . A great fire destroyed the Customs House and eight business establishments.

January 17 . . . The celebrated prima donna, Madame Sontag, gave her first concert in Louisville.

January 22 . . . There was a violent storm which reached tornado proportions on the river; 15 boatmen perished and 110 coal boats were sunk.

January 23 . . . The First Baptist Church opened on the northwest corner of Fourth and Walnut. This is now the *Walnut Street* Baptist Church, curiously located on Third and St. Catherine—Louisville's largest Baptist Church.

January 25 . . . There were 2 big fires this same day; one caused a loss of $10,000 to the Cathedral of the Assumption on Fifth Street, and the other destroyed a tobacco factory on Bullitt. During January there was discussion of proposals for changes and enlargment of the canal.

February 13 . . . The Louisville Female College completed its first session.

February 15 . . . The Louisville Board of Fire Underwriters (now one of the oldest organizations of its kind in the world) was chartered.

February 15 . . . The remodelling program at the Galt House (then located at Second and Main) was progressing nicely. A light was being installed on the top of the building as a guide for river pilots.

February 22 . . . A new public cistern located on Third Street between Green (now Liberty) and Walnut caved in for the second time.

February 22 . . . There was a big celebration of Washington's birthday, and of the 7th anniversary of the Battle of Buena Vista—where

66

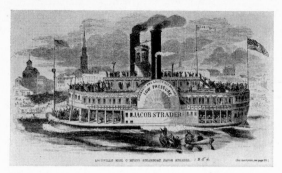

Steamboat Jacob Strader broke record in 1854

our local hero Zachary Taylor distinguished himself.

February 23 . . . A roving reporter reports that "Thieves about town now are as thick as peas, and they pursue their avocations with impunity".

February 23 . . . Much ado is made about a new 3-face clock being mounted in the new cupola of the Galt House, which it is claimed will run a year without winding. One of the dials, it is said, will be a calendar clock, designating the day, month and year.

March 6 . . . The Louisville Water Company is incorporated by an Act of the General Assembly.

March 9 . . . The German Insurance Company receives its charter, which gives it the right to perform banking functions as well as to write fire and general insurance. There were sixteen incorporators, most of them merchants of German extraction.

March 9 . . . The House of Refuge or School of Reform, a house of correction and instruction for juvenile delinquents, was chartered.

March 11 . . . The river was rising fast, the wharf was inundated, and the water was over the Third Street Bridge (the bridge over Beargrass Creek, which then emptied into the Ohio between Third and Fourth, forming a long narrow peninsula from that point east to the present "cut-off".)

March 14 . . . Editorial contains the statement that "The current revenue of the United States is greater than is required." (Happy day!)

March 15 . . . Ex-president Fillmore visits Louisville and big crowds turn out to greet him. The Court House lawn and Jefferson Street are the scene of the reception; guns are fired in salute; a big time was had by all.

March 15 . . . Editorial states that "every 5th person in the United States owns a horse". (Today it's cars—and horse *power!*)

March 27 . . . A grand ball took place at the Galt House, celebrating the opening of the remodelled and redecorated hostelry—the pride and joy of Louisville. (And rightly so, because Dickens and other distinguished Europeans said that it compared favorably with the finest abroad.)

April 1 . . . Newspaper crusading for better streets, reported that "scarcely a day passes that we do not observe in some of the streets the wreck of an unfortunate hack that has been jolted out of existence by the unconscionably rough streets for which Louisville is *famed*". (But that was April Fool's Day!)

April 8 . . . The temperature was 88° in the shade—but 9 days later there was an inch of snow.

May . . . Matt. F. Ward, socially prominent, and the brother of one of Louisville's most beautiful and glamorous society leaders, Sally Ward (later, Downs) was brought to trial for the murder of Wm. H. G. Butler, a teacher in the Louisville Public Schools who had disciplined Ward's younger brother. Public feeling ran so high that the trial had to be held in Elizabethtown. The newspapers, as usual, took opposite view points—some condemning Ward, others defending him. It seems that the majority of the people considered the crime a deliberate and premeditated murder. When the jury at Elizabethtown, no doubt influenced by the most brilliant defense lawyers that money could hire, gave a verdict of NOT GUILTY, the people of Louisville were profoundly shocked and a mob of 8,000 people gathered to denounce the verdict and the jury of the Harding County Circuit Court. They burned (in effigy, of course) all the principals in the case—Matt. Ward, himself; the members of the jury; the defense lawyers John J. Crittenden and Nat. Wolfe; and even the much-respected George D. Prentice, a character witness. The mob then went to the magnificent home of Matt. Ward's father, Robert J. Ward, the finest house in Louisville at that time—an edifice which stood on the north-east corner of Second and Walnut Streets—then a very fashionable neighborhood. These infuriated men threw stones, totally destroyed the large glass conservatory which contained a collection of rare plants of various kinds, and then set the house on fire. Firemen arrived in time to save the house, and the mob was finally appealed to, and quieted down and dispersed.

May 6 . . . The Steamboat Jacob Strader made a notable run from Louisville to Madison in 3 hours 19 minutes, establishing a new record. This was the heyday of the Steamboat, and there was intense competition among the builders and owners, resulting in several sensational races up and down the river.

May 8 . . . The Kentucky Mechanics Institute was chartered, with C. L. Stancliff as president. The Institute, according to a contemporary account, "holds annual exhibitions (of *what* it didn't say) supports a course of lectures, a school, and has a library containing about 5,000 volumes. There are about 1,000 readers, many of whom are ladies and minors".

May 13 . . . Woodland Gardens, a beautiful spot at the head of Market Street, running east from present Johnson Street, was opened to the public for the first time and a vast crowd attended, assuring its success from the beginning. This "family park" with excellent accommodations for food, drink and amusements was Louisville's principal park for many years. It comprised the approximate area now occupied by the Bourbon Stock Yards.

May 15 . . . Forty-four negro slaves, freed by owners in Louisville, were shipped by boat from Louisville down river en route to their native Liberia.

May 26 . . . There was a great annular eclipse of the sun, which attracted a lot of attention in Louisville, as elsewhere.

June 1 . . . There was a race meeting at Oakland Park, located at Seventh and Magnolia.

June 13 . . . The Italian Opera Company presented "Lucia di Lammermoor" and later "Don Giovanni" and other operas, and were warmly received.

June 24 . . . A popular vote was taken on whether or not to build the water works at the expense of the city; 1251 vote *for*, 1751 *against*. (Another victory for private enterprise? No— because on June 30, 1856, an ordinance was passed directing the mayor to subscribe for 5500 shares of stock in the water company to be paid for in bonds of the city. The ordinance was approved in September 1856 by a vote of the people, 1415 to 370. The water company finally became wholly owned by the city.)

June 30 . . . The railroad from Cincinnati to Louisville was completed.

July 6 . . . Another big fire on Main Street.

July 11 . . . Van Amburgh & Co's "Great Menagerie on a River Boat" stopped at Louisville and crowds flocked to see what was advertised as "All the wild beasts of the world!"

July 13 . . . Tolls were abolished on the Portland Canal, possibly because the competition of the railroads as carriers was beginning to be felt.

July 22 . . . There was a strong editorial against the carrying of concealed weapons, supposedly an "old Kentucky custom".

July 18 to August 4 . . . A great drouth, (that's what *they* thought, not having experienced the one 99 summers later). Temperatures stayed between 94 and 102; many were stricken with sunstroke.

August 27 . . . A tremendous storm with winds of 50 miles an hour and "with its rotary movement (tornado type) from 120 to 150 miles an hour" ripped thru Louisville, destroying the half-finished Third Presbyterian Church at 11th and Walnut and killing 18 of the congregation, mainly women and children. Fifty houses and two large warehouses were destroyed, three steamboats sunk, about 30 people seriously injured.

August 28 . . . Mayor James S. Speed proclaimed a day of mourning and services were held for the dead at the First Presbyterian Church by pastor Morrison of the church which had been destroyed the previous day; he was miraculously saved.

At the August election for county offices the "Know-Nothing" ticket was successful in Louisville, which bode no good for the city.

September 28 . . . The new building of the Mechanic's Institute was opened to the public; there was a big exhibition and a large assemblage turned out.

October 10 . . . Another meeting of the horses at Oakland. (Louisvillians always liked the ponies.)

October 19 . . . Beginning about this date there were a series of bank failures in the west, and the panic spread eastward. Louisville banks experienced runs, but practically all of them withstood the financial storm. The good showing made by Kentucky banks established Kentucky bank notes as standard bank funds throughout the Midwest and West.

October 28-9 ... There was a sudden out-break of cholera and eight deaths resulted on these two days.

November 2 ... The State Convention of the "Know-Nothing" Party was in session in Louis-ville.

During this month a great deal of work was done in improving the wharf and its facilities.

November 17 ... A big meeting was held, which the Governor of Indiana attended, to discuss plans for building a *tunnel* under the Ohio to connect Louisville with the Indiana side. It was estimated that the project would cost $1,200,000.00 and would take 12 months to complete. (If the idea got any further than this preliminary stage, we have failed to find note of it.)

November 30 ... A description of "The Charge of the Light Brigade" in the Crimean War (then in progress in Europe) was reported by the local press—a brave action immortalized later in Tennyson's stirring poem.

December 25 ... The Galt House menu for Christmas Day (still preserved by Col. Lucien Beckner at the Museum) describes one of the greatest dinners on record, as well as the biggest bargain in all culinary history!

Here is the Bill of Fare: saddle of venison with currant jelly; rib of beef with Poivards sauce, wild turkey with cranberry jelly, red-head duck stuffed plain, wood-duck with Hunter's sauce, wild goose with pot wine sauce, bridge of buf-falo tongue a la Godar, arcade of pheasants with green peas, venison boar's head. Choice of 4 soups, 2 fish, 9 hot meats, 10 cold ornamented meats, 36 entrees, 6 kinds of game, 7 relishes, 15 vegetables (1 of them baked hoe cake), 30 kinds of confections and cakes (with fancy French and Italian names), 2 puddings, 2 jellies, 5 kinds of nuts and apples for dessert—

Salon of a Palatial Steamboat of the 50's

and charlotte russe, as the top-off with Punch au Rhein! And the price—50 cents!!!

December 29 ... A monument to William H.G. Butler, the school master who was murdered by Matt. Ward, was erected and dedicated in Cave Hill Cemetery—a fitting but sad ending to the year 1854 in which the "big news" locally was this sensational murder trial, which scandalized the city and brought misery and disgrace to one of Louisville's leading families.

Present (1954) Louisville firms, besides Liberty National Bank and Trust Company, which be-gan in 1854 are the following: Louisville Water Company, Carter Dry Good Company, G. Bitt-ner's Sons, Swan-Abram Hat Company, Mul-doon Monument Company, Louisville Board of Insurance Agents (formerly Board of Fire Underwriters), and Liberty Insurance Agency, (formerly Liberty Fire Insurance Company) which had same origin as the bank but is now completely separated from the bank.

Chronology continued on page 72

End of Year 1854

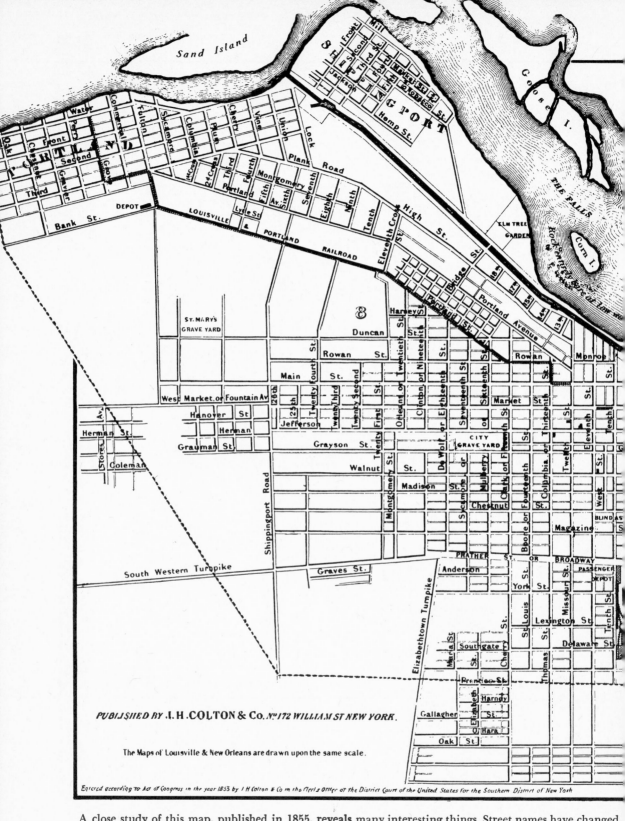

A close study of this map, published in 1855, **reveals** many interesting things. Street names have changed considerably since then and there are several **cases** of duplication. In fact there were *three* Fourth Streets —one in Louisville proper, one in Portland, and one in Shippingport—even though the dotted line shows that all were within the city limits of Louisville. Shippingport was a neat little town with 8 named streets (one was *Tobacco* Street); today it has one road and 2 or 3 houses. Note that there were alternate names for the streets from 14th to 20th; that Fourth north of Main was called *Wall Street* and the proper name of Broadway was *Prather*.

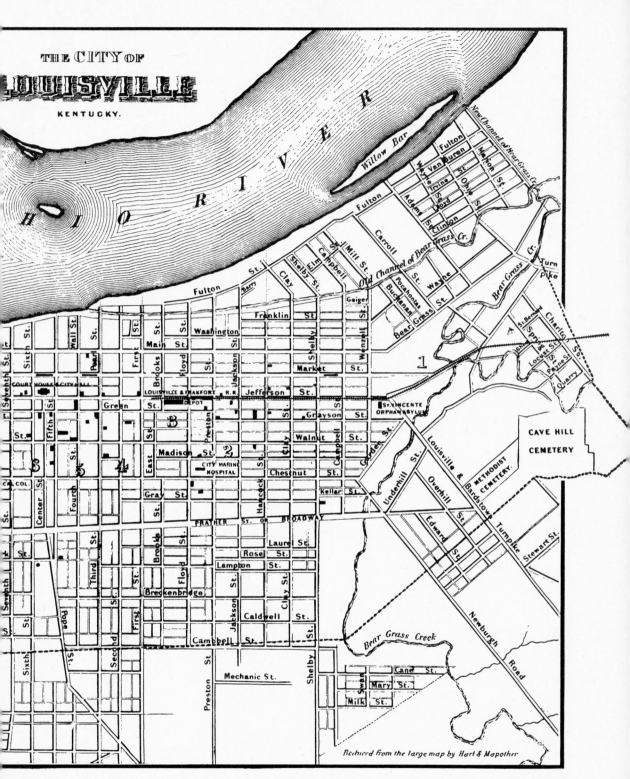

The Louisville and Frankfort Railroad depot was on Jefferson between Brook and Floyd, where the "hay-market" now is; upper Main was called Beargrass—yes, and while Beargrass Creek had a new channel from the "Cut-off" to the river, the old channel was still visible. St. Vincent Orphanage was at the head of Jefferson, the Blind Asylum on west Chestnut; Broadway west of 26th was the South Western Turnpike. There were no bridges across the river and Corn Island was still shown, although farther west than on an earlier map. Had it floated down-stream?

Chronology continued—

Louisville Y. M. C. A. founded.

Louisville and Nashville contract initiated (beginning of end of heyday for river traffic).

Barnum's famous Museum and Menagerie comes to town; featured Tom Thumb, 15 years old, 24″ tall, weight 15 lbs.

For 1854 see pages 61-69.

1855 February 3 . . . Ohio River frozen over for 11 days.

February 6 . . . The largest horse in the world now exhibiting at Louisville, "Magnus Apollo from Perryville, Ky. 20 hands high, of extraordinary grandeur and majesty of proportion and appearance".

February 22 . . . "Know-Nothing" state convention in Louisville.

April 7 . . . Know Nothing ticket successful at city election; John Barbee elected mayor; no opposing candidate. Mr. Speed says he is still mayor—term hasn't expired. Circuit court behind Speed, other departments with Barbee.

August 5 . . . Death at Galt House of Richard R. Robinson, the supposed murderer of Helen Jewett; for several years past he was known as Richard Parmelly.

August 6 . . . Bloody Monday—election day—violence, bloodshed, and houseburning especially in first and eighth wards—between 7 and 1 in the morning—12 houses north side of Main, east of 11th Street and others etc.—just saved new Shelby Street Catholic Church—about 22 were killed or died of wounds.

July . . . First actual laying of rails on L. & N. August 22 . . . reached point eight miles from Louisville.

Louisville Mutual Fire Association started in business.

A. Engelhard & Sons Co., established, wholesale grocers.

1856 February 25 . . . breaking up of ice bridge in Ohio, which had been closed for 53 days.

March 10 . . . death of "Old Ben Duke" a negro, 110 years old.

April 20 . . . Louisville Bridge Co. organized—Thos. W. Gibson, president.

October . . . Falls pilots at their own expense during the low water engaged in deepening and widening a channel over the falls.

October 13 . . . Rain falls, end of a severe drouth.

December 24 . . . Ohio gorged with ice.

December 31 . . . Medical Department of the U. of L. destroyed by fire—library and apparatus also; loss $100,000.

April 7 . . . New Male and Female High Schools were both opened to students this year—Female on Green between First and Second. (1864—Curd House; 1873—First Street Building; early 1900's—Fifth and Hill).

Hillerich and Bradsby Co.—Hillerich first shop on Clay Street near river.

General Box Co., founded as Bell & Coggeshall Co.—main line was steamboat cabins; made the one on the Robert E. Lee; in 1913 became Embry Box Company; in 1922 merged into General Box Company.

First bathtubs in Louisville were installed in the homes of Leven and Thomas Shreve, who lived in the large double-house on Walnut Street where the Armory now stands. Caused a major sensation; people came from miles around to see this marvel of the modern age.

L. S. Dinkelspiel Co. established.

Bradley & Gilbert Co. founded.

M. Sabel & Sons, established; wool, hides, furs.

1857 January 7 . . . river freezes; January 19 . . . 10 below zero. February 6 . . . river open.

February 9 . . . burning of a block of four warehouses and two other buildings on Main near Galt House; loss $250,000.

March 29 . . . complimentary public dinner at Galt House by citizens of Louisville for James Guthrie, Sect'y of Treasury.

May 12 . . . Edward Everett of Massachusetts delivers his great oration on life and character of Washington.

May 14 . . . Four slaves acquitted in Louisville of murder of Joyce family at south of Salt River some time before. Mob attacks jail; one commits suicide—mob hangs other three.

May 27 . . . Two of mob put in jail.

July 20 . . . Editorial street encounter in Louisville between Geo. D. Prentice, of the Journal, and Reuben T. Durrett, of the Courier; the former fired four times, the latter three times with pistols, neither hurt, but one shot from Mr. Prentice wounded G. D. Hinkle. Cause an editorial in the Courier, of a very personal nature. Sharp correspondence preceded and followed the shooting.

October 1 . . . Suspension of several banking houses in Louisville but feeling of confidence prevails—New York, Boston, and Cincinnati bank failures.

October 9-10-12 . . . tremendous runs on banks in New York; Kentucky banks refuse to expend specie payments.

Citizens Guard organized in May.

March . . . Ground broken for Louisville Water Co. Reservoir in a primeval beech forest on the high ground off present Mellwood.

Continued on page 79

SOME HISTORIC CHURCHES
OF LOUISVILLE

Cathedral of the Assumption

On Fifth Street, north of Walnut, stands this impressive Gothic brick Cathedral, its spire towering over all others in the city—the focal point of the Catholic life of Louisville for more than 100 years. Ninety six times a day its chimes have counted the quarter hours of the most eventful century in all history.

Pius IX was Pope, Zachary Taylor was President of the U.S., Benedict Joseph Flaget was Bishop of Louisville on August 15, 1849, when the cornerstone of this Cathedral was laid. (Flaget's body now lies in its crypt).

Designed by William Keely of Baltimore, the building is 200 by 80 by 70 feet in height, with a spire of over 300 feet including a 24-foot cross. In the belfry hangs a 4,500 pound bell, made in Paris in 1858, the gift of the Archbishop of Mexico. The cathedral's most prized treasure is an ancient painting of St. Bernard with the Sacred Host, done in the manner of Van Dyke—now attributed to Gaspar de Crayer (1584-1669).

This photograph was taken about 60 years ago.

73

A BRIEF HISTORY
OF THE EARLY CHURCHES
OF LOUISVILLE

An Episcopalian minister, the Rev. William Kavanaugh, in 1803 had charge of a church in Louisville.

Marriage certificates signed by him as deacon of the Methodist church in the year 1797 are on file in the County Court House, but after that date he signed such papers as an *Episcopalian* minister. According to tradition there was an early church in Louisville near the corner of Twelfth and Main but this was a "general" church in which all denominations worshipped,

Sixth & Green in 1856—Looking south toward[Pres]byterian and (right) St. Paul's Episcopal. Sup[pose] this busy one-way street today! No danger the[re]

First Baptist Church, Fourth & Walnut (where Selman's is now)

not one belonging exclusively to one religious sect. It was a rude structure of logs, 30' x 20'. In 1812 it was sold for taxes and torn down. (Churches paid taxes then?)

In 1811, the first Catholic church was built on the northern end of the half-acre lot on the northwest corner of 10th and Main. The money to buy the lot and erect the building was furnished by citizens generally, but particularly by the French Catholics then resident here. The house was of brick in the Gothic style of architecture and was the handsomest building that had up to that time been erected in the town. Father Badin purchased the ground and planned the building.

In 1812, the Methodists erected their first church on the north side of Market, between Seventh and Eighth Streets. Here Bishop Asburg preached and made an entry in his journal: "I preached in Louisville at 11 o'clock in our new brick house, 34 x 30 feet."

ut. The two churches are (left) First Pres-
ou tried to stand and talk in the middle of

They joined with the Free Masons and erected a large two-story brick building, with the Baptists using the lower floor and the Masons the upper. Contrary to the custom of the early Baptists, who were wont to call their church edifices "Meeting Houses", this church was known as "The Church of Christ."

We quote the following 1852 description, of some of Louisville's churches: "The tasteful and elegant structures which many of these churches have erected are great additions to the beauty of the city. Those most worthy of note are the Walnut Street Baptist, First Presbyterian, Catholic Cathedral, St. Paul's (Episcopal), and the Synagogue."

1816, the Presbyterians erected their first urch on the west side of Fourth, between arket and Jefferson Streets. It was a brick ifice, distinguished not only for its size and od arrangements, but for the silver-toned ll that hung high up in its belfry. The church s burned in 1836, and the loss of this bell s regretted by the people almost as much the church. As the flames consumed the body the church and rose to the belfry, the bell s kept ringing by Nathan Martin until it l among the ruins and was hushed forever.

1824, Christ Church was erected by the iscopalians on Second Street between Green d Walnut.

ie Baptists were the first to preach in Louis- le but they were comparatively late in hav- g a church edifice. They preached in the forts Louisville; in 1815 they organized a church, t had no church edifice for several years after- rd.

First Presbyterian Church, Green & Sixth
(another view of church shown in center above)

75

THE CHURCH THAT BECAME A SCOTTISH RITE CATHEDRAL

St. Paul's Episcopal Church, shown on the left in a woodcut, was one of Louisville's first churches. It was organized November 1, 1834, when the wardens and vestrymen were elected. A building committee met in Christ Church December 10, 1835, to plan the raising of funds for the new church. They decided to seek 20 persons who would give notes for $500 each, to be discounted and used to start the building. A small church 26 x 60 was originally planned, but ended up in a building 80 x 100 feet.

After St. Paul's had served its purpose as a church for many years, it became the Scottish Rite Cathedral with the architectural changes noted in the photograph below. It is now a parking lot.

St. Paul's Episcopal Church
Sixth Street near Walnut—from an old woodcut.

This large impressive structure on the corner of Sixth & Broadway was originally Temple Adath Israel, later the Methodist Temple. It is now a used car lot. (From an early woodcut.)

76

Christ Church Cathedral

**Oldest Church
in Louisville
419 S. Second St.**

Started in 1822, finished in 1824; new facade added in 1872.

The first Episcopal church in Kentucky was Christ Church in Lexington, founded in 1794. The first impulse to establish an Episcopal church in Louisville was felt in about 1820, when the Rev. Asa Baldwin of Western New York preached here.

A group of men including Hancock Taylor, James S. Bate, Richard Ferguson, James C. Johnston, William Croghan and Richard Barnes met May 31, 1822 and organized Christ Church of Louisville. On May 8, 1823, they adopted the plan for the construction of the church.

While the building was in progress, meetings were held in a temporary building, a frame house near 5th and Jefferson, site of the present Court House. Mr. Peter B. Ormsby, one of the original vestrymen, agreed to give the church all the ground needed on Second Street up to 5 acres, but the senior warden, Richard Barnes,

Continued on page 79

LOUISVILLE'S "NOTRE DAME"

The Church of Our Lady in Portland, was originally called *Notre Dame,* because it was the church of the French Settlement in Shippingport and Portland.

The first church on this site was completed in 1839, and the first Mass offered in September 22 of that year, by the Rev. N. J. Perche, the pastor. The dedication services took place on October 8, 1941 with Bishop Flaget participating. Solemn high Mass was sung by the Rev. S. T. Badin; the Rev. James McGill preached the sermon; the chorus was from the church of St. Louis. The second Church of Our Lady was dedicated November 13, 1866 by Bishop McCloskey and the Rev. J. L. Spalding.

The damage done by many floods has made it necessary to rebuild this church twice. The present structure was completed in 1873; the interior has recently been redecorated; and it is one of the most attractive of the older churches of Louisville.

"Notre Dame"—The Church of Our Lady on Rudd Avenue in Portland—founded by the French colony.

When the First Christian Church was at Fourth & Walnut. These columns are now in new church at 4th & Breckinridge.

REV. STEPHEN THEODORE BADIN
Louisville's second Catholic Priest.

In the spring of the year 1787, there were already about fifty Catholic families in Kentucky. The Rev. Mr. Whelan, a zealous and talented Irish priest, was the first pastor in Louisville. He remained until 1790 when he returned to Maryland. The Catholics of Kentucky were without a pastor until the Rev. Stephen Theodore Badin was sent them.

The first Catholic church was built by Father Badin "near the river bank and in the western part of the town." The second Catholic church was erected by the Rev. Robert Abell and was opened for divine service in 1832.

Christ Church Cathedral *continued*—

failed to have the ground surveyed and the deed executed. Financial reverses later caused Ormsby to lose this land and the church lost all except the ground on which it was built. The burial ground, which was then in the rear of the church, belonged to Ormsby's daughter Mrs. Mary O. Gray, and was later presented to the church. Christ Church was completed before the end of 1824.

In 1872, the church was enlarged, the front wall of the original building was removed, and a new facade of native limestone was erected in Neo-Gothic style. Two towers, one topped with a spire and a cross, were included in the latter facade. Christ Church was consecrated as a Cathedral in 1894.

Chronology continued—

September . . . Construction of pumping station in river begun.

Great National Agricultural Fair here.

Masonic Temple begins.

1858 Fire Department reorganized; all voluntary before this time; now have steam fire engines, with 65 men and 23 horses.

Woodland Race Course—a few gentlemen formed Woodland Association; stock $50,000; purchased beautiful place on Frankfort Railroad five miles from city; regular spring and fall races provided; on what is now Crescent Hill.

Bourbon Stockyards opened its doors.

Woodland Course fell into disuse at close of 60's.

Wm. Preston of Louisville, Minister to Spain '58-'61.

April 11 ect. . . . Very heavy rain with much damage—statewide and through Mississippi valley. Remarkable revival of religion; 428 accessions to five Methodist churches in Louisville.

October 13 . . . Brilliant comet known as the "Great Comet of 1858" has been visible to the naked eye since August 29 and observed through telescopes since June 28.

United States Government Building at Third and Green completed.

DuPont completed Artesian Well on Twelfth Street between Main and River; wanted clear water for paper mill at 120 N. 10th Street; at depth of 2086 feet sulfur water was struck (330,000 gallons per day). (Well was capped and flow stopped several years ago.)

American Printing House, chartered in 1858, located on grounds of Kentucky School for Blind, (today is largest braille publishing house in the world).

Work resumed on Court House after twenty years.

Old "Union Station" dedicated; city celebrated; wood burner carried first official load of freight.

The Bradley & Gilbert Company, paper box manufacturers, founded by Thomas Bradley and James C. Gilbert.

1859 Joseph Holt of Louisville, Postmaster General, 1859-1860.

April 25 . . . James Porter, seven-foot-nine giant dies at Shippingport.

Court House completed; cost $500,000.

Tobacco sales 18,452 hogheads (up from 7500 hogheads in 1850).

Sixty miles of paved streets.

First horse cars put into service from Portland

wharf to 12th Street, connecting with omnibus which ran east on Main to Wenzel.

Course of Beargrass Creek changed—now entering two miles up at "cut off"; old bed filled.

October 27 . . . First train, a special, left Louisville and in ten hours arrived in Nashville.

Darwin's Origin of Species published.

Falls City Tin Tag and Lithograph Company, founded, under name of German & Brother. Washington Mutual Fire Insurance Co., founded.

1860 March 27 . . . City Council set apart the tract of land south of the city, known as Oakland Cemetery, for the purpose of establishing a House of Refuge.

September 1 . . . Merchants Bank of Kentucky, incorporated.

January 24 . . . Legislatures of Tennessee and Kentucky meet at Louisville and are eloquently entertained by the city and citizens.

May 21 . . . Most destructive tornado ever known along valley of Ohio for 900 miles; passed from Louisville to Portsmouth, Ohio (245 miles) desolating a space forty miles wide in two hours; 75 lives lost on river boats alone.

May 27 . . . Violent windstorm, 1:00 A.M., much property damage, no lives lost.

August 7 . . . Earthquake shocks at Henderson, felt slightly at Louisville.

December 5 . . . United States Treasury suspends specie payment.

December 8 . . . Kentucky Banks determine such a measure would afford no commercial relief, continue to pay specie as usual.

Chas. Rosenheim & Co., established, crockery and glassware wholesale business.

Citizens Guard becomes part of State Guard.

Water turned into city mains.

Railroad tunnel through Muldraugh Hill completed.

Mr. Theodore Ahrens, Sr. started brass foundry on Market between Preston and Jackson—the beginning of The Standard Sanitary Corporation.

Court House occupied.

Struck Construction Company began business.

Fulton, Conway & Co. founded from a partnership with W. Fulton & T. L. Clark.

1861 Fort Sumter fired on.

Long & Brother Manufacturing Co. started; American Bent-wood furniture.

Cave Hill National Cemetery established in Cave Hill.

April 18 . . . Union meeting at Louisville. James Guthrie, Archibald Dixon, Wm. F. Bullock,

and John Young Brown address meeting and favor a "Mediatorial position".

April 23 . . . Louisville City Council appropriates $50,000 to arm and defend the city.

July 3 . . . A brilliant comet visible from dark to 10 P.M.

Louisville Transfer Co. started; now the Louisville Taxicab & Transfer Co. (Yellow Cabs).

Carriage or "hack" of Louisville Transfer Co. Reprinted from an early advertisement.

October . . . 16 Hon. Simon Cameron, United States Secretary of War, and Brig. Gen. L. Thomas, Adjutant General of U.S. army visits Louisville to consult with Gen. Sherman, Gen. Wood and Hon. James Guthrie as to the conduct of the war in Kentucky.

December 22, 23 . . . 145 tons of ammunition received at Louisville in two days for United States troops.

Levy Bros. NE corner of Third and Market, established by Moses Levy and Henry Levy. Louisville known as City of Flags.

Mozart's Society musical library was burned; (in 1862 they gave their final concert).

August 31 . . . First parade of Home Guard, 2000 strong, under General Pope.

Fort construction begun—eleven forts with earthen breastworks in semicircle around city, from Paddy's Run to Clifton on the Brownsboro Road.

Nicola Marshall a Louisvillian, designed Confederate flag.

February 22 . . . Washington's birthday celebration in front of Court House.

1862 January . . . Gen. Buell's Union Army reaches Louisville.

January 23 . . . Flood of 1862, higher than at any time since 1847.

R. Mansfeld & Son, incorporated, started under name of R. Mansfeld on March 15th, 1862.

March 25 . . . Board of Trade organized by leading merchants, manufacturers and business men of Louisville who had become convinced that it was necessary for their mutual protection. First president, George W. Morris. First office, Main W. of 6th.

June 6 . . . 930 soldiers have died in the military hospitals at Louisville since September 16, 1861,—less than nine months.

July 12, 13 . . . Immense excitement and alarm at Louisville from exaggerated reports of Morgan's force and exploits.

July 13 . . . General Boyle at his Louisville headquarters issues an order "that every able bodied man take arms and aid in repelling the marauders; every man who does not join will remain in his house 48 hours, and be shot down if he leaves it" most stores closed.

July 16 . . . Arrest of citizens charged with disloyalty increasing; 13 arrested this day alone.

August 2 . . . Steamboat "Commodore Perry" burns at Louisville dock; three dead, two hurt.

July 22 . . . Two religious Louisville newspapers closed.

September 3 . . . Legislature in session at Louisville resolved "that the invasion of the state by the rebels must be resisted".

September 17 . . . Louisville fortifying against the expected approach of Gen. E. Kirby Smith's forces.

W. S. Mathews & Sons, tobacco firm, established.

W. A. Stratton and Jacob Thome, Jr., started firm now known as Stratton & Terstegge.

September 22 . . . General Nelson orders the women and children to be sent out of Louisville preparatory to a battle with the Confederates.

September 25 . . . Gen. Buell's Federal Army reaches Louisville having outmarched Gen. Bragg.

September 29 . . . Gen. Wm. Nelson shot in Galt House in a personal difference with Brig. Gen. Jeff. E. Davis of Indiana—died in fifteen minutes.

October 1 . . . Confederate pickets within six miles of Louisville but main body 25-30 miles away; Gen. Buell leaves Louisville in pursuit; Gen. McCook's corps, the left wing on the Taylorsville Road; Gen. Gilbert's on the Shepherdsville; and Gen. Crittenden's, the right wing, on the Bardstown pike.

October 8 . . . Battle of Perryville, after which train of 700 wounded arrives in Louisville.

November 5 . . . Gen. Boyle orders all confederate prisoners in Kentucky to Louisville to go to Vicksburg.

November 25 . . . Louisville 'Courier' printing establishment sold at auction, in the absence of owner in south, to Louisville 'Democrat' Company for $6,150.

August and September . . . Two pontoon bridges constructed across Ohio; one where Big Four is now, another between New Albany and Portland.

Union gunboats patrol river.

Louisville & Nashville tracks built to water's edge at First Street; ferrys used to take across river.

Athenaem, Male High Literary Society founded,—oldest of its kind in the nation.

Landing of Ohio Troops at Louisville.

T. B. Duncan & Sons, established, first under the names of Duncan & Brooks.

1863 January 1 . . . Lincoln issued Emancipation Proclamation.

First of famous Magnolia hams cured by McFerran & Menefee, 7,500 cured. In 1887—375,000 hams!—Firm: McFerran, Shallcross & Co.; R. J. Menefee, and W. P. Clancy.

Joseph B. Gathright, details mechanic for Kentucky Cavalry saddles; forerunner of Harbison & Gathright.

Philip Fink & Sons, roofers, established.

January 15, 16 . . . One of heaviest falls of snow ever known in Kentucky—18 inches.

February 2 . . . A letter from Col. Laban J. Bradford, of Augusta, shows that Kentucky is largest tobacco growing state.

The Louisville warehouses in 1857 sold a little over 8,000 hogsheads, in 1861 about 29,500—one house alone selling more than the entire sales of Liverpool, England.

February 8 . . . Richard Springer, a 104-year old Revolutionary Soldier, still living in Louisville, fought at Brandywine, wounded at Germantown, never received a pension from the government.

March 4 . . . Kentucky bank notes at Louisville at 14% premium.

March 18, 19 . . . Union Democratic State Convention at Louisville.

April 5 . . . William Kaye elected mayor by 710 majority over Thomas H. Crawford, both 'Union', the former supported by the 'Democrat' and the latter by the 'Journal' newspaper.

April 17 . . . Suspension of tobacco manufactories at Louisville, throwing 3,000 operatives out of employment.

April 30 . . . President Lincoln set aside this day (Thursday) "as a day of national humiliation and prayer".

May 27 . . . $1,600 for premium tobacco distributed at the Kentucky State exhibition at Louisville.

July 6, 7, 8 . . . Morgan's forces enter Indiana.

July 8 . . . Great alarm in Louisville caused by approach of Gen. Morgan's Confederate cavalry. City Council orders "enrollment of all males between 18 and 45 into companies for service, if required, and all refusing to be enrolled shall be sent to the north." Nearly 5,000 enrolled and actively drilling.

July 11 . . . Saturday night about 100 of Morgan's cavalry attempt to cross the Ohio at 12 Mile Island above Louisville on a woodboat; but the gunboat 'Moose' shells the island, and Gen. Manson with a large force on 10 steamboats arrives in time to capture many of them.

July 12 . . . At a sale in Louisville, bank shares brought $100 for Northern Bank; $96 each for Bank of Kentucky and Bank of Louisville.

July 18-20 . . . Morgan defeated.

Epping Bottling Works established by H. Epping.

Jacob Schulz started florist business.

August 6 . . . In U.S. District Court here, Judge Bland Ballard sentences Thomas C. Shacklett, convicted of treason, to 10 years imprisonment in the Louisville jail, a fine of $10,000 and to have his slaves emancipated.

December 24 . . . First lot of sugar and molasses received here by the river from New Orleans since the Confederates established a blockade of the Mississippi in 1861.

December 30 . . . Sale of slaves near Louisville; man aged 28, $500; boy aged 11, $350; women aged 18, $430, and 19, $380.

The "Louisville", an ironclad steamer that fought on the Mississippi, made its appearance here.

1864 Population—over 80,000.

Masonic Savings Bank chartered—the scheme was to make the bank a savings institution for the Masonic fraternity. Did not work out.

Public Schools are "the pride of the city".

January 18 . . . Col. Bruce closes number of "coffee shops" for selling liquor to soldiers.

March 1 . . . Shacklett (sentenced to 10 years in 1863), takes amnesty oath and is freed from jail.

May 22-July 24 . . . Severe drought.

July 1 . . . Great fire in Louisville on Main between 8th and 9th; loss $1,500,000 of which $800,000 government stores.

July 15 . . . Over 12,000 negroes have been taken out of Kentucky and enlisted elsewhere.

July 16 . . . Two negro regiments have been organized here.

July 18 . . . Twenty four women and children reach Louisville military prison, being arrested and sent there by Gen. Sherman.

August 10 . . . Louisville 'Democrat' says: "A large number of political prisoners are confined in the military barracks here, and the number is being increased daily by the arrival of prisoners arrested in other portions of the state."

August 25 . . . Trade restrictions removed in city on marketing.

November . . . Many political prisoners released here after oath and bond.

December 31-January 1 . . . Temperature fell from 45 degrees to 20 degrees below zero with blinding snowstorm.

Louisville City Railway Co., first road to operate by horsepower; first lines built were the 'Main' Street, running from 12th to Beargrass, and the 'Portland' from 12th to Portland Ferry Landing.

Otis Hidden Co. established by H. Herold, Market Street between 2nd and 3rd.

A few companies of Union soldiers were on Corn Island which was city's most popular resort for old-fashioned fish fries, picnics, boating, restaurants, beer gardens, etc.

Bosse Funeral Home established by Henry and Joseph Bosse, brothers.

Dearing Printing Company began.

1865 January 11 . . . Early morning, Galt House was burned; two dead; over $1,000,000 loss.

Falls City Bank chartered; this bank was later robbed of $300,000.00.

Thomas C. Caummisar begins making brooms in stable at Hancock and Walnut.

January 27 . . . Military prison burned.

March 1 . . . A dash was made into a part of Louisville by a small party of guerrillas, who carried off two valuable horses owned by Capt. Julius Fasses, Assistant Inspector General of cavalry; only time during the war that enemy penetrated the corporate limits of the city.

April 18 . . . (Four days after Lincoln's death) —Speeches, resolutions, and a funeral procession three miles long was formed and moved sadly through the principal streets.

July 19 . . . First recorded game of baseball— 19th and Field (Duncan) Street, between Cumberlands of Nashville and an unnamed 9 of Louisville. Louisville won 20-5.

Harbison and Gathright established by Josiah B. Gathright. (John J. Harbison organized first YMCA in Louisville).

June 3 . . . Louisville Bridge and Iron Co. incorporated; 11th and Oak.

Farmers Home Journal began publication.

Robert Rowell established first stereotype company in city.

Continued on page 94

Good Shepherds for 112 years

THE SISTERS OF THE GOOD SHEPHERD have been known in Louisville for 112 years for the good work they have done in rescuing and caring for outcast girls and women. The order was founded in France, but in 1842 five Sisters were selected to establish the order in America. This devout group reached Louisville, December 1, 1842, at a time when there was great antagonism to both foreigners and Catholics. They were sheltered by the Lorettine Sisters until a house could be found.

Bishop Joseph Flaget of Bardstown purchased a lot on Eighth Street between Walnut and Madison, and by September 4, 1843, the Sisters were installed in their new convent, where they have carried on their good work ever since, taking care of the physical and spiritual needs of female delinquents, derelicts and others who need loving care and understanding.

This venerable and yet attractive building is one of Louisville's oldest landmarks; it is known as the "cradle" of the order in the United States, and for many years was the Provincial House of the Order in America. On September 8, 1943 the Sisters of the Good Shepherd celebrated the completion of a century of their mission of mercy to both white and negro penitents—without benefit of state, county or municipal funds or the Community Chest.

The graceful, winding stone staircase behind cloistered walls gives an Old World atmosphere to this venerable building at 518 S. Eighth Street, which is the Mother House of the Sisters of the Good Shepherd in Louisville.

The old Masonic Home for Widows and Orphans. The new Home in Crescent Hill is a model of modern planning.

The original section of the old Baptist Orphans' Home on First Street at St. Catherine.

The Young Men's Christian Association (YMCA) was located in this old residence at Fourth & Broadway before the present fine building at 3rd & Broadway was constructed. Previously had been at 5th & Walnut.

History of the Louisville Baptist Children's Home

The Louisville Baptist Orphans' Home, (now Spring Meadows) had its beginning in The War Between the States as "The Orphans' Aid Society." This organization of Baptist women aided the children made orphans by the War, by finding homes for them.

Dr. George C. Lorimer, pastor of the old Walnut Street Baptist Church, and father of the famed editor of the Saturday Evening Post, was responsible for the establishment of the first Baptist Children's Home in Louisville. On June 30, 1869, "The Home for Helpless Children" was opened in a rented house at 828 W. Walnut Street. Miss Mary A. Hollingsworth was the first superintendent and served for thirty-six years—till 1905.

On March 21, 1870 ground was broken at First and St. Catherine for a permanent home on a site given by Dr. and Mrs. J. Lawrence Smith; the children and staff moved to the new building in December 1870. At this time Louisville was much smaller and the corner of First and St. Catherine was on the outskirts. Fifty years later it was in the center of a crowded midtown section.

On January 21, 1950, the Home left the antiquated building and moved to a complete new plant, called Spring Meadows, built on the

COMMUNITY CHEST—OVER THE TOP IN 1953
Lyman L. Dawson headed the campaign.

cottage plan, on a beautiful 87-acre tract at Middletown. This plant is one of the finest in the country and embodies the latest ideas for the care of dependent children.

Sam Ed Bradley is superintendent; V. V. Cooke president of the board of trustees.

St. Joseph's Orphans' Home (founded 1849) moved to their Crescent Hill Home in 1886.

St. Joseph's Orphans' Home was established in August, 1849, when there were only two German Catholic parishes in Louisville, St. Boniface and St. Mary's—both poor, and both having many orphans to take care of. Fifty men of the two parishes met with the Rev. Boeswald and established St. Joseph's Orphans' Society, now the oldest layman group of its kind in Louisville.

The first St. Joseph's children's home was at St. Mary's. The first officers were Jos. Bossant, president; Nicholas Vorndron, vice-president; Jacob Pfalzer, secretary; and Bernard Reiling, treasurer. By 1859 larger quarters were needed and the Society bought the large colonial home of Jason Rogers at Jackson and Fehr, where it remained till 1886, when the large new home shown in this old cut was built on the 24-acre tract in Crescent Hill.

This building, greatly enlarged and remodeled is now the home of 122 orphaned children. Latest addition to the facilities will be a $65,000 junior-size gymnasium for which funds are now being raised. Actually the first orphanage in Louisville was started by Mother Catherine Spalding in 1832 in a building next to the present Cathedral of the Assumption.

This original building of the German Protestant Orphans' Home was located on West Jefferson Street; it was unroofed in the severe 1854 storm. Home is now on Bardstown Road.

All these buildings—on Madison and Chestnut east of Brook have been razed to enlarge Louisville

THE JEWISH HOSPITAL was 51 years old last February; it was organized on February 6, 1903; incorporated April 1, 1903. The original building at Floyd and Kentucky, with 6 wards and 8 private rooms was dedicated May 15, 1905. The entire building cost $26,456. The first administrator was paid $60.00 a month! The Bernheim family paid for a remodeling program in 1929 which increased the size to 100 beds and gave the hospital a nurses' home.

Norton Memorial Infirmary

This is the original section of the Norton Infirmary which today forms only a small part of the hospital —the infirmary being extremely modern in every respect. This location at Third and Oak is the site of Civil War Barracks.

86

Medical Center" and make room for the new $2,650,000 Jewish Hospital now under construction.

The idea for the new Jewish Hospital, as part of the Louisville "Medical Center", started to take shape in 1944—and a drive for funds in 1946 realized $800,000 in pledges. The new hospital, now under construction, adjacent to General Hospital, will cost a total of $2,649,473.00—$1,284,065.88 provided by United States Government Hill-Burton Funds. Capacity will be 118 beds—to be increased to 250 when two more floors are added at some future time.

The Grand Old Medical College of U. of L.

The old pump on the corner dates this picture—it was taken about 1900, possibly earlier — but the building has not changed at all in 50 years in external appearance. Ideally located at First and Chestnut it is an essential unit of Louisville's growing Medical Center.

DR. DANIEL DRAKE
Famous 100 years ago in Louisville & Cincinnati,
Dr. Drake wrote a monumental medical work.

DR. L. P. YANDELL
Professor of Physiology at Louisville Medical
Institute (1845) and Medical Dept. U of L (1849)

The old City Hospital, preceding present General Hospital, was opened February 18, 1870. On same 7-acre location, it was one of the most imposing buildings of its day.

The children of the Kentucky pioneers—and early Louisvillians—went to schools like this.

THE STORY OF GRADE AND HIGH SCHOOLS

MANN BUTLER
Louisville's first school principal

There were two eminent educators of early Louisville named Butler; Mann Butler, first principal of Louisville's first public school—and Noble Butler (apparently no kin) who was an outstanding grammarian, teacher, and author of textbooks.

Mann Butler is known to us principally (no pun intended) as the author of a quite interesting and extensive Sketch of Louisville which appeared in the first Directory of Louisville (1832) and occupied more than a third of that small volume.

Noble Butler came to Louisville as a Professor of Greek and Latin in 1839, joining the faculty of the new Louisville college. At this time there were seven "free" schools in Louisville, but nearly 40 private schools—all conducted by "gentlemen of great reputation." Butler soon opened a private school of his own for girls, and also found time to write a new English grammar, which became the standard accepted textbook for all Kentucky schools. Later he revised a whole series of "readers" on which several generations of Louisville boys and girls grew up.

Noble Butler was the older brother of Will Butler, who was killed by Matt. Ward in one of Louisville's most sensational murder cases.

PROF. "RUBE" HALLECK
One of the great Louisville educators of the past 50 years. Principal of Male High—"in the good old days."

In 1917 Male High merged with duPont Manual in this beautiful building; but it didn't last.

Louisville Military Institute

Surprising Facts About Our Schools

Eight buildings, each over 100 years old, are today used by 4000 students of Louisville's Public Schools. (See photographs 2 pages further on.)

Twelve buildings, 75 years old are used by 6000 students.

Fifteen Public School buildings 50 years old house 7000 students.

More than 8,000 Public School students are housed in portable buildings.

Only four new public schools have been built in Louisville in 20 years: duPont Manual High School in 1934; Hazelwood and Sallie B. Rutherford in 1951; and Central High School in 1952.

HISTORY OF OUR PUBLIC SCHOOLS

In 1829, one year after the City of Louisville received its first charter, the Town Council adopted an ordinance which established a school to be free to all white children between the ages of 6 and 14. Control was vested in six trustees, to be elected annually by the Mayor and Board of Councilmen.

The trustees rented the upper story of the Old Baptist Church on the southwest corner of Fifth and Green (Liberty), and on August 17, 1829, opened the school. The attendance soon reached 250 pupils, all of whom were housed in a single room. With so large an enrollment the school could not long continue to be housed in the church.

Therefore, the first public school building was erected on the corner of Fifth and Walnut Streets, at a cost of $2,100. It was opened in September, 1830. By 1840 there were 14 public schools, exclusive of the Louisville College (later to become the University of Louisville) which had been started in 1837. These 14 schools had a total attendance of about 1,000 pupils.

By 1850, there were 5 grammar schools, one for girls and one for boys in the building at Fifth and Walnut Streets; a male and female grammar school in a building on Jefferson Street between Floyd and Preston; and a male grammar school on Tenth between Walnut and Grayson. In addition, there were 18 primary schools.

A second charter, granted the city in 1851, placed all the schools in the city in charge of an elected Board of Trustees, two from each ward. In 1911, the law was changed to provide for a five-member Board of Education, elected at large.

The first public schools for Negroes were opened in 1870. These schools were established in the Center Street Church and the Fifth Street Church. In 1872 elementary schools were opened at Fourteenth and Broadway and at Campbell and Chestnut Streets. Then followed: the Central School at 6th and Kentucky in 1873; the Eastern School at Jackson and Breckinridge Streets in 1874; and the Western School on Magazine Streets between 15th and 16th in 1875. In 1887 a branch of the Western School was opened at Ninth and Walnut.

The first high school for Negroes was established at Central in 1882. The Normal School was established in 1897. Between 1882 and 1896 there were established California, Main Street, Maiden Lane, Portland, Eighth and Kentucky Streets, Douglas, Wilson Street, Grayson Street, and Lincoln Schools. In 1895 the high school for Negroes was moved to Ninth and Magazine and in 1912 it was moved to the old University Square on Chestnut between Eighth and Ninth. In 1952 the magnificient new Central High, at 12th and Chestnut was completed.

A Famous Girls' School in Portland Over One Hundred Years Ago

St. Benedict's Academy, also called "Cedar Grove Academy", was located across the street from The Church *of Our Lady* in Portland (see section on Early Churches of Louisville).

The Catholic Almanac of 1843 gives the following information on St. Benedict's Academy:

"On the first of September 1842, an Academy, for the instruction of young ladies was opened under the patronage of The Reverend Bishop, within a few miles of Louisville and adjoining the town of Portland. It is conducted by the Sisters from the Institution of Loretta, Marion County, Ky., whose qualifications and long experience in the instruction of youths will insure the rapid progress of all who shall be entrusted to their direction.

"The site chosen for this institution, and known as Cedar Grove, is elevated and beautiful. The house, which has been recently fitted out at great expense, is well suited for its present destination. It will afford comfortable accommodations to a large number of boarders."

Cedar Grove continued as a highly-thought-of school for girls until 1925, when the Sisters of Loretta bought an estate near the foot of Broadway and established Loretta High School there.

St. Benedict's Seminary—Cedar Grove

The School for the Blind

Printing House for the Blind

1836—GEORGE D. PRENTICE SCHOOL

1853—PAUL DUNBAR SCHOOL

1852—GEORGE W. MORRIS SCHOOL

All of these Louisville Public Schools are over 100 years old

The Lucie N. Duvalle School, 8th & Chestnut (old U. of L. building) is 118 years old

-and all are in daily use!

1853—S. COLERIDGE TAYLOR SCHOOL

1853—EMMA DOLFINGER SCHOOL

1853—MARGARET MERKER SCHOOL

1853—PORTLAND SCHOOL

Female High School— Later Became Male

This handsome building was planned in 1870 by the School Board as the new Female High School, and it was built and ready for occupancy at the beginning of the fall term, 1873. It was an imposing stone structure located on First Street just north of the Medical College. It served as Girls' High for many years; then for a short period became Male High after that school moved from 9th and Chestnut and *before* it moved to Brook and Breckinridge in 1917, to become for a few years the Louisville Boys' High School— a consolidation of Male and Manual that did not work.

First, Newcomb Home; then Louisville Female Seminary; now St. Xavier High School.

Originally the "palatial Newcomb Place" on the entire block between 1st and 2nd on Broadway— in 1890 this was the exclusive Female Seminary, better known as "Miss Annie Nold's School." Purchased in 1892 by the Xaverian Brothers it became St. Xavier's College—now "St. X" High School. Six Xaverian brothers, of the teaching order founded in Belgium in 1839, came to Louisville in 1854—"to teach the Indians in America."

Introduced here by Bishop Spalding, they started several grammar schools. Their first high school was established in 1874 on Fourth where Loew's is now; 18 years later they acquired their present location, above. Note change in the facade of this building, which was moved forward and wings and a third story added.

1866 May 31 . . . National Tobacco Fair was held here.

Mutual Life Insurance Company of Kentucky organized.

July 24-29 . . . First National Saengerfest in the West held here; a sectional one had been held here in 1850. Special building erected on corner 5th and Broadway, seating 5,000; first time Louisville heard selections from Lohengrin.

October 5 . . . Died in Breckinridge county, Fred A. Kaye, mayor of Louisville for 16 years; native of city and was born in the first brick house ever built here.

The infamous murder of Rev. Thos. Jefferson Fisher who came to Louisville to collect a $2,000 debt.

Louisville Board of Health established.

Fisher Leaf Company started business. (Bought out in 1926 by Hart Manufacturing Co.)

Woodland Race Course begun on Louisville-Frankfort Railroad, 6 miles east of city, now Crescent Hill. After few years, financial trouble closed it.

Publishers Printing Co. started.

Andrew Cowan & Co., started on 3rd between Main and Market.

Bensinger Outfitting Co. established.

Henry Ott formed partnership with Theodore Ahrens, Sr. (Later became Ahrens & Ott Manufacturing Co., which grew to the giant Standard Sanitary Manufacturing Co., now (1954) American Radiator & Standard Sanitary Corporation).

1867 Masonic Widow and Orphans Home established.

Insurance firm of Barbee & Castleman formed, 5th and Main.

C. T. Dearing adds printing department to his book store.

May 30 . . . Great marble statue of Henry Clay (by Joel Hart, famed Kentucky sculptor) unveiled in rotunda of Court House; 100 trained voices sang a song written specially for occasion.

Two large wings erected to the City Hospital.

Cholera swept city.

December 25 . . . Throckmorton, famous manager of the Galt House, died.

Peaslee-Gaulbert Corporation started as Louisville Lead & Color Co.

Macauley's Theater erected.

J. Zoll & Son, shoe merchants, started; (still in business—1954—oldest in state).

Quast & Schulten, boot factory, also started.

Louisville Banking and Insurance Co. chartered; open for business March 2, 1868.

Security Bank organized, NE corner Preston and Market.

Louisville Transit Co. established.

August 1 . . . One of most notable events in history of city; cornerstone laid for great railway bridge across Falls.

1868 Merger of *Louisville Journal* and *Courier and Democrat* under the editorship of Henry Watterson as "Courier-Journal". Walter N. Haldeman of Courier is made president; venerable Prentice is retained on the editorial staff; Watterson made managing editor.

Loevenhart's, men's clothing store, founded in Lexington by Lee Loevenhart (moved to Louisville in 1898).

Louisville Daily Journal—1830 (in 1832 absorbed *Focus*) established by Prentice; *Louisville Daily Democrat*—1843; *Louisville Morning Courier*—1844, established by Haldeman. Locations: 110-112 Jefferson between 3rd and 4th (1869); 4th and Green (1874); 3rd and Liberty—(November 17, 1912); 6th and Broadway—(September 19, 1948). Reverses came in early 1868; change made in organization; Henry Watterson became one-third owner and business and editorial manager in May.

Louisville Theater became Louisville Opera House (until '73 when Macauley's competition put it out of business).

Act established Board of Police of Louisville and Jefferson County.

Tandems race on levee, a popular sport.

C. C. Bickel Co., tobacco firm, started.

Blatz Paint Co. started.

Wintersmith Chemical Co. founded.

W. D. Gatchel, photographic materials concern (started in 1862 in Cincinnati), established in Louisville.

1869 James Guthrie, one of the most influential men in the history of Louisville, died.

Remains of George Rogers Clark removed to Cave Hill Cemetery.

The Farmers and Drovers Bank, organized.

Falls City Mutual Fire Insurance Co. chartered.

Ewing-Von Allmen Dairy Co. established.

August 7 . . . Eclipse of sun.

January 7 . . . Gen. Rousseau, Louisville's best known soldier in the late war, died.

May 20 . . . Observed as Confederate Decoration Day.

Baptist Orphans' Home established.

April 5 . . . Second Galt House completed (1st and Main); designed by Henry Whitestone; having eight elegant Corinthian columns and great dignity.

The Louisville Daily Commercial, later *The Louisville Herald*, began publication at 102 Green Street.

Louisville Gas Co. charter renewed for 20

Continued on page 98

Engine No. 77—Early L & N Woodburner, built at the L & N Shops at 10th and Kentucky. Designed by Thatcher Perkins and used until 1911.

HISTORY OF THE L&N RAILROAD

THE Louisville and Nashville Railroad secured its charter from the Commonwealth of Kentucky on March 5, 1850, thus crystalizing the by-then flourishing sentiment for a railroad between the metropolis of Kentucky and the capital of Tennessee. That sentiment had been active as early as 1832 and had blossomed in 1849 and 1850 into mass meetings at Glasgow, Bowling Green, Louisville and in other cities which might profit from such a railroad.

The meeting at Louisville was an enthusiastic one and resulted in the City pledging to invest $1,000,000 in the project. With this moral support the backers of the line were encouraged to secure the charter mentioned, and also one from Tennessee for that portion of the road that would lie in that state.

Then subscription books for the sale of the road's stock were opened at Louisville and at various other points. Louisville soon fulfilled its million-dollar pledge (years later it disposed of its stock at a substantial profit) and its lead was followed by the various counties along the proposed route, the purchases being made through the issuance of County bonds.

A century ago it took rare foresight and courage to envision a rail transportation system that would link up the promising areas of the South and the incident development of the natural riches of an inland empire. From the modest undertaking to join Louisville with the state line of Tennessee (140 miles) the L. & N. has by consolidation, purchase and construction extended its mileage to nearly 5,000 and now serves 13 states. From the employment of 1,200 men with an annual pay roll of $750,000, it now has about 27,000 employees with annual wages of $100 million. Its rolling stock and motive power has increased from two locomotives (in 1855), one of them with a "broken tyre", and a mere handful of other equipment, to today's mighty armada of 757 steam engines and 104 Diesels.

The Old Reliable has plowed back millions into property development and has paid conservative dividends for 70 years of its useful existence. When the Old Reliable—after a period of some nine years replete with financial difficulties and the struggles attendant upon wresting a passageway from nature—operated

An old wood burning engine of the Louisville and Frankfort Railroad pulling into the new station at Pewee Valley, on opening day in 1867. This depot is still standing. The line was acquired by L & N in 1881.

its first through train between Louisville and Nashville on October 27, 1859, wood supplied the power for the engine.

L. & N. DURING CIVIL WAR.

Wood held this dominant position until after the close of the War between the States. With much of its trackage (a branch to Lebanon, Ky., and one to the state line at Guthrie, Ky., were also in operation at the time) in the path of the opposing armies of the North and South, the Railroad was considerably damaged during the conflict. As the war grew older and as the Northern forces moved further southward, the little commandeered road became an important factor in the supplying of the Federal armies with material and replacements.

The retreating Confederates invariably destroyed bridges, trestles and track with great thoroughness, providing plenty of additional work for the Road's employees, who frequently performed their duties under armed guard.

In the 1880's, three other momentous events also took place which were to link the L. & N.

more effectively with other railroads, thus increasing the usefulness and importance of all, and making possible America's mighty integrated rail transportation system of today. It had long been evident that an efficient exchange of traffic with connecting roads required maximum standardization. Accordingly, in 1883, the railroads inaugurated the standard time zones which have remained virtually the same to this day. In 1885, the L. & N. dedicated its Henderson Bridge across the Ohio River at Henderson, Ky., breaching a substantial barrier between North and South, and, in 1886, the L. & N. and other lines in the South adopted the standard track gauge of four feet 8½ inches, the Old Reliable alone changing some 2,000 miles of track from a five-foot gauge in one day's time.

MILTON H. SMITH

Much of the expansion outlined was done under the inspired leadership of Milton H. Smith, famed L. & N. executive head, who was president of the road from June 11, 1884 to October 6, 1886 and again from March 9, 1891 until his death on February 22, 1921. (In the five year interim between his two terms of office, he was vice president.) In all, "M. H." was dominant in L. & N. affairs for nearly 37 years. More than any one other man he was responsible for the L. & N.'s emergence from a small local carrier into one of America's major transportation systems.

THE L. & N.'S PART IN WORLD WAR II.

Pearl Harbor, intensified an activity that really had its inception in Hitler's invasion of France in the spring of 1940. A few comparative freight and passenger statistics tell the story best of L & N's participation in World War II:

YEAR	PASSENGERS	TONS OF FREIGHT
1939	3,202,442	42,093,172
1940	3,140,586	49,429,151
1941	3,589,198	58,504,512
1942	6,421,218	71,021,454
1943	11,905,645	72,607,969
1944	12,440,022	73,374,452
1945	10,074,188	70,235,754

Thus, it will be seen that the peak years of the L. & N.'s contribution to World War II were 1943 and 1944, with much of its passenger traffic consisting of members of the armed forces (it handled 4,228 special military trains in 1943 alone) and with a great part of its freight traffic directly related to the war effort.

LEVIN LAWRENCE SHREVE
First President of the Louisville and Nashville Railroad, 1851-1854

The early seal of Louisville contained cut of an old wood-burning engine.

MILTON H. SMITH
Famed President of L & N for 32 years—1884-1886 and 1891-1921

97

years. Made gas continuously except for two nights in February 1883, when flood put out fires and left city in complete darkness. City owned ⅓ stock; got its light at actual cost.

Chris Miller opened undertaking establishment on Market between 16th and 17th.

1870 January 2 . . . Heaviest snowfall ever known in Louisville; 3 to 4 feet deep.

Brown Forman Distillers Corp. founded.

January 21 . . . Death of George D. Prentice, whom Henry Watterson said exerted more influence than any other political writer; buried in Cave Hill.

February 18 . . . New City Hospital opened.

February 18 . . . Dedication of first Louisville bridge across Ohio (at 14th Street); now known as Pennsylvania Railroad Bridge; designed and built by Albert Fink; first train taken across February 18; open to traffic on March 1; cost $2,000,000; 5294 feet long with 27 spans.

August 16 . . . Louisville College of Pharmacy organized. Chartered 1873.

Construction of new City Hall begins; to cost $464,778; Mergell and Andrewatha, architects; Stancliff & Co. complete plans; $500 public contest in 1866 for plans.

Liederkranz Society, founded 1846, erected large building on Market between 1st and 2nd (cornerstone laid 1870).

Joseph Denunzio brought largest amount of tropical fruit (50 bunches of bananas etc.) seen in Louisville to that date, to store on south side of Market near 3rd.

Edinger & Co., wholesale grocers, begin business. W. H. Edinger later became president of German Insurance Bank.

1871 Gen. George Custer, with 7th Cavalry, came to Elizabethtown and stayed two years; sent to control Ku Klux Klan and carpet baggers.

Ku Klux Klan active in Louisville.

Drive for funds to help Chicago fire sufferers.

February 15 . . . First number, Louisville Daily Ledger.

The great event of this year was the initiation of the movements which culminated in the founding of the Public Library. Col. Durrett obtained permission from legislature to raise funds for library by holding a series of five "gift concerts" or lotteries; $6,250,000 taken in; $3,142,500 profit. Library got only $422,392 with which it purchased Weisiger Hall on 4th Street, now the site of Kaufmans, along with 50,000 volumes and some art works. The cost of raising the money was a public scandal which

reflected on some of the promoters. Henry Watterson resigned from committee in indignation. This was the nucleus of today's public library. Widened Portland Canal opened.

Louisville Cement Co. built mill at Speed, Indiana.

First Caron City Directory.

John Wannamaker opened clothing store at NE corner of 4th and Jefferson, "Oak Hall."

M. Cohen & Sons, tailors, started at 306 W. Market.

House of Pilcher, organ manufacturers, established in Louisville (original company started in Dover, England, in 1820).

1872 Public Library and Museum opened January 30, 31 . . . Grand Duke Alexis of royal family of Russia visited the city.

July 18 . . . Liederkranz opens new hall; complete operas Tannhäuser and Lohengrin heard for first time in city.

July 20 . . . National Industrial Exposition opened at 4th and Chestnut; Gov. Bramlette addressed large audience; first exposition held September 3—October 12. Expositions held there until Southern Exposition opened.

September 21 . . . Horace Greeley visited here.

September 22 . . . Unfinished brick store on Market Street collapsed; four killed, three injured; walls made too thin; architect and contractor jailed.

October 25 . . . Relics of extinct animals, 15 feet long, exhumed in digging Broadway sewer, 22 feet below the surface.

November . . . 100 cases of chicken pox.

December 12 . . . Large and brilliant detonating meteor, "one-fourth size of moon!"

First presidential nominee who was a Catholic, Charles O'Conor of Louisville.

J. J. B. Hilliard and Sons, investment bankers, began as A. D. Hunt Co., a private bank.

Chambers Seed Co. started by Samuel R. Chambers and John R. Watts.

J. P. Will Co., building materials, started in Portland.

1873 Great financial panic of 1873.

Jacob Schulz opens florist shop on East Broadway (now Cherokee Road).

DuPont & Co., 10th and River, among largest mills in U.S. making newsprint.

First negro school in state opened in Louisville.

25,000 houses; 70 churches; 5 distilleries in city.

February 18 . . . Remington streetcar, propelled by steam, had successful trial here.

University Law School graduated 10; Louisville Municipal College graduated 51.

Continued on page 102

THE LOUISVILLE GAS COMPANY'S WORKS—AS THE PLANT LOOKED IN THE '80'S

THE DEVELOPMENT OF LIGHT AND POWER

JUST TWO DAYS after Louisville received its charter as a city (February 13, 1828) the Louisville Gas and Water Company received its charter. L. L. Shreve (the fellow with the white bobbed hair and the chin whiskers—but very shrewd and virile looking, none-the-less) was the first president of this company, which like German Insurance Company (chartered 26 years later) had certain banking privileges and functions. The authorized capital stock was $1,200,000.00, and the company was given the right to construct and establish gas and water works, to borrow and lend money, and deal in exchange and bank notes. It was stipulated that the gas works should be established in three years, the water works in five. The incorporators besides L. L. Shreve were J. I. Jacob, James Rudd, and Robert Tyler.

On January 3, 1842 the owners—or perhaps the State—decided that supplying water, gas and banking facilities were three separate businesses. Anyway, a new charter was granted confining the company's activity to producing and selling gas, and the name became Louisville Gas Company. During the next 25 years gas mains were installed covering the important streets of the city. In 1869 the mains were extended to Portland.

With the introduction of an arc-dynamo, publicly displayed for the first time at the Louisville Industrial Exposition in 1877, experiments began for the commercial use of electric lighting. Dr. C. L. Mees, a professor of physics and chemistry at old Male High School, installed the arc-light on a river steamboat, as an experiment, and caused a sensation. Another successful river trial of the same lamp was made on the Steamboat "General Lyle" between here and Cincinnati, with a locomotive reflector borrowed from the L. & N. The intensity of the light frightened other steamer crews as well as the people along the shore.

The first commercial use of the arc in Louisville proper was at Kelly's ax factory on Portland Avenue. During this experimental stage it was also used to illuminate the stage at the old Opera House.

The first plant in Louisville to produce electricity for lighting was the Brush Electric Light Company, organized in 1881 by Jacob Smyser and James S. Lithgow, who operated the Lithgow Foundry at Clay and Main.

Forty three "40 light" dynamos were installed. The company applied for a franchise to light the streets by electricity, but the city officials wanted proof that the new-fangled invention was practical. Smyser and Lithgow then installed a line of poles from their plant south on Clay to Market and west on Market to Twelfth.

Among the first commercial customers for the sensational new lighting were Denunzio Fruit Company; two large clothing companies—Winter & Deppens and the Tower Palace; the Galt House; and the Buckingham Theater—let Dad or Grandad tell you about the "Buck"! The levee was soon lighted by six arc lamps mounted on a tower at the foot of Fourth Street. The company charged $1.00 per night—from dusk till midnight. These lights were the open-arc type.

The first company here to use Thomas A. Edison's invention—the incandescent lamp—was the U.S. Electric Light Company organized in 1882 by James Clark and associates. It had no plant of its own, but produced current in the plant of the Louisville Gas Company, which later absorbed it.

Four years after Edison invented the incandescent lamp his company installed the electric lighting system for the Southern Exposition (1883). Henry Byllesby, a great name in electricity, had charge of the installation and operation. The contract for 4,600 Edison lamps of 16 candle-power each, was largest made in the U.S. to that date. The cost of the plant was $100,000—and it took 100 men an entire month to string the wires and get the plant in operation.

The advantages over gas lighting were so tremendous, that electric lighting was accepted at once. It was pointed out in the Courier-Journal of March 2, 1883, that if the same amount of

illumination had been supplied by gas, the oxygen required would have been equal to the volume used up by 75,000 people. And of course Edison's light, being sealed in an air-tight bulb could use no oxygen, and it created very little heat.

The next important firm to enter the electric light business was the Louisville Electric Light Company, chartered in December 1882. Incorporators were Silas F. Miller, W. C. Hall, Edward Fulton, Leon Bamberger, Edward E. McKenna, Wm. L. Breyfoyle, George Wolff, W. N. Haldeman and W. H. Johnson. A plant was built on Third Street between Green and Walnut, the site of the old interurban station, which is now (1954) an ultra-modern car parking building.

Natural gas came to Louisville in 1889 when the Kentucky Rock Gas Company laid a pipe from the gas fields in Meade County.

Soon there was a clamoring for electric street lighting and the era of the picturesque "lamplighter" was coming to an end. In 1890, the Louisville Gas Company consolidated with the Louisville Electric Light Company, and a new power station was started at 14th and Magazine. The Legislature this same year granted them the right to make artificial gas.

THOMAS A. EDISON

LOOKED LIKE THIS AS A YOUTH OF 19

WHEN HE WORKED IN LOUISVILLE

In 1893, four "10,000 light dynamos" were installed—then the largest of the type in the country.

The advent of electric street lighting and the growth in the number of commercial and home consumers tremendously increased the number of wires needed to carry the current. Downtown Louisville, as you can see by some of the pictures in this book, became a labyrinth of telephone poles with hundreds of stretched wires.

In the early 1900's the City Council passed an ordinance that all wires in the central district be placed under ground. By this time there were a number of electric and gas companies in the city, which resulted in confusing duplication of service facilities and higher rates. Through the efforts of H. M. Byllesby & Company, all the local firms were merged into one organization on July 1, 1913—the present Louisville Gas and Electric Company. The far-reaching planning of this company to keep pace with, and indeed *ahead,* of Louisville's industrial growth, is covered in the latter part of this book.

EDISON LIVED IN LOUISVILLE FOR TWO YEARS AS A YOUNG MAN

NEAR THE CLOSE of the Civil War, Thomas Edison, then a youth of 19, was a telegraph operator in the Louisville office of Western Union, and said to be one of the fastest receivers in the country.

One day, while working on one of his countless experiments, he spilled some nitric acid on the Manager's desk, scarring it badly. As this was the culmination of a series of mishaps and pranks charged to Edison, the boss decided he wanted "operators, not experimenters" and Edison was fired. Young Tom then left Louisville and thus our city lost the greatest inventor of all times.

When Edison worked here he had already developed the personal traits for which he later became famous. He worked late at night, often *all* night; slept very little; ate an apple or two for lunch, never more; wore a $1.50 suit every day; was habitually absorbed in his own thoughts and theories. Louisvillians considered him "daffy", but while here he greatly improved the stock-ticker and worked on numerous other devices which he later perfected in New Jersey.

Many years later, in 1883, Edison came back to Louisville, a man of world-wide fame and fortune, to install the dynamos and other electrical equipment at Louisville's great Southern Exposition where the people of this section first saw his incandescent lamp illustrated on the previous page.

Edison, while he worked here, lodged in this cottage at 729 E. Washington.

March 10 . . . One of the most sensational bank robberies in south took place at old Falls City Tobacco Bank; burglars worked way through ceiling into vault; got over $300,000 in gold, jewelry and negotiable bonds.

March 10 . . . Tent of Great Eastern Circus blown down on 7,000; 2 dead.

May 27 . . . Tornado, with terrific lightning, passed over city.

June 12 . . . Concert in Exposition Building by band of King of Saxony.

June 12 . . . (night) Three big fires; one came near destroying Public Library; total loss $84,000; plot suspected, never proved.

September 15 . . . Two men swindled two banks of $11,000 with forged letters; one caught.

By end of September, most Louisville Banks had suspended cash payments; resumed October 13.

October 13 . . . Macauley's Theater opened with "Extremes" by J. Austin Sperry. Theater built on old Prather Square on site of old burial ground; cost $200,000; 1500 seating capacity.

City Hall completed at cost of $474,778; occupied in June.

October 16 . . . City Hall damaged by gas explosion.

New Female High School on 1st Street completed and dedicated.

Joseph Imorde and Ben Melter started general store at 3rd and Ormsby.

Joseph and Sebastian Hubbuch (brothers) started House of Hubbuch, 11th and Market. Joseph Hubbuch, Sr., & Sons, home furnishings.

1874 February 16 . . . Jean Louis Rodolphe Agassiz, famous literary figure, delivered lecture before Louisville Library Association.

March 29 . . . Vaudeville Theater burned.

Organization of Louisville Jockey Club and establishment of Churchill Downs under leadership of Col. Lewis M. Clark; 320 members subscribed $100 each.

June 1 . . . SS. Mary & Elizabeth Hospital opened (12th and Magnolia) for factory and railroad workers at first.

New Alms House opened in fall; 5 miles south of courthouse.

Henry Pilcher opens organ company in Louisville.

Churchill Downs established.

Government purchases Portland Canal.

J. F. Wagner & Sons Co. founded.

Edwin Booth (John Wilkes Booth's brother) at Macauley's.

"Eclipse" baseball team established a park at 28th and Elliott; played its first major game on a diamond located on present site of St. James Court; at this location in '76 and '77.

1875 Plan made to utilize water power at Falls of the Ohio.

Glenmore Distillers Corp. incorporated.

First Kentucky Derby won by Aristides; 15 horses started; Matt J. Winn, age 14, saw it.

February 7 . . . Sunday Globe is started.

February 9 . . . First celebration of Mardi Gras in city.

April 18 . . . Heavy snowstorm—ice one inch thick.

June 2 . . . Heavy windstorm, blows down central part of Masonic Home; $30,000 loss; no deaths.

July 4 . . . Steamer James D. Parker sinks, but is raised again.

November 17 . . . City Hall tower nearly consumed by fire—loss about $10,000.

November 24 . . . Louisville Clearing House established; began operations January 3, 1876—Clinton McCarty manager; 22 banks in Louisville all joined; opened at the old National Bank of Kentucky, Main, east of 3rd.

November 27 . . . Mary Anderson, Louisville actress, makes debut at Macauley's as Juliet.

December 2 . . . Partial burning of Broadway Baptist Church.

J. V. Reed & Co. began business.

S. Goodman & Sons founded.

National meeting of The American Medical Association here.

1876 Second Derby; Dom Pedro, emperor of Brazil, attended.

Electricity first used as a commercial product in Louisville.

May 16 . . . Splendid new Courier-Journal Building formally opened at SW corner of 4th and Green (Liberty).

July 17 . . . Eye and Ear Infirmary incorporated.

September 24 . . . Slight shocks of earthquake felt.

November 2 . . . Contract given to build Crescent Hill reservoir.

December 9 . . . Organization of Polytechnic Society.

Logan Co. started (as Dow's Wire Works).

1877 Enormous ice gorge in river—broke on January 14.

"Home & Farm" agricultural paper started by B. F. Avery & Sons.

Southern Baptist Theological Seminary was removed to the city from Greenville, South Carolina.

April . . . Work begun on reservoir (100,000,000
Continued on page 105

Early Photograph of the Original Waterworks and Tower on the River—a Classic Group.

THE LOUISVILLE WATERWORKS

All the public utilities are essential to modern city life—water, gas, electricity, sewers and transportation—but the one that is absolutely indispensable is water.

In the earliest days of Louisville's history, water was supplied by the river (it was *clean* then, and needed no purification). As the town grew inward, away from the water-front, springs and wells supplied the water. Then the "corner pump" came into being. Less than fifty years ago there were still pumps of this character in almost every block. They were deep wells, and the water tasted good and was delightfully cool in the summer. The neighborhood pump was a gathering place for all the urchins of the block, because it was necessary for each home to send to the pump several times a day to supply the household needs. This "bucket brigade" was usually composed of the children;

it was a never-ending chore which would not appeal very much to the youngster of today.

The corner pump was a romantic institution. (Nathaniel Hawthorne has written a panegyric about it). But it was *unhealthy*. Pollution from the gutters of the street, (it was the horse and buggy era) seeped underground; a large amount of slop water and sewage was thrown into the street by householders before sewers were installed, and even for many years after, until sewer connections became obligatory upon all property owners. Thus the pump water became polluted and malaria and other diseases resulted.

As early as the middle of the last century, the city fathers realized that a city water system had to be installed. In 1854, the same year in which the "sponsor" of this history got its charter, the Louisville Water Company was incor-

Courtesy H. M. Gerber and Louisville Water Co.

Rare photograph never before published showing digging of the Reservoir in Crescent Hill about 1877

porated under an Act of the State Legislature, with a capital of one million dollars, divided into 10,000 shares of a par value of $100 each. The city did not own all the stock until 1906 but controlled the company through the board of directors appointed by the Sinking Fund Commissioners. Since March 21, 1906, the full management and control has been vested in the Board of Water Works.

The actual construction of the water works began in 1856, and the first water was delivered by the Pumping Station on the river to the reservoir situated on the hill behind what was then the Country Club, in October 1860.

The initial distribution system consisted of 26 miles of mains. The cost of the entire project was only $829,455.81. The original plant including all buildings and equipment was designed by Theodore R. Scowden assisted by Charles Hermany, who became Chief Engineer of the Water Company and remained so until his death in January 1908.

Below: Woodcut of the Reservoir when completed about 1880; Reservoir Park is still a show place.

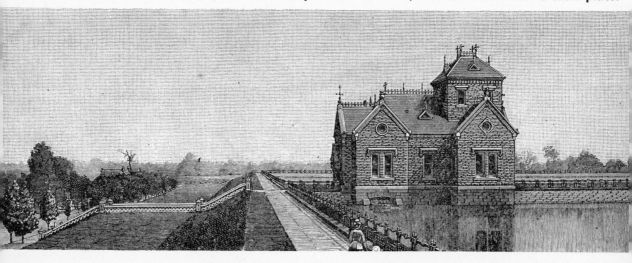

Note that this gigantic job is being done by hand and mule power. It was before the day of mechanized equipment. This comparatively modern project was built in the same manner that the ancient Egyptian pyramids were built, with sweat and brawn, toil and tears, almost.

The Pumping Station on River under construction

No city ever started out with a better water works. This is proved by the fact that the original machinery was in active daily operation until 1909 and is still capable of being utilized if necessary in times of emergency.

With the growth of the city a larger reservoir became a necessity, and the Crescent Hill Reservoir was contracted for in 1876 and completed in December 1879.

The most prominent landmark of the Water Company is the immense water tank which towers above the Crescent Hill Pumping Station and Filter House on Frankfort Avenue; it is visible for miles around. This tank was designed to afford the pressure necessary to carry the water over the entire system. The present head of the Water Company, President Henry M. Gerber reveals that when the tank was filled and the water released the pressure was so much greater than expected that it broke water mains in all sections of Louisville. After the completion of the improvements begun in 1909 the value of the Water Works rose to over 8 million dollars. There have been continuing improvements and enlargements since.

Chronology Continued—
gallon capacity). Charles Hermany chief engineer.

April 9 . . . First Elks Club in state established in Louisville; "Benevolent and Protective Order of Elks"; eighth such club in U.S.

July . . . Employees of L & N strike, riot; unsuccessful attempt to set fire to railway station. L & N moves into general office building at NE corner of 2nd and Main (still standing, 1954).

September 27 . . . President Hayes and cabinet visit Exposition.

Mengel Co. founded by Col. C. C. Mengel.

North American Saengerbund 5-day Festival in old Exposition Building; 4th and Chestnut; 1,000 in chorus, 75 in orchestra.

1878 Yellow fever epidemic swept city.

Hubbuch Bros. & Wellendorf begin business.

American Printing House for the Blind established.

January 9 . . . First telephone communication with Nashville.

January 22 . . . First Handel & Haydn concert in Louisville.

April 1 . . . Cornerstone of St. Vincent's Church laid.

October . . . Detachment of Louisville Legion on guard at jail to protect a prisoner from a mob.

October 8 . . . Opening of Louisville College of Pharmacy.

October 24 . . . Dedication of Masonic Widows' and Orphans' Home.

October 25 . . . Opening of Masonic Grand Lodge.

December 2 . . . Introduction of electric light into Kelly's ax factory.

December 5 . . . Ben Casseday, Louisville historian, died.

December 10 . . . New workhouse accepted by city.

December 16 . . . New hall in Phoenix Hill Park opened.

December 19 . . . Opening of Davis's new theater.

December . . . Lithgow Foundry on Main Street near Clay housed first electric arc lamp manufactured in Louisville (for Brush Co.).

Dennis Long & Co., Manufacturers of cast-iron pipe, incorporated.

Maurice Barrymore (father of John and Lionel) at Macauley's with John Drew.

Marret & Miller, florists, founded.

1879 February 1 . . . Fire in Almhouse; building destroyed. (Built 1824)

Continued on page 108

Mary Anderson, most famous Louisville actress; made her debut at Macauley's Theater in 1875.

First bath tub in Louisville was installed in Shreve mansion—where Armory now stands.

Eugene J. Straus, Fred Haupt & Hewett Brown on 500-miles-in-3-days endurance test in 1908.

Most historical playhouse in Louisville today is U of L Little Theater, directed by Boyd Martin.

Phoenix Hill Park, a glorified beer garden, was favorite spot in Gay Nineties and early 1900's.

Lexington Road at Baxter—possibly oldest stone building in city. Said to have been toll house.

The park system of Louisville was started by Mayor Jacobs. Iroquois was for many years called "Jacob's Park." It's the largest Louisville Park (550 acres), and was the favorite haunt of nature poet Madison Cawein, inspiring many of his loveliest poems.

Cherokee Park (306 acres) is beautiful and more accessible. A familiar landmark near the entrance is the equestrian statue of Col. John Castleman—who, incidentally, had the rare pleasure of attending the unveiling in 1913.

Some years ago, before Charles Farnsley was Mayor, (and he was one of the best) there was a movement to remove the Confederate monument to facilitate traffic on Third Street. "Confederate Charlie", of string-tie fame, was immediately on guard (see below). That's one battle Charlie won!

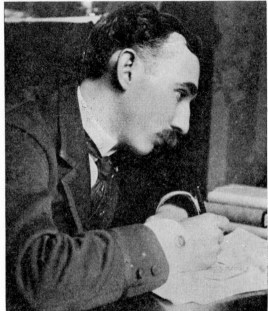

Madison Cawein, Louisville's greatest nature poet

Gen. Castleman & Horse guard Park entrance.

Charlie Farnsley guards Confederate monument.

Chronology Continued—

July 29 . . . Judge Bland Ballard, prominent jurist, dies.

December 10 . . . Gen. Grant visits Louisville; large public demonstration for him; came from the west on trip around world.

December 14 . . . New reservoir completed and water let in for first time.

December 17 . . . New Almshouse built on site of old burnt one.

Edison Telephone Company organized.

First telephone exchange in Kentucky established in Louisville, less than 4 years after new device invented. Owned and operated by American District Telegraph Co.; James B. Speed, president; first conversation within Louisville was between Speed's office and Portland Co.; started in little second story room over 213 3rd Street; 200 subscribers; the wires ran over the rooftops.

Board of Trade acquires building at 3rd and Main; stock and grain exchange was operated there in those days—"Going on Change" was then the traditional luncheon pastime of business leaders of the community. They met at Exchange Hall annex, built on rear of building, which still stands.

Horn Transfer Co., and R. Baude Company, Jewelers, established.

Henry Kaufman, with $200 in cash and $1200 credit starts the dry goods business which today (1954) as Kaufman-Straus Company, is one of the largest department stores of the South.

1880 Sarah Bernhardt and many other celebrities made their appearance at Macauley's Theater; Bernhardt's first American tour.

L. Strauss, haberdasher; Durkee Famous Foods; Theo. Tafel Surgical Instrument Co., founded.

Ballard & Ballard flour mills began operations.

March 13 . . . Unsuccessful attempt to assassinate Mayor Baxter.

May 1 . . . Louisville celebrates her centennial anniversary with an elaborate address by Col. R. T. Durrett and other exercises. This address, amplified, was published as a book by the Filson Club.

September 10 . . . Total destruction of Finzer Brothers Tobacco factory, largest in the world, by fire.

December 28 . . . River closed, extreme cold.

Hay Market originated in '80's in abandoned railroad yard on Jefferson Street between Floyd and Brook.

YMCA enters new home (old residence of A. A. Gordon) on north side of Walnut near 5th.

U.S. gains complete control of Louisville & Portland Canal.

Henry Vogt opens first machine shop.

Baxter Park, Louisville's first, established in old graveyard on Jefferson between 11th and 12th.

Central office of telephone exchange set up in Board of Trade Building.

1881 Elizabeth Robbins of Louisville, who won international fame as an actress, started her career here.

Kentucky Public Elevator Co., founded.

Louisville, Evansville & St. Louis line completed.

February 21 . . . Sarah Bernhardt in "Camille" at Macauley's.

May 2 . . . Public opening of Phoenix Hill and Riverside Parks.

May 30 . . . Dedication of Tabernacle (Warren Memorial Church) at 4th and Broadway.

Early July . . . many deaths from heat.

December 10 . . . Visit of Jefferson Davis.

December 24 . . . Start of 80,000 candle power circuit by Brush Electric Light Co.

Letter written which started Pendennis Club— Major James W. Wright was the first president.

First Public Electric Utility Service commenced in Louisville.

State Prohibition Party organized here.

Continued on page 112

Engine Company No. 6, named in honor of Louisville's First Fire Chief Johnson—24th and Portland—1874.

LOUISVILLE FIRE DEPARTMENT

THE organization of a fire department in Louisville dates back as far as 1798, when the General Assembly authorized formation of fire companies on the same basis as volunteer militia.

The early fire companies were decidedly primitive in their operations at fires. A row of men was formed extending from the fire to one of the numerous ponds in the town. They then passed from one to another buckets filled with water to be poured on the fire, and again passed back the empty buckets to be refilled and returned, and thus the process went on until the fire was out or the house consumed, for there was no danger of exhausting the ponds—there were so many in those days.

In 1812 persons owning houses that rented for as much as forty dollars per year were required to furnish a pair of fire buckets for each house. In 1816 all citizens attending the fires were required to obey the officers of the companies or pay a fine, and in this way the revenue of the companies was also increased. They soon became strong enough to supply themselves with

hand engines and suction hose, and before the trustees went out of office in 1828 they had three of these engines manned by forty or more persons. The engines were drawn to the fire by the men instead of horses, and were worked by hand.

The volunteers served without pay, and fought many thrilling blaze battles including the burning of the steamboats Sentinel, Rambler, and Delphine at the Louisville Wharf, and the great fire of 1840. This fire which was perhaps the most disastrous in the city's history, started in a chair factory on Third Street, between Main and Market, and spread rapidly through the business district. It destroyed a total of 30 buildings at a loss of over $300,000.

In 1858, the hand engine and volunteer system was supplanted with steam fire-engines and a professional force consisting of a chief, 65 men, and 23 horses, all maintained by the city. Fire losses then decreased 75%. Ever since that time, Louisville has had one of the finest fire departments in the nation for a city of its size.

First Three Fire Chiefs of Louisville

A. Y. JOHNSON
1856-1861

GEORGE LEVI
1861-1862

MICHAEL J. PAUL
1862-1864

A. Y. JOHNSON
1864-1868

A. Y. JOHNSON
First Fire Chief of the City of Louisville
The Fire Department was founded in 1858.

Relics of the early Fire Fighters

These objects are in the Fire Department Museum at 27th and Broadway: First, a section of the first *leather* hose, used here before canvas (or rubber) was used for this purpose. Second, a flambeau dated 1838 which was carried blazing at night before the hand-drawn fire truck in the days of the volunteer firemen. Third, a quaint old leather and metal hat worn by one of the volunteer firemen. The firemen's museum has an extensive collection of early photos, a few of which are printed on these pages.

In front of the Charles D. Jacob Engine House No. 1 in 1874. Note the early 3-wheeled steam engine.

A Big Fire at Fourth and Liberty

The coal-fired steam engines, used to pump water before the advent of modern gasoline-driven pumps, added drama and excitement to fires in earlier days. Here are two of the smoking, throbbing engines—presumably at the fire which badly damaged the Courier-Journal building in the early 1900's.

Fire engine house of the Volunteer Firemen—before day of paid firemen. This building still stands on First Street.

1882 "A great flood came in February, working more mischief on the river front than any other that ever visited Louisville. It reached its highest on the 22nd; it was accounted the most disastrous inundation that ever visited the Ohio valley." Portland, severely damaged.

March 5 . . . Steamer 'James D. Parker' wrecked on falls.

March 12 . . . Cornerstone laid of new Colored Baptist Church on Center between Chestnut and Broadway.

March . . . Legislature chartered "Louisville Canal and Water-Power Co. to build canal of 6 miles to bypass falls (from point near water works to mouth of Paddy's Run is proposed).

September 12 . . . Great public celebration on completion of 4 new railroad lines.

(McCoy-Hatfield feud flares with renewed vigor this year in Kentucky mountains.)

December 8 . . . Louisville Electric Light Co. inaugurated, with Leon Bamberger as President; public city franchise granted.

Louis Appel Co. incorporated.

Foundations of Union Station dug.

1883 Cyclones brought devastation to Louisville.

Ohio Valley Telephone Company organized.

E. S. Tachau & Sons formed.

Southern Exposition opened in Louisville on August 1st, closed November 10; (story: p.144.)

Ohio Valley Telephone Co. organized with 1400 subscribers.

Courier Journal Lithographing Co. and Job Printing Co. began.

Louisville Electric Light Co. began operations.

New City Hospital started.

Helena Modjeska in first American performance at Macauley's; Nora in "The Doll's House"; Louisville was the first American city to see one of Ibsen's plays.

Population 155,600; 29,631 buildings of which 24,366 were dwellings.

Louisville Police and Fire Departments had parades.

1884 The Filson Club founded by Reuben T. Durrett and nine other prominent Louisvillians. (Filson was Kentucky's first historian).

Flood called "greatest local flood of modern times" in February 17 Courier-Journal; followed by great storms (a disaster second only to the flood of 1937).

Louisville Safety Vault and Trust Co., incorporated.

John Rose Co. founded; cigar dealer.

Kentucky Mutual Security Fund Co. chartered.

Louisville Public Machine Company founded —208 W. Main.

City covers 16 square miles.

Louisville ranks as "healthiest city of its size in U.S.

May 1 . . . Louisville Times first edition on May Day; editors Emmett G. Logan and E. Polk Johnson.

First baseball bat made by "Bud" Hillerich.

Reorganized Ohio Valley Telephone Co. erected 2 fine buildings at 424 W. Jefferson; first building in South to be used exclusively as a telephone exchange.

Kentucky Normal & Theological Institute, founded in 1873, became a university and was renamed the State University of Kentucky; in 1918 became "Simmons University", 722 W. Kentucky Street.

Warren Memorial Presbyterian Church completed.

Louisville Public Warehouse opened for business.

1885 Louisville was 3rd city in U.S. to have underground conduits and cables for telephones; originally all the wires had to go overhead.

LIEDERKRANZ HALL.

THE

"Mark Twain"—Cable Readings,

Monday Evening, January 5th, 1885.

PROGRAMME.

1. FROM DR. SEVIER,—*Narcisse and John and Mary Richling.*
 "Mistoo 'Ichlin', in fact, I can baw that fifty dolla' f'om you myself."
 GEO. W. CABLE.

2. ADVANCE SHEETS FROM "THE ADVENTURES OF HUCKLEBERRY FINN."—*"King Sollermunn."*
 MARK TWAIN.

3. FROM DR. SEVIER,—*Kate Riley, Richling and Ristofalo.*
 GEO. W. CABLE.

4. *Tragic Tale of the Fishwife.*
 MARK TWAIN.

5. FROM DR. SEVIER,—*Narcisse puts on mourning for "Lady Byron."*
 GEO. W. CABLE.

6. *A Trying Situation.*
 MARK TWAIN.

7. FROM DR. SEVIER,—*Mary's Night Ride*
 GEO. W. CABLE.

8. *Selection.*
 MARK TWAIN.

Maj. Pond begs to announce that "MARK TWAIN" and MR. CABLE will appear in Liederkranz Hall, on Tuesday Evening, January 6th, with an entirely new programme.

J. B. POND, MANAGER, EVERETT HOUSE, NEW YORK.

CARRIAGES AT 10.

C. Heimerdinger Co. formed.

Hirsch Bros. & Co. began making pickles.

Almstedt Brothers, brokers, established.

Norton's Infirmary completed (4-story brick building).

The "Fair" opened a "super-market" of its day on Market Street.

April 2 . . . Courier-Journal quote: "There were several ladies in the stands". (Baseball game)

Continued on page 116

"Keystone Cops"? No—Keepers of the peace in Louisville in the "Gay Nineties."

The original of the above picture belongs to Mr. George J. Mueller. It shows part of the Louisville Police Department in 1895, photographed in front of Police Station No. 1., on Clay Street between Jefferson and Green. Gen. Thomas H. Taylor was chief of police.

In the back row, from left, are: Ed Scharre, Edw. St. John, Charlie Kyne, Frank Butell, John Senn, John Snyder, Jim Cassell, Charles Reese, Lon Miller and John McHugh. Standing, front row, are: Dave Nolan, George Elbers, M. J. Ahearn, Louis Hulzweed, Emmanuel Weinstock, F. Hilliand, Ed Powell, John Hess, John Reese and Jack Sipe. Seated in front are: George Praether and Lt. Harrison Browning.

HISTORY OF OUR POLICE

JOHN FERGUSON and Edward Dowen were Louisville's first two policemen. They were appointed in 1810 as "public watchmen" at an annual salary of $250.00.

The first President of the United States to be escorted by Louisville police officers was President James Monroe when he visited Louisville in 1819.

The first bank robbery that Louisville police officers were called on to investigate occurred September 18, 1829. Thieves broke into the Commonwealth Bank sometime during the night and stole $25,000.00. The robbers were never apprehended.

Juvenile delinquency in Louisville in the middle of the last century was so bad that the

Continued on page 115

1909—The Louisville Police Department Gets Its First Automotive Equipment.

Hard-tops on Parade! Can you identify this downtown corner?

LOUISVILLE POLICEMEN'S "BIBLE" OF 1868

THIS interesting manual of the Louisville Police Department, was published in 1868. It is the only copy known to be in existence today, and is reproduced through the courtesy of Col. Carl E. Heustis, Chief of Police.

It was designed as a pocket-book with leather cover and flap, to be carried by policemen at all times. It contains 87 sections and chapters on the legal powers and duties of the police officers of Louisville, and on City ordinances. Among these was one on the observance of the Sabbath, which today might be considered an old "blue law."

The following things are forbidden on SUNDAY:

"Playing at marbles, pitching quoits, or engaging in any other game or sport on Sunday, by any minor or other person; sporting, rioting, quarreling, hunting, fishing, shooting, trading, bartering, or selling or buying any goods, wares or merchandise, or at any common labor (works of necessity and charity excepted,) by any person of the age of fourteen years and upwards, excepting as to common labor those who conscientiously observe Saturday as a Sabbath; exposing clothing, or any other article of merchandise, by hanging the same outside of the door of any house where such article is kept for sale, or by placing the same upon any of the side-walks; exposing or offering for sale any article in a market-place on Sunday."

The Louisville Police "Black Maria" on the job at Fourth and Jefferson—perhaps in the 1890's? We don't know the cause of the trouble—but it wasn't an auto accident—(no automobiles!)

Photo courtesy Capt. John Cunningham

Police Story continued

School of Reform was instituted in Louisville in 1854. Today Louisville's reduction in juvenile delinquency is one of the outstanding records in the United States.

The first riot that Louisville police were called to quell was August 6, 1855. The "Know-Nothing" party went on rampage and killed 22 people mostly foreigners. This day is known as "Bloody Monday" (see story in another section).

All police officers of the Louisville Department were called in for emergency duty on the night of March 27, 1890, when the tornado struck Louisville. This was Louisville's worst disaster, in loss of life and in *complete loss* of property—far exceeding the 1937 flood.

The largest parade that Louisville police were ever called on to handle, with the exception of the American Legion parade of 1929, was during the week of September 9-14, 1895, when the G.A.R. held its National Encampment in this city.

On the night of July 14, 1914, Louisville police were called out to guard the fire lines at one of the few general alarm fires ever to strike Louisville. This big fire was at the Bourbon Stock Yards.

In 1917, volunteers for the armed services for World War I seriously depleted the ranks of the Louisville Police Department.

The first automotive transportation in the Louisville Police Department was put into service in 1909. Today there are 81 automo-

biles, 19 two-wheel motorcycles and 10 three-wheel motorcycles in the department.

In 1929, one of the greatest steps of advancement was seen in the Louisville Police Department. Civil Service was instituted that year for the divisions of police and fire.

Modern invention was brought into the Louisville Police Department when police radios were installed in police cars. The first official call transmitted was on October 4, 1930 at 8:00 P.M. Car 11 was given a call to a break-in. The police arrived in record time and caught the culprit who had fled to the alley. Louisville was the fifth city in the United States to have police radios.

During the 1937 flood, all police officers were put on 24-hour emergency duty. One police officer, Patrolman Lawrence Claycomb, lost his life in the flood.

There were 109 men from the police department who either enlisted or were drafted in World War II for the duration of the war. Three police officers Henninger Pile, George Van Meter, Jr., and William Hedrick were killed in action.

Something new was added to the Louisville Division of Police in 1949 when 25 women were hired part-time as School Traffic Guards. Since then 50 more have been added.

Today, 1954, the Department of Safety's budget allows for 519 police officers (including 12 police women), 75 school traffic guards and 41 civilian employees. The 1953 budget was $2,200,000.

Finest Police Building in U. S. under construction

In 1953, the voters of Louisville approved a two million dollar bond issue by ⅔ majority to provide a modern home for Louisville's 520 police officers and 100 civilian employees. The new 4-story structure which will contain 100,000 square feet of floor space, will be located on the NE corner of 7th and Jefferson.

The most advanced ideas in planning and construction will be incorporated. The building will be connected with Police Court by underground tunnel, which will prevent prisoners escaping. Plans for the handling of the holdovers, including unique use of the "electric eye", will whisk prisoners to the top floor on a special elevator shaft that has no doorways on the other floors. Other features of the sensational new building will be I.B.M. equipment to microfilm the tons of police records; a central information desk connected by phone, P. A. system, wire and tube with every department for immediate handling of all questions and complaints; a three-quarters standard size gymnasium; and a school.

Physical training is now handled at the Y.M.C.A., but with the new building *all* activities will center under one roof. Almost unbelievably, there are no showers or lockers in the present police quarters. A policeman hasn't a place to hang a raincoat or keep a change of socks. All this will be corrected in the new building; besides, there will be a 25-yard revolver range in the basement where five policeman can practice at one time; there will be a refrigerated property-room for furs and perishables recovered by the police or kept as evidence; the building will be about 75% air conditioned; and it will be *pigeon-proof!*

Chief of Police Col. Carl E. Heustis for 18 months has been checking modern police buildings in various cities and he promises that the new one will surpass all others in the U.S.

> The late George Tilden Ragsdale, Professor at Male High, was given permission to start a police training school for recruit police officers in 1919. Much of the modern police training school is patterned after the school set up by him. Prof. Ragsdale collapsed suddenly and died of over-exertion during the 1937 flood.

Chronology Continued—

Louisville policemen furnished clubs to defend selves.

This was the era of hourglass figures, red woolen underwear, mule cars, high bikes.

October 11 . . . First number of a new weekly newspaper called "Truth" was published. Established by Young E. Allison, George W. Smith and Ben H. Ridgely. Isaac Dinkelspiel was manager.

1886 Writer on the "Spirit of the Times" referred to Louisville track as Churchill Downs —was beginning of its march to fame.

The Five Brothers Tobacco Works—John Finzer & Bros.; Nicholas Finzer was director of the German Insurance Bank.

Standard Oil Company chartered in September.

August . . . "Last Days of Pompeii" presented Mr. James Pain, London pyrotechnist, at the famous fireworks amphitheater between 4th and 5th at Hill Street. Stage 250 x 400 feet, seated 10,000, covered 4 acres; 250 lavishly costumed performers. Ran every Thursday and Saturday from August through October. Later Louisvillians saw "Burning of Moscow" and the "Siege of Sevastopol"; adults 25¢, children 10¢.

Sales of tobacco reached 127,026 hogsheads, always a good barometer of city's progress.

Customs House in progress.

"Daisy Line" via Kentucky and Indiana Railroad bridge to New Albany streetcar, opened. Operated first as a steam-driven train from First and Water Streets, electrified May 1892, discontinued March 1, 1908.

1887 First Louisville free kindergarten opened February 1st.

Astoria Veneer Mills and Lumber Co. founded.

Commercial Club incorporated; (1891 membership 1,272), was original Board of Trade.

April . . . Jennie Bowman, an innocent girl, murdered by two negroes, Turner and Patterson, in residential part of town. Public up in arms. Apprehended, taken to Frankfort; returned April 27. Louisville Legion guarding the jail; mob attacks jail but is repulsed; later, the two hanged by law.

New stockyards of Kentucky and Indiana Co. opened at 28th and Broadway. Beef 5-10¢ lb.; flour $4/barrel; other commodities in proportion.

August 2 . . . J. F. Kurfees Paint Co. founded.

November 24 . . . Louisville Legion celebrated Thanksgiving with sham battles at the old fort at the end of Preston Street.

November 30 . . . Mass meeting at Liederkranz Hall to prevent bribery on election day.

Continued on page 118

Drunken Rioters attacking Private Residences in the Streets of Louisville.

BLOODY MONDAY

1855—Terrible riot in Louisville, on election day; then designated, and still most painfully remembered as "BLOODY MONDAY". Fighting and disturbance between individuals or squads, in various parts of the city. The most fearful and deplorable scenes of violence, bloodshed, and house-burning principally in the First and Eighth wards. Between 7 and 1 o'clock at night, twelve houses were set fire and burned, on the north side of Main, east of Eleventh, two adjoining on Eleventh and two on the south side of Main opposite. Patrick Quinn, the owner of most of them was shot, and his body partially consumed in the flames. Numerous shots were fired by foreigners from windows in some of the buildings which killed or wounded Americans in the streets; this fact, with the exaggerated report that arms and powder were concealed there, excited to frenzy a mob of Americans (Know-Nothings) already crazed with similar excitement; shooting and bloodshed on both sides at other points; several persons who were concealed in the buildings, or fled to them for refuge from the mob, were burned to death; several were shot as they attemped to escape from the flames; Ambruster's large brick brewery and his dwelling, at the head of Jefferson were burned; also two Irish copper-shops on Main above Woodland gar-

den; frame grocery corner of Madison and Shelby; many houses were riddled or gutted.

The mob which ranged through the streets and set fire to the houses was composed of Americans, part of them with a cannon at their head; the foreigners fought from their houses and lost life and property together. About twenty-two were killed or died of wounds, about three-fourth of them foreigners, one fourth Americans; many more were severely wounded but recovered. Mayor Barbee, Marshall Kidd, and a portion of the police and the personal efforts of Hon. William P. Thomasson, Captain L. H. Rousseau, George D. Prentice, Colonel William Preston (the anti Know-Nothing candidate for Congress) Joseph Burton, and others, at different times and places, stopped the effusion of blood, and saved the then new Shelby Street Catholic Church (St. Martin's) and other valuable property from the rapacity and violence of the mob. Bad blood on both sides, aggravated and intensified for several days previous by distorted representations of preparation for serious work, culminated in a most terrible and disgraceful riot. For several days after, fears of a renewal of the desperate conflict and work of destruction hung like a funeral pall over the city. A card from R. Rev. Bishop Martin J. Spalding, and the steady efforts of many good citizens gradually restored a feeling of quiet and security.

December 4 . . . Nine men arrested in a raid on a cockfight at 10th and Market.

December 6 . . . Charles Dickens, Jr. read selections from father's works at Masonic Temple; critics disappointed.

December 22 . . . Helena Modjeska played "Camille" in the afternoon and that night played "As You Like It".

Handsome new building of Southern Baptist Seminary begun at 5th and Broadway (completed 1888).

Kaufman-Straus moves from Jefferson Street to present Boston Shoe Building on Fourth Avenue.

1888 Great annual event in late '80's and early '90's was spectacular "Satellites of Mercury"; immense parade similar to world-famous New Orleans Mardi Gras. One year there were 493 elaborately decorated and illuminated floats; parade over 5 miles long; climaxed by grand ball at Galt House.

Louisville Textiles incorporated.

Louisville Gas Co. amends charter to include manufacture and distribution of electricity.

Nine hundred thirty four buildings erected this year.

Clearing House showed a business of over $300,000,000.

First city ordinance in Louisville regulating electric wiring of homes.

Jennie Benedict opens store on Fourth "Avenue".

Australian Ballot first used in U.S. in Louisville.

Louisville Tin & Stove Co. founded.

January 27 . . . Rooms for rent; SW corner 4th and Green, $8 to $11 per month.

Seelbach's "European Style" Hotel opened about this time at 6th and Main (Old Inn now, 1954).

1889 April 30 . . . Louisville Legion marches in New York; Centennial Celebration of Washington's first inaugural as president.

F. M. Perkins & Sons established.

Frey Planning Mill Co. began operations.

September 21 . . . First horseless streetcar, on Green Street. Great excitement; everyone turned out to see this new wonder of the world!

1890 Louisville's greatest disaster—Tornado of March 27th. One hundred twenty killed; destroyed property of $2,500,000. There were light rains during the day with some wind but no cyclonic symptoms. Struck at 8 P.M. going in a northeast direction; started in Parkland; path 6 blocks wide; passed over to Jeffersonville and back across river at water works. Terrific damage and destruction to the 7th and

River Railroad Station, 5 churches, 2 public halls, 3 schools, 324 manufacturing plants, 10 tobacco warehouses, 532 homes; $115,000 raised in a few days for relief.

The following Louisville companies, still in business were established this year: Gould-Levy Company, Henry Bickel Co., J. J. Repetto Broom Works, Peter and Burghard Stone Co., Norman Lumber Co., Nill's Bakery.

Louisville Railway Co. formed (2 firms consolidated).

Louisville played Brooklyn in World Series! Influenza epidemic.

Power Station to supply carlines erected at Campbell and Jacob; its 200 foot smokestack was outstanding landmark until recent years.

First Louisville "skyscraper" completed—Columbia Building, 4th and Main; tornado missed it by 2 blocks; cost $1,000,000.

City Park Act passed—plans made for 3 major parks, Iroquois, Cherokee and Shawnee. Capt. Thomas Speed launched campaign in 1887. Act passed under leadership of Col. John Mason Brown; internationally famous artist, Frederick Law Olmstead, laid out the parks.

Louisville Gas Co. becomes Louisville Gas and Electric Co.

Ewald Iron Co. moves to Louisville.

Smith Memorial Library built (5th and Broadway, part of Baptist Seminary).

Louisville Woman's Club organized.

1891 First horse breeding society, National Horse Breeders Association, organized in Louisville.

J. C. Heitzman's Bakery started in business.

Ohio River Sand Company was incorporated.

J. J. Mueller Tailoring Co. founded.

September 7 . . . Union Station formally opened; cost $400,000; F. W. Mowbray, architect (foundation dug in 1882).

George G. Fetter Co. organized.

October 21-22 . . . "Carmen", "La Traviata" and "Lohengrin" given in Louisville by the Metropolitan Opera—first grand opera in Louisville.

St. Xavier moved to Broadway from St. Patrick's on 8th Street.

1892 Kentucky Centennial Celebration—great crowds.

"Free Silver" and "Sound Money" campaigns kept country in turmoil from '92-'96, era of William Jennings Bryan.

Federal Building completed at 3rd and Liberty.

Oertel Brewing Co. established by Louis Hartmetz; then called Butchertown Brewery.

January 17 . . . Children's Free Hospital opened doors.

Continued on page 131

The masterpiece of Henry Whitestone—the last of three famous Galt Houses
(Below) The second Galt House—destroyed by fire in 1865; the first Galt House is shown on page 57

SOME FAMOUS HOTELS OF LOUISVILLE

Early drawing of Patton's Inn or Hotel

Capt. James Patton (1748-1815) one of the founders of Louisville, and proprietor of its first hotel.

Alexander's Hotel, s-e corner of Jefferson and Center apparently changed name later to Willard Hotel (see below).

WILLARD HOTEL.

The beautiful main dining room of the Seelbach Hotel, one of Louisville's most exclusive eating places 40 years ago.

GALT HOUSE WAITER
(from an old engraving)

(Below) Seelbach's original "European Hotel" on the corner of 6th & Main in the days of the mule cars. (Note gas-lit display sign at left connected with street lamp). The Old Inn is still operating at 6th & Main. Louisville Hotel was adjacent.

THE FIRST "MISS LOUISVILLE"

Sallie Ward was born in 1827 at the family mansion at Second and Walnut. Her father was a descendant of an English Lord. Educated at a French finishing school in Philadelphia, Sallie married Bigelow Lawrence of Boston, at the age of 17. She scandalized many people by marrying four times—the last time to Maj. George Downs. Sallie was the only member of her social set who painted her lips and cheeks. She was most unconventional. Once, on a dare, she rode up the Galt House steps on horseback and into the lobby, an unthinkable thing for a Victorian lady to do. But she was never ostracized because of her great personal charm, her wit and intelligence and the position of her family—in fact, she was envied and emulated.

She was always a striking figure and one of the most fascinating of all the beautiful women who have lived in Louisville. Her fame spread to the East and even to Europe. Once she visited France upon the request of the Emperor. All she wore or did was imitated by loving admirers in all walks of life.

Sallie Ward (Downs)

FAMILY GROUP in the gay nineties— ☞ taken in the front yard of the large fashionable T. L. Jefferson home on Gray Street near Floyd. Among those in the picture are Dr. J. M. Holloway and his son, and the Suddeth children. Dr. C. W. Jefferson, who is practicing in Louisville today, is the intense looking youngster on the right in the front row; his mother, Mrs. C. W. Jefferson, who is still living, is the lady in the back row in the very fancy hat. When this picture was made, Gray Street was Louisville's most fashionable residential street. Other prominent families who lived on Gray Street were Bishop Noye, the Dr. Thomas Satterwhites, the Preston Rogers, Whitneys, Knotts, Middletons, Johnsons, Almstedts, Fincks, Whites, Fetters, Bakers, etc. Mary Anderson, lived in this block in these proper days of Victorian society, when each socially acceptable street had a "Receiving Day." For Gray Street this was Thursday.

TAKEN at South Park about 1890—hotel ☞ in background. Man in foreground is Mr. Goodwin, an executive of the Standard Oil Company of Kentucky. Seated next to him is Sam Chambers; Bertie Goodwin is standing behind his father; others in the picture are Mrs. Lithgow Smith, Mrs. Chas. W. Jefferson, Mrs. Q. D. Vaughn, Judge Stone, and other prominent Louisvillians of that day. The season at South Park was from June to September. Among the guests this particular season were Henry Watterson and Dr. and Mrs. Larabee (famous physician.)

Louisville's First Newspaper—
Its Editor and Publisher

ON the 18th of January, 1801, *The Farmer's Library*, a weekly paper edited by Samuel Vail, was laid before the citizens of Louisville. It was a folio sheet, nineteen by eleven inches, printed with long primer type on coarse paper made at Georgetown, Kentucky. The types with which it was printed had been formerly used by Col. Matthew Lyon to print his "Scourge of Aristocracy and Repository of Political Truth," published at Fair Haven, Vermont. Lyon lent his types and printing press to Vail, who transported them over the mountains and down the Ohio to Louisville, and used them in the production of the first paper in the town. The Farmer's Library was continued until 1808, when Vail grew weary of journalism and joined the U.S. Army. He was promoted through the ranks and finally was made a Major; he later retired to his deep-South sugar plantation.

SAMUEL VAIL
EDITOR AND PUBLISHER
"THE FARMER'S LIBRARY"
1801

COLLECTOR'S ITEM

EARLY ISSUES ARE EXTREMELY SCARCE—NO COPY OF THE FIRST NUMBER IS KNOWN

HISTORIC HOME

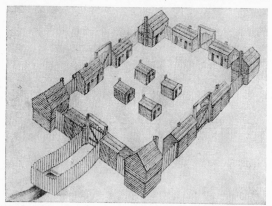

"Spring Station," 3241 Trinity Road, residence of Mr. & Mrs. R. J. Herrmann; restored in 1920.

There are scores of beautiful century-old homes in and around Louisville. The oldest is "Spring Station", originally a fort (1780); present house built in 1795. "Mulberry Hill" (no longer standing) on Poplar Level Road was home of George Rogers Clark's parents; he lived there from 1783 to 1803. He died and was originally buried at Locust Grove, now home of Col. and Mrs. John S. Waters.

Farmington, the old John Speed home on

"Mulberry Hill"—G. R. Clark lived here for 20 years after his Revolutionary War campaigns.

Early drawing of Spring Station; note the wall extending around source of spring—which still runs as Beal's Branch of Beargrass Creek.

Locust Grove, Blankenbaker Lane. Clark died here, the home of his sister Lucy.

Early mansion still standing near "hay-market."

Famous pioneer, Col. John Floyd built "Spring Station" in 1780; was killed near the fort by Indians.

OF LOUISVILLE

Bardstown Road, was designed by Thomas Jefferson; and Abraham Lincoln ("The Tall Kentuckian") slept there! The two oldest river residences still standing are Jonathan Paget House (circa 1800-1838) opposite Towhead Island; and the Judge Earick home (circa 1800) at 34th and Rudd, now residence of Mrs. Lilly H. Guembel. The land grant on the Reed home, 2837 Riedling Drive, was signed by Thos. Jefferson, then governor of Virginia.

Farmington on Bardstown Road was recently restored by Mr. & Mrs. Porter Smith and their son.

Grayson Home (1806-10) oldest in downtown section. Originally situated on beautiful pond.

This is the couple Abraham Lincoln visited at Farmington—his friends Mr. & Mrs. Joshua Fry Speed. (Filson Club has original portrait.)

Oldest house in Portland, built in 1800 or earlier. Contained court and lock-up of early judge.

"Mansion House"—oldest in East End overlooks boat harbor. Facade copied in recent residence.

The octagonal hall and living rooms at Farmington are typical of architect Thos. Jefferson.

120-year-old residence of Mr. & Mrs. Henry M. Reed, Jr. Land grant signed by Thos. Jefferson.

"Ridgeway" (1808) home of the Churchill Humphreys. A classic example, in St. Matthews.

144-year-old residence of Mrs. Paul J. Hughes; 1212 Castlewood; built by B. Lammers.

Jonathan Clark's "Tecoma" — Trough Spring Farm, 1802. Now home of Geo. H. Imordes.

The Gil Whittenberg home "Hayfield" was started in 1795; is in beautiful condition today.

Home of Dr. & Mrs. Jas. R. Hendon, in Crescent Court. Similar to old house in Kennedy Court.

The Montfort home, 4th & Broadway, razed in 1953. Impressive residence by Whitestone.

Cardinal Hill, once home of C-J editor Col. C. E. Sears; now the R. C. Riebels. Restored in 1928.

Early view of the Louisville Country Club, Louisville's oldest and socially most prominent Country Club.

The Woman's Club on South Fourth Street is a center of social, civic, intellectual and artistic activity.

Louisville's Rock Creek, an excellent Riding Club, holds outstanding annual horse show.

Ex-Mayor Wilson W. Wyatt apparently has the floor in this group of prominent Louisvillians photographed in the 235 Club on Fifth Street.

The Filson Club, Louisville and Kentucky's famous historical society. This building is the clever combination of two old homes into one building; central hall built between.

This was the famous Kentuckiana library of Col. Reuben T. Durrett, founder of The Filson Club, located in his home (still standing) on the S-E corner of Brook and Chestnut. Near the end of his life Col. Durrett sold this library to the University of Chicago, thereby starting a controversy which has not yet terminated. It has been claimed that the collection contained many rare and unique historical items from the Louisville Polytechnic Library and The Filson Club.

BULL BUILT THIS "BLOCK"

Doctor Bull, that is—the patent medicine tycoon of his time, the man who in 1867 reported an income of over $100,000 to the U.S. Internal Revenue Department (see story below). If this was a typical year, he could have rebuilt *Louisville*, considering the comparative cost of building then and now! Incidentally "Bull Block", as this building was called (now considerably remodeled and modernized) is still going strong as the Southern Trust Building, affording offices for many business and professional men.

INCOME TAXES 87 YEARS AGO!

We think of the income tax as a development of the past three or four decades, but actually there was an income tax levied in the years after the Civic War (all wars have to be paid for) and it seems that, in Louisville, at least, the names of all income tax payers were published, together with their annual incomes. Most of the front page of the Daily Courier of May 11, 1868 is devoted to this "Income List" for the year ending December 31st, 1867.

It is interesting to note that one resident, the famous patent medicine man, Dr. John Bull, owner of "Bull Block", headed the list with the amazing income (for that time) of $105,625.00. B. F. Avery, the great Louisville industrialist, and founder of the world-famous plow company, was a poor second with $62,324.00 (although that wasn't "hay" *then*!)

Because we thought it would interest everyone (particularly the descendants of these "big money" men) we reprint the names of all whose income exceeded $20,000.00 as reported by the Daily Courier:

Dr. John Bull	$105,625.
B. F. Avery	62,324.
E. Bustard	46,744.
Mrs. M. L. Tyler	38,230.
T. T. Shreve	36,121.
H. Verhoeff, Jr.	33,736.
R. Burge	30,859.
W. C. Hite	30,396.
M. Kean	28,616.
R. Houston	26,593.
W. B. Belknap	26,127.
J. A. Faulds (Att'y J. A. Dunlap)	24,982.
B. Dupont	23,985.
L. L. Warren	23,447.
Theodore Schwartz	22,298.
R. Houston (Adm'r)	22,095.
H. V. Loving	21,319.
Joseph Monk	20,860.
J. F. Speed	20,899.
Edwin Moore	20,650.
J. W. Henning	20,207.
S. S. Nicholas	20,162.

JAMES GUTHRIE — "MR. LOUISVILLE"

BUSINESS AND ITS LEADERS

WE think it appropriate to begin this chapter on the history of business in Louisville, with a tribute to James Guthrie.

Unquestionably the man who did the most to build and develop Louisville in its critical, formative years was James Guthrie—a leader in government, in business and industry, in education, in banking, and in all civic affairs; a *big* man who has done more for Louisville than any other man in its history.

The extent and diversity of his achievements is phenomenal. Under the inspiration of his

leadership Louisville grew from a sleepy river hamlet of 4,000 souls, the "graveyard of the West"—so called because of its many stagnant ponds—to become a great city of the South, of nearly 100,000 people, all in the lifetime of James Guthrie.

Guthrie came to Louisville from Bardstown as a young lawyer. From the start he recognized the great potentialities of Louisville, and set about to realize them. First of all, as Commonwealth's attorney, he cleaned up the city and established law and order, even among the roughneck rivermen. Then he attacked the unsanitary conditions of the town and made a drive to fill up the scores of unhealthy ponds and quagmires that had caused many epidemics. He saw that strict sanitary regulations were incorporated in the city's charter of 1828, and he became a member of Louisville's first city council.

Having faith in the growth of Louisville he invested in real estate—bought the entire block between Second and Third and Walnut and Chestnut—where he eventually built himself a fine mansion.

Guthrie, like other far-sighted men, realized that a canal was necessary to relieve the traffic "bottle-neck" at the falls, and vigorously worked for this objective, succeeding in getting a $100,000 Federal Government appropriation; later he had the canal widened and deepened, to accommodate larger craft.

About this time Guthrie became interested in banking, realizing that Louisville could not grow commercially without strong banks. In 1834 he got a new charter for the Bank of Kentucky, became a director, and later president.

Then he turned his interest to education. Louisville needed a public school system. Guthrie organized it. Then he worked to make the Louisville Medical Institute the nucleus of a municipal university, and was therefore instrumental in creating the University of Louisville. In 1847, he became its second president. No man in Louisville's history has been president of so many important institutions.

Turning back to governmental matters, he helped to plan the Court House, with the view that it might be the State Capital. It was planned so much larger than the needs of the county of that day, and it was so long in building, due to lack of funds, that it became known as "Guthrie's Folly." But Guthrie was finally vindicated, for the Court House is still functioning and is still Louisville's noblest structure.

Guthrie now turned his attention to that great new development in transportation, the "Iron Horse", which was just appearing in the North. Quick to see the significance of the railroad, Guthrie began planning for a line into Louis-

ville. He was principally responsible for the road from Louisville to Frankfort, connecting with the Lexington line. The next step was a railroad to Nashville, and Guthrie was one of the instigators of the mass meeting held in Louisville in 1850 which resulted in the establishment of the L & N Railroad—of which he later became president.

In 1853 Guthrie went to Washington as Secretary of the Treasury where he also did a good job of eliminating extravagance, rooting out incompetence and improving treasury regulations.

In 1857 he resigned and came back to Louisville to guide the L. & N. through some hard times. He re-established the company on a sound basis so when the panic of '59 came and railroads everywhere were going bankrupt, Guthrie was able to sell $1,000,000 worth of L. & N. bonds at par to complete the road to Nashville. In 1860 he was elected president of the L. & N., a position he held until June 11, 1868.

Then came the Civil War—and James Guthrie, good Southern Democrat that he was, was too good a *business man* to advocate Kentucky's joining the Confederacy. On the contrary he saw the commercial advantages of Kentucky's staying neutral—and doing business with both sides. The geographical position made this feasible.

So again, in spite of the clamoring of Southern sympathizers, business man Guthrie won out— and Louisville became the war-profiteering center of the country. The war which impoverished the South actually made Louisville stronger and richer. By the close of the War the population was nearly 100,000 and many neat fortunes had been made.

Forty-nine of James Guthrie's 77 years were devoted to Louisville. Keeping the city and state out of the war was his last big contribution. Guthrie apparently had little glamor; he was not an orator or a "dynamic personality" in the modern sense; he limped badly because of a leg wound received in a duel in his youth; yet he was perhaps the *greatest* Louisvillian.

893 On advent of 1893 everyone very hopeful of a renewal of business activity; however, there was the "Panic of 1893"; great depression; several banks in state closed.
1885-1893—great civic awakening and unusual business activity in Louisville).
Postoffice at 4th and Chestnut completed.
Jos. Denunzio Fruit Co. incorporated.
R. C. Schlich and William Mayer established first commercial photo engraving business in city.
Norton Hall built, 5th and Broadway, with myriad of spires.
Du Pont Manual began as a manual training school; dedicated May 1st; 16 days later the benefactor, du Pont dies.
U.S. Life Saving Station established here, mainly because of dangers of the rapids.
1894 City Hospital further remodeled.
Medical School Building erected at 1st and Chestnut from private funds of the faculty.
C. F. Snyder Coal Co. and E. T. Slider Co., incorporated.
Steamboat "City of Louisville" built.
Bicycle track completed in Fountain Ferry Park—called "Mecca of the Wheelman". 1895 witnessed the greatest encampment of record breakers that has ever been known to be at one place at one time.
1895 Democratic State Convention met in Louisville in June to nominate state officers for the November elections. The currency question, the important issue, split the party. John C. Carlisle, of Kentucky, and Secretary of National Treasury, made three speeches in the state in favor of the gold standard. P. Watt Hardin, democratic candidate for governor, was an advocate of free coinage in silver. Bradley defeated him and was Kentucky Governor, '95-'99.
Isaac Rosenbaum & Sons, established.
Kentucky Children's Home conducted by a society, founded 1895 by Judge R. H. Thompson of Louisville.
One hundred-fifty miles of streetcar tracks (110 electrified, 40 horse or mule power).
Biggest week in Louisville history (?). Louisville entertained the 29th Annual Encampment of the Grand Army of the Republic; more than 150,000 attended from Union and Confederacy.
New Louisville Jockey Club reorganized.
New grandstand with twin towers (nucleus of present) erected at Churchill Downs.
Confederate Monument erected—designed by Louisville born sculptress, Emil Yandell.
1896 Mrs. Sallie Ward Downs died at Galt House, 66 years old.

Continued on page 137

131

Theodore Ahrens

One of the greatest Louisville industrialists of the past 100 years was Theodore Ahrens, founder with Henry Ott of Ahrens & Ott (1866) which in 1900, after merger with ten other manufacturing concerns, became The Standard—Sanitary Corporation, and is now the American-Radiator Standard—Sanitary Corporation. Without capital but with great skill as a mechanic, Theodore Ahrens started a brass foundry in 1860 (see early ad below) on Market Street between Jackson and Preston. From a modest shop the business became one of the largest industries in America—all in the lifetime and under the direction of one man. The Theodore Ahren's Trade School is a permanent and practical memorial to this truly great Louisvillian.

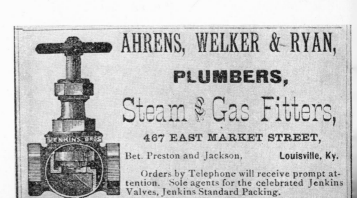

Main Street between Second and Third—100 years ago. Reproduced from an old chromo in colors belonging to Lemon & Son. Note that this firm, Louisville's oldest, was then located in this block.

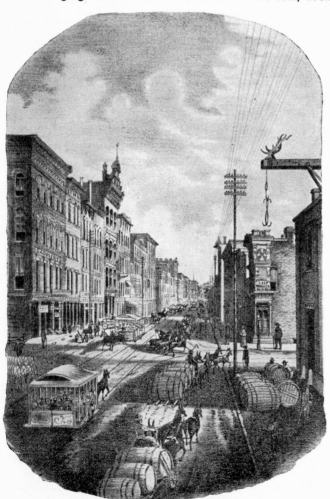

Main Street 75 years ago—note tobacco hogsheads & open mule cars.

Louisville was once largest tobacco market

100-yr.-old Carter Dry Goods Co., 50 yrs. ag

The Brewmaster and his staff at the Shelby Street Brewery—one of many in the 1880's.

Distilleries like this (Wathen's) established Louisville as "the Whiskey Capital of the U. S. A."
(Below) Peter-Burghard Stone Company—Lettering and Engraving Department, from 1899 photo.

The "Kentucky DuPont's" famous Artesian Well at their paper mill on 12th Street.

Digging a commercial well in 1858 for pure water needed to manufacture paper, the DuPonts hit an artesian well at 2,086 feet, and released a stream of sulphur water that flowed steadily at the rate of 230 gallons a minute and sent a column of water 40 feet into the air. This most famous of all Louisville wells and fountains made Louisville a noted watering place for a number of years. A bath house with 100 tubs was built; but eventually (possibly because of lack of promotion) the well was forgotten, though it gushed on at the same rate until plugged up in recent years.

Edw. H. Marcus Paint Company started in 1853.

TWO OF MARKET STREET'S OLDEST BUSINESS FIRMS

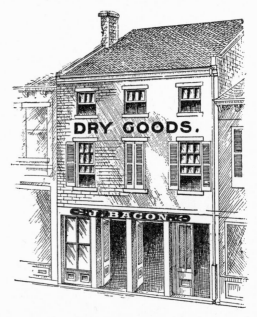

Started on East Market Street 109 years ago.

om the small busi-
ss of 114 years ago
een in an earlier
ew of Third and
ain) the Belknap
rdware and Manu-
cturing Company has
come one of the
ants in its field. Its
ain office now occu-
es the site of the
ird Galt House.

e National Seed
mpany is another
Louisville's historic
mmercial firms, and
e of the oldest
Main Street. This
ilding has changed
tle since the Civil
ar, when it served
a hospital.

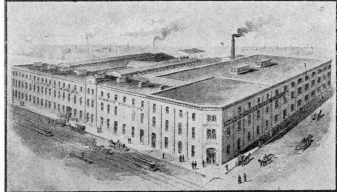

MENNE'S CANDY FACTORY

is no longer in ex-
istence but at the
turn of the century
is was the largest
candy factory in
the world (Wenzel
and Main).

e Exchange Room of
e old Board of Trade
Third and Main
reets was a busy
ot in the old days.
is was the dignified
a when businessmen
ore silk hats, morn-
g coats, and carried
nes.

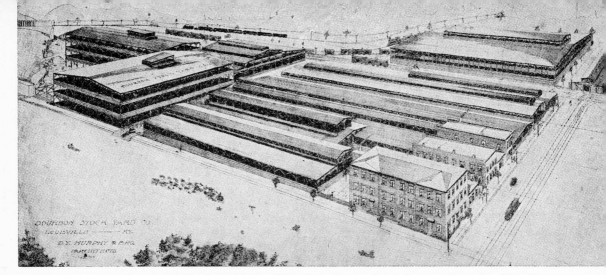

Bourbon Stock Yards in 1907—"The best livestock market south of the Ohio."

IN 1834 when Louisville was a thriving town of less than 20,000, a stockyard was established on the south side of Main Street between Campbell and Woodland Gardens.

Steamboats came to Louisville from the South laden with cotton and sugar, and returned carrying Kentucky pork and lard and other Kentucky products.

Kentucky and Tennessee were at that time the two largest hog-producing states. By 1870 meat packing was the largest industry in Louisville —there were 13 such provision companies.

On July 1st, 1875, the present Bourbon Stock Yard Company was incorporated, now the only daily livestock market in Kentucky. It has seen the movement of livestock change from being driven on foot, or transported by river, to being moved in tremendous volume by railroads; and now principally by highway motor trucks. Today Bourbon Stock Yards is the largest livestock market south of the Ohio River.

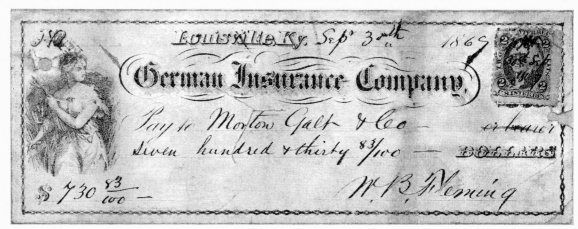

Check dated 1869 drawn on German Insurance Company, showing that the Company was operating as a bank before the German Insurance Bank was incorporated. *(Courtesy Judge Ben F. Washer.)*

BALLARD'S FLOUR MILL ABOUT 50 YEARS AGO

Most of these elevators and buildings are still standing although the plant has been tremendously enlarged since. The overpass would now run thru the foreground of this picture.

136

Gamble Bros. incorporated.

Smith & Dugan, founded.

Louisville is largest tobacco market in world (over 175,000 hogsheads).

Four toll gates still remain in city.

Kentucky Derby changed from 1½ miles to present 1¼ miles.

Stoll Oil Refining Co. established (one of oldest independent oil companies in the south).

"Phoenix Hill" at the apex of its glory. The lights from this gay and glorified beer garden could be seen and the music heard over a good part of the east end, because of its high location overlooking downtown Louisville.

1897 Turnpike disturbances and toll gate raiders.

Bridges-Smith Company (Paint Co.) and Ferncliff Feed & Grain Co. founded.

Louisville Credit Men's Association established in old Southern National Bank Building, 322 W. Main.

July 19 . . . In Courier-Journal appeared Klondike Gold Rush story.

"Allegro", special open streetcar, brilliantly illuminated (by storage batteries) and with Victorian art, could be chartered by private parties for rides all around the town; many ended at Phoenix Hill Park. This was one of the items which made the "gay-nineties" gay in Louisville.

August 8 . . . Robert Wedekind, M.D. established Wedekind Optical Co. on NW corner 3rd and Chestnut—first lens grinding in Louisville; in 1906 became Southern Optical Co.

YMCA building dedicated in November (in old Avery residence, SE corner 4th and Broadway).

1898 (Maine blown up in Havana Harbor) War with Spain; Louisville Legion, commanded by Col. John B. Castleman, took part.

Last year gas street lights used by city.

October 4 . . . First automobile in Louisville, electrically powered.

First picture play in Louisville, February 18th at Library Hall; title was "Miss Jerry", a picture by Alexander Black.

1899 Music Hall Convention at Louisville for nomination of state Democratic ticket. Much bitterness felt and expressed by candidates P. Watt Hardin, W. J. Stone and Wm. Goebel. The withdrawal of Hardin and Stone left Goebel as the nominee of the convention, but the friends of former governor John Young Brown held a convention and nominated him. The three sided fight resulted in the election of W. S. Taylor on the face of the returns; he was inaugurated in December 1899, but the election was contested by Mr. Goebel and thrown into the House of Representatives.

Ahrens & Ott of Louisville consolidated with the Standard Manufacturing Company of Pittsburgh to form the Standard Sanitary Manufacturing Company (now the American Radiator—Standard Sanitary Corporation).

The Mengel Co. established.

The Louisville Fire Department this year was called, "One of the most efficient metropolitan fire departments in the world."

1900 Wm. Goebel, governor, assassinated (shot); died January 30.

Following firms established this year: Linker Cigar Co., Jobson Printing Co., Louisville Title Insurance Co., Ehrman's Bakery, and Louisville Chemical Co.

Ohio Valley merged with Cumberland Telephone and Telegraph. Name changed to Cumberland Telephone and Telegraph Co.

Fourth Avenue known as "Street of Churches"; there were two at Fourth and Walnut.

Miss Lucy Belknap donates public drinking fountain, installed in front of YMCA, 4th and Broadway.

May 14 . . . Wells Fargo comes to Louisville.

1901 Last mule drawn streetcars were seen on Louisville streets this year.

Caxton Company, printing, and Richard G. Tafel & Son started in business.

Bacon's moves to present location on Market Street between Third and Fourth—from Preston and Market.

First music store established in Louisville—"Smith & Nixon Co."

Julia Trabue—First woman to be sentenced to hang in Jefferson County.

1902 First fair known as "Kentucky State Fair" held at Churchill Downs. 40,000 attended; main attraction was head-on collision of two large locomotives.

Becker & Durski, Grocers Baking Co., and Burwinkle-Hendershot Co., established this year.

'Louisville Public Library' established (outgrowth of Polytechnic Society on Kaufman site.)

Eclipse Ball Park opened at 7th and Kentucky.

Jewish Hospital founded.

Haldeman Hall of Presbyterian Theological Seminary completed.

1903 (First flight of the Wright Bros. at Kitty Hawk)

Chas. R. Long, Jr. Co.; Boston Shoe Co.; and Liebschutz Book Store started in business this year.

Adler Royal Manufacturing Co. moves to Louisville.

Continued on page 140

Old woodcut of Speed Market (Market St. bet. Preston & Floyd.) There were 6 like this on Market Street in 185-

Kentucky Market, 5th & Liberty. One of city's oldest market houses; just razed (March 1954) for parking lot.

Same street today as in top view: 👉 Market, looking east from Floyd. Note how much wider street is in block where the Market House stood.

Market Street's Famous Street Markets

One hundred years ago Market Street was really the *market street*. There were six huge market houses located right in the center of the street in six different locations. These market blocks can still be identified because the street is wider in these places (traffic had to pass on both sides). We gather that practically all the food sold in those days was dispensed through these "super-markets." Strange, how we've come back to this type of food market in *1954!*

138

☜ **Louisville's "HAY MARKET"**

50 years ago . . .

TODAY ☞

MOST OF THE MARKET IS COVERED BY SHEDS

Here's the place to find local color, odd personalities and good bargains!

P.S.: As our second edition goes to press we note that Louisville's new $2,250,000 Produce Market, between New-burg and Poplar Level Roads, has just opened for business (December 5, 1955).

Kaufman-Straus Company erects new building and moves into new quarters, 427-437 S. 4th

1904 John Philip Sousa gave his last concert at old Louisville Auditorium.

W. E. Shacklett Co. and Kosmos Portland Cement Co. established.

Beckmann Photographers opened studio.

First moving picture shown in Kentucky was in Hale's Touring Car; screen was at the front end of the car; seats were on the side; was on 4th Street in Louisville.

April 6 . . . First moving picture house built here; called the "Dreamland", Market near 5th, was the third moving picture house in the U.S. (The first was in Los Angeles and the 2nd was in New York).

Sacred Heart Academy building was erected.

Editor's Note: As a matter of historical record we have attempted in this chronology to list all firms still in business in 1954 which were established 50 years ago or more. Firms established since 1904 may appear for other reasons.

1905 Beginning of tobacco war.

July 12 . . . Fire gutted inside of Union Station.

August 14 . . . Ground broken for Louisville Free Public Library.

Falls City Brewing Co. incorporated.

New Seelbach Hotel finished.

Library opened in temporary quarters in Kaufman-Straus building.

Louisville-Tuberculosis Association organized.

Louisville & Nashville shops completed.

1906 Columbia Theater on 4th Street has opening.

(San Francisco earthquake—April 18th and 19th, 1906)

Horace Wild makes first plane flight over Louisville.

1907 Five medical schools of city united.

Casino Theater (4th Street) and Orpheum (Jefferson) commenced business (movies).

Present site of Stewart's finished and occupied.

January . . . L & N began to move its general offices into its new building at 9th and Broadway.

April 1 . . . Mary Anderson Theater opens.

1908 Fairgrounds acquired when Kentucky State Fair became permanent institution; $100,000 livestock pavilion erected, largest in the world at that time.

Financial panic in U.S.

Present Library building completed at 3rd and York—Andrew Carnegie gave $250,000; city gave land; Carnegie later gave $200,000 for branches. 300,000 books checked out first day.

December 25 . . . Majestic Theater (4th opposite Guthrie) opened.

1909 (State capital building erected).

Henry Fisher Packing Company opened for business.

Crescent Hill filtration plant completed on July 13; ground broken October 8, 1898.

1910 Waverly Hill Sanitorium opened July 24, dedicated October 12.

Publication of the Flexner Report on Medical Education.

1911 Majestic Theater enlarged and became one of the first "Palace" Movie Houses; was the amusement center for the younger set.

1912 July 23 . . . First Rotary Club in state, organized in Louisville, the fifth in the world.

Cumberland Telephone and Telegraph Co. absorbed by Southern Bell Telephone and Telegraph Co.; continues operating under name of Cumberland Telephone and Telegraph Co.

Woodrow Wilson elected President—Teddy Roosevelt, "Progressive" candidate, defeated.

November 10 . . . Thomas E. Shea appeared in "Dr. Jekyll and Mr. Hyde" at Walnut Theater.

November 11 . . . Oak Street crosstown carline opened.

November 27 . . . New K & I bridge completed and first train ran over.

November 17 . . . Times and Courier-Journal plant moves from 4th and Green to 3rd and Green without missing an edition.

December 21 . . . Prentice statue taken down from Courier-Journal Building.

December 31 . . . Old K & I bridge began to be torn down.

Mengel moves to Louisville (original structure erected).

YWCA organized February 12, at 229 S. 4th, upstairs.

Colonial Dames of America erect the Fort Nelson Monument at 7th and Main—a rough stone column, with bronze plaque.

Walnut Street Christian Church (NE corner, 4th and Walnut) razed in spring; handsome stone pillars moved to present site at 4th and Breckenridge.

In July the first section of the Starks Building was begun; finished July, 1913.

1913 Louisville Gas and Electric Co. completes merger of all local lighting companies into the Louisville Gas & Electric Co.

Ford car bodies were mounted on chassis in two small shops, one of them where the present Summers-Hermann dealership is located.

YMCA building completed and dedicated the first week of August.

Continued on page 147

Landing of Ohio Troops at Louisville—January 11, 1862

LOUISVILLE IN THE CIVIL WAR

A Story in Pictures—reprinted from magazines and newspapers of that day

General Buell's Bodyguard parading through the streets of Louisville

The Wharf during the war—Many inhabitants are leaving the city

Gen. Curtis's Division passing the Louisville Hotel to meet Gen. Bragg

GENERAL DON CARLOS BUELL AND HIS HEADQUARTERS IN LOUISVILLE, 1862

Women and children leaving the city in October, 1862, by order of General Nelson preparatory to expected bombardment by Confederate General Bragg (which fortunately never happened).

"The Louisville," a Battleship of the Civil War—one of the original Eads' Ironclads.

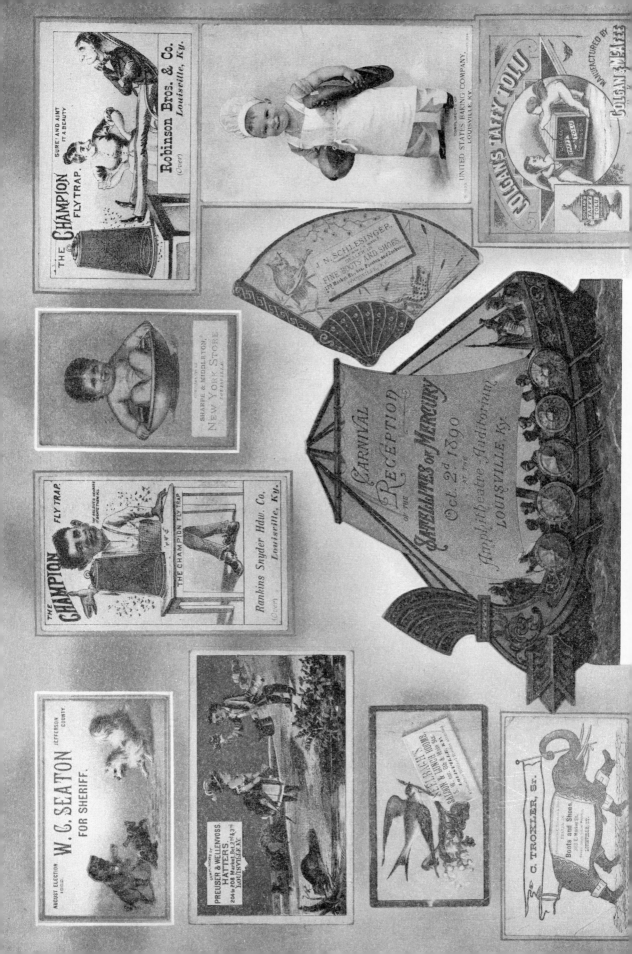

"THE LOUISVILLE EXPOSITION," FOURTH & CHESTNUT

ON THE 20th of July 1872, an Industrial Exposition Building, situated at the corner of Fourth and Chestnut Streets, on the ground later occupied by the Post Office, was opened with appropriate ceremonies in the presence of a large audience. "The structure is of attractive design and liberal dimensions", said a contemporary account, "extending three hundred and thirty feet on Fourth street, and two hundred and thirty on Chestnut."

"Annual expositions were held in it successfully, and with advantage to the city for a number of years. The expositions held here were mainly local in their scope, and intended to show simply the stage of development which the industries and general business of the city itself had reached, and to advertise to her customers the character and variety of her wares and her capacity to supply all their wants."

However, some elegantly attired crowds turned out, judging by the contemporary woodcuts which we have reprinted to the right. The figures in the foreground might have stepped out of Godey's Fashion Book —but do you see that hill-billy character in the background?

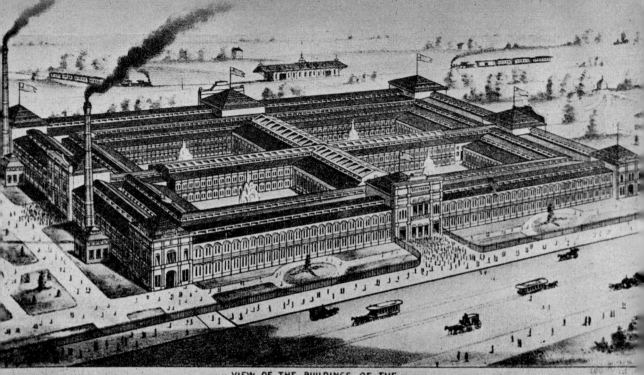

VIEW OF THE BUILDINGS OF THE

Southern Exposition, at Louisville, Kentucky.

OPENS AUGUST 1ST 1883 AND CONTINUES ONE HUNDRED DAYS.

Note the Railroad Station west of the building and trains coming from North and South

The Memorial History of Louisville (1896) states that . . . "The most important event which has transpired in Louisville for a long time, and one which gave great impetus to its progress, was the inauguration of the Southern Exposition, under the management of Major J. M. Wright, then superintendent of the Board of Trade. It was opened on the 1st of August, 1883, in the presence of a vast throng, by Chester A. Arthur, President of the United States.

"The grounds, on the west side of Fourth and south of Weissinger Avenues inclosed forty acres, including Central Park. The buildings were of frame, comprising a handsome two-story structure 900x600 feet, with carriage, saw-mill and boiler annexes, besides an art gallery, pavilion and restaurant, and other structures in the park. The cost of the plant was $300,000. There were 88 exhibition days, with a total attendance of 770,048. The machinery and electric light system were driven by the engines of 2,225 horse-power, requiring

twenty-one boilers. The premises were lighted by electric lights, then of recent introduction, and the display was far in advance of anything seen up to that time.

"There were over 1,500 exhibits, covering every variety of produce and manufacture. The display of textile machinery was particularly fine, while the art gallery, filled chiefly with paintings from the private galleries of Eastern connoisseurs, was the most valuable loan exhibition ever displayed in the West. But the display which was of greatest practical merit was the exhibit of the natural resources of Kentucky, in minerals, timbers, and agricultural products. The advertisement thus afforded led to large investments in the State by capitalists from other sections. The exposition was held annually for several years."

The Courier-Journal of August 2, 1883, reports that: "The Southern Exposition Building is, in point of immensity, among the foremost in the world's catalogue of big structures of the kind. At night the entire building will

146

Thousands went to the exposition by mule car —Note S-E buildings in background.

be illuminated by the incandescent electric light furnished by the Edison Company of New York. The building and annexes are lighted with 4,600 Edison lights of 16 candle-power each. In other words, the plant will furnish more light than any other plant ever did. It is even larger than the combined plants used at the great electric light exhibit at London last year. The cost of the entire electric plant was about $100,000, and the power is sufficient to supply a village with 20,000 lamps.

"These grounds are some two miles from the central part of the city, but the facilities for reaching them are abundant and convenient. The Central Passenger Railway Service on Fourth Street has tracks running right up to the gatehouse at the eastern approach, and in similar manner are they approached on Sixth Street by the City Passenger Railway Company, which lets off passengers at the door of the western gatehouse.

"The L&N Railroad ran a switch from its main stem northward through Sixth Street."

Swiss Chalet—One of several foreign exhibits.

January 3 . . . Louisville led nation in the number of packages mailed under new parcel post system with 927.

January 4 . . . George M. Cohan at Macauley's in "The Little Millionaire."

March . . . Old L & I bridge coming down.

1914 February 7 . . . Present City Hospital dedicated.

July 27 . . . Bourbon Stock Yard fire; 40,000 saw it; $200,000 loss; eight acres of yards destroyed; the cry of the animals and the stench were overpowering—a terrifying holocaust.

October . . . Old Ford residence at 2nd and Broadway becomes home of YWCA. A Whitestone masterpiece, it is still one of Louisville's beautiful buildings.

November 14 . . . Federal Reserve Banks open for business; (branch of St. Louis Bank established here in 1917).

Ford plant at 3rd and Eastern Parkway—dozen cars a day jumps to "200" a day.

In '14 H. C. Kelting was conducting a produce house in Louisville. His business had outgrown his pick-up and delivery system of horse and wagon. He purchased one truck and started what perhaps was the first truck line established in the state and the nation. From this small beginning grew the motor express transportation of today.

1915 First local transportation by "jitney" buses—5¢ per ride.

May 7 . . . Lusitania sunk; one of the reasons U.S. entered the World War I.

Male High moved to Brook and Breckenridge.

1916 Lewis D. Brandeis appointed member of Supreme Court.

December 7 . . . German Insurance Bank announces that the School Board has approved School Savings Plan recommended by bank; to be put in effect at once at Second Ward School; other schools to follow at request of principals.

Louisville Commercial Club consolidated with Board of Trade.

August 9 . . . First Kiwanis Club organized in state.

Louisville's first Better Business Bureau; functioned till 1934 when funds gave out.

Semaphores introduced on city streets.

Basil Duke died in Louisville.

Maj. Thomas Allen Moore is first to "go calling" by airplane—landed on Cherokee Road.

1917 March . . . Louisville chapter of American Red Cross organized.

July 2 . . . German Insurance Bank announces it is now member of Federal Reserve System; first State bank in Kentucky to join.

Continued on page 149

This is just half of the gigantic tent—Main attraction in Louisville's first big fair

THE FAIR—THAT GREAT AMERICAN INSTITUTION
HAS BEEN POPULAR IN LOUISVILLE SINCE 1853

The greatest saddle horses of the world have been crowned in the Kentucky State Fair Ring

THE ORIGIN OF THE KENTUCKY STATE FAIR

GOES BACK OVER 100 YEARS

The first Kentucky Fair in any way representative of the entire state was held in 1853 in an area which now comprises part of Crescent Hill. It was sponsored by the Southwestern Agricultural and Mechanical Association and ran for five days ending with a "Grand Cavalcade" at the Galt House.

One of the largest of the early fairs was held on the same grounds in 1857—called the Fifth Exhibition of the United States Agricultural Society.

The first fair known as the "Kentucky State Fair" was made possible through the energy of the Kentucky Livestock Breeders' Association and the merchants of Louisville. This was held at Churchill Downs in 1902. There were not complete facilities for a fair; and cool, wet weather was another handicap, but nevertheless this fair was successful. Forty thousand people passed through the gates in one day alone, when the unusual feature attraction was a head-on collision of two full-size locomotives.

When the present fair grounds, in the west end, were purchased in 1908, The Kentucky State Fair became a permanent Louisville institution. It was in this same year that the $100,000 livestock pavilion, then the largest in the world, was erected, and the street car lines were extended to the fair grounds. In 1921, the mammoth Merchants' and Manufacturers' building, which is larger than Madison Square Garden, was completed.

With its famous World's Champion horse show, prize cattle, incomparable produce exhibits, historical and industrial displays, midway attractions and thousands of other features, the State Fair is truly Kentucky's annual "big show." The future plans for the State Fair of Tomorrow are truly magnificent. An air view of the new Fair grounds is printed in the final section of this book.

Chronology Continued—

April . . . U.S.A. declares WAR against Germany and her allies.

Camp Taylor . . . 2,730 acres on Poplar Level and Preston Street Roads provided training accommodations for 40,000 men. 45,000,000 feet of lumber used. "Louisville changed overnight from a big little city to a little big city."

Kentucky Home School, at 1220 4th since 1904, moves to 1649 Everett.

Federal Reserve Bank of St. Louis established its first branch in Louisville on December 3, 1917 on 2nd floor, Columbia Building, 4th and Main.

1918 Robert Worth Bingham became owner, president, and publisher of the Courier-Journal and Louisville Times. He said: "Its power must be used justly and wisely. Its influence must be exerted unselfishly and honorably for the welfare of all those who come within its scope".

Winter 1917-18 worst in 50 years; Ohio frozen over; schools closed; streetcars stop running.

Foreign Trade & Travel Bureau is established at Liberty Bank, first department of its kind in city.

November 11 . . . 1:50 A.M. Armistice—bedlam, people went wild all over America and particularly on Fourth Street in Louisville!

Flu epidemic hit Camp Taylor—824 died, especially in the 84th Division; many civilians also died.

Kentucky suffered over 5,000 casualties in World War I.

Woman's Missionary Union (WMU) Training School of Southern Baptist Theological Seminary building, "House Beautiful", on SW corner Preston and Broadway dedicated (now home of WAVE).

Sacred Heart Academy destroyed by fire—pupils all saved.

1919 American Legion Auxiliary of Kentucky organized at Louisville.

Liberty Bank is first bank in Kentucky to receive deposit by airplane; flown from Shelbyville by famous pioneer aviator Robert Gast and dropped on roof of Bank.

Liberty Bank begins first of a long series of flower shows; educational, commercial and industrial lobby exhibitions.

January 20 . . . Liberty Insurance Bank moves into its newly remodeled building; during renovations bank had operated in building at SW corner Third and Main.

First actual motor truck freight line in the state established here.

(January 29—Prohibition).

Reynolds begins "foil" business in Louisville.

Enro Shirt Co. established at 331 W. Main.

Continued on page 155

Mardi Gras Procession thru Louisville Streets, 1875—Illustrating Follies of the Day

Satellites of Mercury Parade

OLD LOUISVILLE LOVED A PARADE!

AFTER the season of 1887, the Southern Exposition Company was liquidated and its handsome edifices were torn down. The next fall it was determined to have an industrial procession in which all lines of business in the city should be represented by appropriate floats, to be supplemented by a flambeau parade at night; and further, by a pageant after the order of those which have so long made the Mardi Gras festivities at New Orleans famous. The Fall Celebration Company was organized to conduct in an orderly way the multitudinous operations necessary to the success of such demonstrations and a secret association or club called the "Satellites of Mercury" was formed to manage the mystic and allegoric pageant. The parade and the pageant took place and were immensely successful in drawing crowds of visitors to the city. The Club of the Satellites after their successful debut in 1888 incorporated themselves, "built a large and substantial depositary for their elaborate properties, to furnish the public with refined and attractive entertainment for years to come."

THERE'S BEEN
BASEBALL
IN LOUISVILLE
SINCE 1865

According to A. H. Tarvin, who is perhaps the best authority in these parts on the gentle game of baseball, the first Louisville team was organized in 1865 by Alexander Galt Booth, and played its first game July 19 in an open field at what is now 19th and Duncan. It defeated the Nashville "Cumberlands" 22 to 5.

That was the first baseball game played under Standard rules west of the Alleghenies. Cincinnati began a year later.

Mayor Lithgow attended this opening game, a custom which is still observed by Louisville's mayors. Whether Lithgow threw out the first ball is not known. Although several hundred attended the game only a few knew who had won before the announcement was made at the close of the game, so new was our "National pastime" in that *past time,* if you'll pardon the pun. Apparently early baseball players were "men of distinction", men of social, business and professional importance—the "who's who" of the era from 1865 through 1869.

Mr. Tarvin reports further that the first box-score ever published here appeared in The

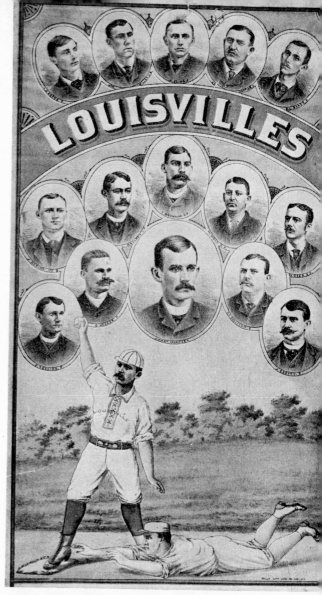

ONE OF LOUISVILLE'S EARLY TEAMS OF "GENTLEMEN BASEBALL PLAYERS"

from left to right;

Top row—A. D. Cross, catcher; Joe Miller, 3rd. base; J. Kline, fielder; Ed. Whiting, catcher; N. Baker, pitcher.

2nd. Row—J. Kerins, 1st. base; L. Maskrey, left-field; L. Browning, center-field; W. Wolf, right-field; W. Geer, short-stop.

3rd. Row—P. Reccius, pitcher; R. G. Hecker, pitcher; P. J. Hart, manager; D. C. Sullivan, catcher; J. Crotty, catcher.

Above is reproduced from an old colored lithograph belonging to Hillerich & Bradsby Company.

They took their baseball "serious" in those days. Fans at Eclipse Park about 1900.

JIMMY "CHICKEN" WOLF
Great Louisville Outfielder 1881-91

BABE RUTH AT PARKWAY FIELD

Courier, March 18, 1866—the record of a game played the day before on the Louisville Club's new grounds, Cedar Hill, situated between Third, Fifth, Oak and Park. The "Colonels" were then called the "Eagles".

The next ball park was on the present site of St. James Court and was the playing field of Louisville's first National League Club in 1876. One of the amazing things about early baseball was the size of the final score. In 1867 the "Atlantics" of *Brooklyn,* the outstanding teams in the nation, played and beat Louisville 66 to 11. Other typical scores of that era were 57 to 20; 72 to 11; 55 to 14; 39 to 23, etc. (72 runs is still the record for Louisville!) Louisville often played the Cincinnati *"Red Stockings"* (!) in those days, and many gala steamboat trips were taken between the two cities by players and fans.

The Louisville Club was uniformed from the start—gray flannel shirts trimmed with scarlet, blue jean pants, shoe-top length, high shoes with cleats but no spikes, black and white checkered caps, and patent leather belts. Baseballs were scarce, hand-made, and expensive in those days; there was seldom more than one ball for each game. Incidentally the balls were made in a factory in Cincinnati conducted by two sisters—Mary and Margaret Truman. There were three Trumans on early Louisville teams—H. C., George, and O. M. The year Louisville won the pennant in the old Association the name of its third baseman was Harry S. Truman!

Honus Wagner, generally considered the greatest baseball player of all time, played on the Louisville team in the late nineties. He joined the team in the middle of the 1897 season when Barney Dreyfuss, then owner of the club, bought his contract for $2,000! Wagner played here until the franchise went to Pittsburgh in 1900.

Perhaps the most amazing thing about baseball in the early times was that the players received no pay. In fact, they had to pay *dues* to belong to the club.

The old auditorium at Fourth & Hill. Some athletic events took place here; it had what was perhaps the first large public roller-skating rink in Louisville.

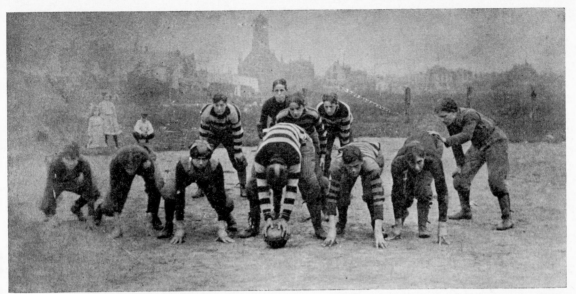

Rare photo of Manual's team, 1902.   Line from left: Sam Matlack, Meriwether Baird, Wolsey Caye, Norman Arthur, Emmet Logan, Bud Cherget, Selby Sale.   Backfield: Elliott Haynes, Walker Hancock, Marion Terry and Nat Cartwill.

Track Meet at Male High, 1911.   Runners, left to right: Abe Rosty, Earl Grabfelder, George Ewald. Coach (looking like young F. D. R.) Prof. Ralph Hill.

Big turn-out for the team—Male High (about 1912) Let's hear from you, boys!

LOUISVILLE'S
Churchill Downs

HOME OF "THE KENTUCKY DERBY" AMERICA'S GREATEST AND MOST HISTORIC HORSE RACE

Aristides—First Derby Winner—1875

HERE'S OFFICIAL STORY OF RUNNING OF THE FIRST KENTUCKY DERBY:

MAY 17, 1875. 1½ miles. Time 2:37¾. Track fast. The field was away on the first attempt. Volcano went to the front, followed closely by Verdigris, Aristides, and McCreery. Chesapeake was away poorly. On the backside, Aristides moved into second place, was lapped on Volcano at the end of the mile, went to the front shortly thereafter. The field was strung out for a hundred yards in his wake. Aristides continued to increase his lead as Volcano was steadied for the final drive. At the head of the stretch, Owner McGrath, who had expected to win with Chesapeake, waved Jockey Lewis on. Immediately, Aristides moved out to win by a length. Volcano came strongly through the stretch, but could not reach the winner. Volcano finished second; Verdigris finished third.

The Original "Club House" pictured in 1889

Churchill Downs in 1903—Note new Club House

One Tower—Two Roof Pavilions—in 1889

1933—Sensational Derby "shot"—Broker's Tip won.

CHURCHILL DOWNS, DERBY DAY 1954

Chronology Continued—

Kentucky Color & Chemical Co. incorporated. Jones Dabney Co. Laboratory began.

June 19 . . . Federal Reserve Bank moves to NW corner 5th and Market—building owned by German Bank.

1920 Galt House abandoned as a hotel.
Nazareth College founded.
Animal Rescue League founded.

1921 Louisville and America lost her most famous journalist, Henry Watterson—beloved "Marse Henry".

Merchants' and Manufacturers' building at State Fair completed, larger than Madison Square Garden.

Airport opened at Bowman Field.

Galt House razed for warehouse for Belknap Hardware Co.

A & P comes to Louisville.

May 12 . . . Rialto opened.

October 6 . . . Kentucky Theatre opened.

Southern Baptist Seminary buys land on Lexington Road.

1922 WHAS—first radio broadcasting station in Kentucky goes on the air July 18, (500 watts)—Mr. Credo Harris, manager; broadcast time from 4–5; 7:30–9 P.M. weekdays.

Liberty is first bank to broadcast a radio program and commercials from WHAS, Louisville's first radio station.

July 24–29 . . . First "Radio Exposition" in lobby of Liberty Bank; exhibits by local dealers; lecturers on radio; Mayor Huston Quinn made address.

October 16 . . . Branch Agency of Liberty Bank opened at Seventh and Hill; first bank in Louisville to establish a branch office.

October 26 . . . Statue of Lincoln unveiled on Library lawn; called the "Candidate".

November 18 . . . Liberty Bank opens 2nd branch on Shelby Street, south of Oak.

Over 200,000 attend Kentucky State Fair.

December 29 . . . Liberty Bank opens another branch—at corner of 18th and Oak Streets.

Year's Banking Transactions $3,730,401,266.00. Louisville is 24th city in size in U.S.

Barnes Bros. Bus Line (Louisville to Lexington) established.

1923 Kentucky Ornithological Society organized at Louisville.

Liberty Bank opens Fourth Avenue office at 660 S. Fourth Street.

Parkway Field built; 13,000 seats.

June 24 . . . First motor bus street car line in state starts in Louisville.

Ground broken for new Southern Baptist Seminary—cornerstone for new Norton Hall laid in 1924.

July-November . . . Beargrass Plant of Louisville Gas & Electric Co. built.

Members of Kosair Temple planned to build 7-story building on site of Gypsy Smith Tabernacle, sometimes called Municipal Tabernacle or the Louisville Auditorium. Wrecking didn't

Continued on page 160

Fontaine Fox got the inspiration for his "Toonerville Trolley" here—but later.

Quiet, peaceful, residential Second Street (s. of Bdwy.) in mule-car days.

CHRONOLOGY OF THE STREET RAILWAY SYSTEM

1844 — Louisville and Portland Railroad-Steam Railroad was in operation from 12th and Main Streets to Portland ferry landing.

1864 — Louisville City Railway began with mule-drawn cars on same line as above. 2,000 mules used in early days (1864-1890) to carry traffic. Cars were 18 feet long, seats lengthwise, fare 5¢.

1865 — Central Passenger Railroad organized with lines on Walnut from Garden to 18th, and Fourth from Main south.

1866—Citizens Passenger Railway Organized.

1867—Louisville Railway Company incorporated, but inactive until 1890. Jefferson Railway Organized.

1868 — Beargrass Railway incorporated.

1882 — Crescent Hill Railway Company and Kentucky Street Railway organized.

1886 — The boast in 1886 was that "no other city of similar size in the world has half as many lines of street railway track as Louisville."

1890 — Unification of all the foregoing systems except the Crescent Hill Railway Company, by the Louisville Railway Company. Electrified in 1890—one of first electrical railway systems in U.S. First electric trolley cars were 45 feet long, seated 28.

1899 — Crescent Hill Railway taken into Louisville Railway Company.

1901 — Last mule car operated November 14, 1901.

1910 — Cars were instructed to stop on Fourth Street at "Baseball Alley" to pick up fans hastening home from games at the old Eclipse Ball Park at 7th and Kentucky. First hot-air and hot-water heaters installed in Fall.

Green Street was first line to be electrified (1890). Note open-car trailer.

Refreshment at the end of the line—called "rushing the growler."

1913 — First center-entrance trail cars were put into service November, 1913. Louisville was first city to have pay-as-you-enter fare collection and first to have fare box, the invention of Tom L. Johnson, a Louisvillian, who became Mayor of Detroit after leaving Louisville.

1914 — First organized "Safety First" Campaign conducted in May.

1920 — Cars averaged 8.41 miles per hour. (Today, gas and diesel busses average 15.18 miles per hour.)

1926 — Louisville Railway Company received Anthony N. Brady Award for safest street railway in U.S.A.

1926-1940 — Normal operation.

1940 — John H. Bickley, consultant on public transportation and utilities, after a survey, recommended a $6,000,000 modernization program to be completed by 1948. In 1940 all equipment was electrical trolley cars except for gas busses on a few feeder lines.

1947 — The company operated equipment 15,273,000 miles over 175 miles of bus routes carrying 126,000,000 passengers; peak year for passengers.

1948 — Mr. Bickley became president upon retirement of F. H. Miller. Final 4th St. trolley car retired.

1950 — Frederick J. Johnson became president, July, 1950.

1951 — Completion of the modernization program begun in 1940 at a capital expenditure of $8,250,000. End of electrical operation with the abandonment of all trolley busses. The company operated equipment over 13,357,396 miles of bus routes. It used 1,766,512 gallons of gasoline, 411,774 gallons of fuel oil and 35,949 gallons of lubricating oil.

TODAY — The company operates a fleet of 409 busses—207 gas and 202 diesel. It employs 949 people; annual payroll: $3,558,384.

Earliest known photograph of a Louisville telephone exchange. At first all the operators were young boys, but it was soon found that young women were more courteous and efficient.

BRIEF HISTORY OF THE TELEPHONE COMPANIES IN LOUISVILLE

Below: Women had taken over completely when this picture of the Louisville Exchange was taken in the 90's.

Russia? No—Louisville Telephone Exchange in 80's!

CHRONOLOGY

1874
In 1874 the American District Telegraph Co. was organized in Louisville to do a general messenger business in connection with a local transfer, carriage and messenger service. It was not the intention to do a general telephone business at that time.

1879
In the spring of 1879 the Edison Telephone Co. was organized. Before the year closed the Edison Co. in Louisville was consolidated with the American District Telegraph Co.

1883
In 1883 a reorganization was effected. The Western Union Telegraph Co. took over the messenger department of the American District Telegraph Co. and the Ohio Valley Telephone Co. took over the telephone business. The number of subscribers was now about 1,400.

1886
On December 31, 1886, the company was again reorganized under special charter as the Ohio Valley Telephone Co. The number of subscribers was now about 2,000.

1900
In January, 1900 a consolidation was effected and the Cumberland Telephone and Telegraph Co. took over all the property of the Ohio Valley Telephone Co., and the name was changed to the Cumberland Telephone and Telegraph Co.

1912
In 1912 the property of the Cumberland Telephone and Telegraph Co. was absorbed by the Southern Bell Telephone and Telegraph Co., who continued to operate under the name of the Cumberland Telephone and Telegraph Co.

1924
On March 26, 1924, by an act of the General Council and the approval of Mayor of Louisville, the unification of the two telephone systems in Louisville was granted. By this act and its approval the sale and transfer of all the property which was owned and operated by the Louisville Home Telephone Co. was made to the Cumberland Telephone and Telegraph Co.

1925
At midnight December 29, 1925, the consolidation of the properties of the former Home Telephone Co. and the Cumberland Telephone and Telegraph Co. was effected and a universal telephone system was placed in service.

1926
On July 1, 1926, the name of the Cumberland Telephone and Telegraph Co. was changed to the Southern Bell Telephone and Telegraph Co.

1932
On November 26th the Jackson-Wabash dial exchange was cut into service. This cut retired from service the old Main, South and City exchanges. The old main building was the first building in the world built exclusively for telephone purposes.

Early type telephone switchboard ☞

159

start because Billy Sunday was giving revival.

1924 One hundred ninety-two industries established in Louisville during the early 20's. City had several manufacturing plants the largest of their kind in the world. (Six largest in U.S.—18 largest in south).

June 16 . . . Liberty Bank opens branch at 23rd and Market Sts.

Cumberland Telephone and Telegraph Co. and Louisville Home Telephone Co. merge.

New Ford plant established at 1400 Southwestern Parkway.

A & P bought out Quaker Maid Stores.

January 28 . . . Atherton High School opened.

Cornerstone of Kosair Temple laid May 3, 1924—now is the Farm Credit Administration Building.

November 17 . . . Baptist Hospital opened.

Kosair Hospital opened.

Cornerstone of first building laid at Southern Baptist Theological Seminary on Lexington Road.

New Sacred Heart Academy built.

1925 J. B. Speed Art Museum started— Arthur Loomis, Architect; Cost $800,000; gift of Mrs. J. B. Speed in honor of her husband.

WHAS has first commercially sponsored program.

Last performance at Macauley's Theater on August 29—razing began August 30—(also in 1925 the 'Evening Post' building was razed.)

Second section of Starks Building begun July 1925; completed July 1926.

70,000 new citizens since 1920.

Shackleton Piano Co. opens.

Work on the dam is begun.

Cornerstone of new St. Joseph Infirmary laid March 19th.

Last horse-driven fire apparatus retired.

1926 Pendennis Club moves to present site at 2nd and Walnut, from Belknap residence, where part of Stewart's now stands.

Liberty Bank opens branch at corner Bardstown Road and Deerwood.

Kentucky ranks 2nd in tobacco production.

Yellow Taxi Airline Co. flew passengers from Louisville to Cincinnati.

Consolidation of the Home and Cumberland Companies to Southern Bell System.

1927 J. B. Speed Memorial Museum opened at Louisville on University of Louisville Campus.

September 19 . . . Liberty Bank opens another community branch at 26th and Broadway.

Personal Loan Department (now Consumer Credit Division) established at Liberty Bank; among first of kind in U.S.

Airline, Louisville & Cleveland—later became American Airlines.

February 1 . . . Ground broken for Heyburn Building.

August 8 . . . Lindberg visits Louisville in his "Spirit of St. Louis"; 10,000 at Bowman Field; 100,000 on hand for 4th Street parade; celebration at Brown Hotel.

September 1 . . . Large Brown & Williamson Tobacco Corp. factory begun.

The dam is finished.

Columbia Hall (Knights of Columbus) completed.

September 13 . . . First all freight air delivery to Louisville from Indianapolis; it was a load of typewriters.

Kentucky Masonic Widows and Orphans' Home on Shelbyville Road is completed; cost $2,000,000; over 500 residents now.

1928 Centenary Exhibition of Matthew Jouett's portraits at Speed Museum.

Liberty Bank is first bank in city to provide free parking for customers—at Fourth Avenue office.

American Legion held 11th National Convention here.

Bowman Field purchased by city for an Airport.

Present Sears-Roebuck building erected.

March 18 . . . Site selected at 16th and Hill for Brown & Williamson plant.

September 1 . . . Loews opened; 3,274 seats.

New Building at Norton's Infirmary erected.

1929 April 8 . . . Board of Trade sells 3rd and Main Building, moves to 421 W. Market Street.

April 15 . . . Work begins on the new Telephone Co. Building

October . . . WALL STREET CRASH.

Filson Club moved to new home—first meeting Monday, October 7—118 W. Breckenridge.

Memorial Auditorium, 4th and Kentucky, dedicated on Decoration Day; 3,000 seating capacity; cost $1,250,000; classic Greek design, great dome, larger in diameter and almost as high as Pantheon in Rome.

October 16 . . . Liberty Bank opens branch at 209 S. Fifth Street, near Market.

Dedication of the Municipal Bridge (now the George Rogers Clark Memorial Bridge) connecting Louisville and Jeffersonville; cost $5,000,000; one and one tenth miles long; Frank M. Masters and Ralph Modjeska architects.

Mayor Huston Quinn said, "Louisville has the thrift of the East, the hustle of the North, and optimism of the West, and the hospitality of the South."

Continued on page 168

THE OLD COURIER-JOURNAL BUILDING, 4TH & LIBERTY, OVER 50 YEARS AGO

A TRIP THROUGH THE
OLD FAMILY NEWSPAPER

We are grateful to The Courier-Journal for permission to publish the group of photographs that appears on the two pages which follow. These interesting pictures which show all of the operations in the writing, publishing and distributing of a leading American newspaper of a half-century ago, have never to our knowledge been reproduced or published before.

The Courier-Journal building of that day was located on the corner of Fourth and Green (now Liberty). Built in 1873, it was a large, handsome structure and the "last word" in a newspaper publishing plant. That it was a sound structure is proved by the fact that it still stands (as the Will Sales Building), but hardly recognizable due to the new fronts and other remodeling. Note the marble statue of George D. Prentice over the corner doorway. This statue now stands on the lawn of the Louisville Free Public Library. Note also the cobblestone streets, the gas lamp-posts, the awnings projecting to the street, and the newly installed telephone poles. Light, power, and telephone wires apparently had not yet been stretched. (The Courier-Journal generated its own light and power in the early days.)

These pictures hardly require explanation. On the first floor was the "Paper and Subscription" counter and the place where advertisements were accepted. The composing room and printing presses were also on the ground floor.

Upstairs were the executive and editorial offices; the wrapping and shipping department was in the basement. The dispatch room where news came in by wire is shown at the top of the column to the left; the man with the leggings was all ready to carry the dispatches—whether by bicycle, horseback or possibly motorcycle.

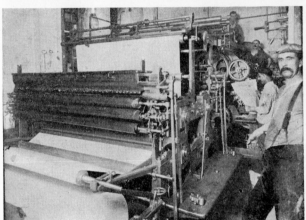

There's an interesting difference in the two groups of writers shown in 2 lower pictures in column one. Note papers on floor, workers in shirt sleeves, one with hat on; in the other office all is neatness and decorum. Was it the editorial sanctum or the Society department?

The two close-up views in the composing room are also in sensational contrast; one looks like "all hands on deck" working desperately to get an "Extra" on the street; the other looks like Sunday afternoon.

We think the last picture on this page is interesting, because there were few female secretaries in those days, and then—look at the desk with the pigeon-holes!

Incidentally the old Courier-Journal building was pretty well gutted by a fire in 1907, but it didn't put them out of business. They published in this building until 1912, when they moved one block east.

163

GEORGE D. PRENTICE, 1802-1870

Poet, Wit, Editor, and Publisher of The Louisville Journal

George D. Prentice, a new Englander, came to Louisville in 1830, at the age of 28, because he had heard favorable reports of Louisville, and began the publication of *The Louisville Journal*. In 1832 *The Focus* was merged into *The Journal*. The papers became famous for their wit, humor, and fine literary style. Prentice was therefore not only an editor but also one of Louisville's early authors. His *Poems, Prenticiana* (witty paragraphs from his editorial writings); and his *Life of Henry Clay* are still read and collected. Prentice was a fitting predecessor to the more famous Henry Watterson, as a great Kentucky journalist.

Founder of The Courier-Journal and The Louisville Times

The newspaper men who created The Courier-Journal were Walter N. Haldeman and Henry Watterson. Mr. Haldeman was a good business executive who had then been in the newspaper business ever since 1843, when he bought the *Daily Dime;* to this he added the experience which a quarter of a century at the head of the old *Louisville Daily Courier* had given him. He had the foresight to know that a combination of *The Journal, The Courier* and *The Democrat* would prove successful, particularly with the brilliant Henry Watterson as its editor. He also saw that a good evening paper was needed in Louisville, and on May 1st, 1884, began to publish *The Louisville Times.*

WALTER N. HALDEMAN

"MARSE HENRY" WATTERSON . . .

He made The Courier-Journal America's Leading Newspaper

HENRY WATTERSON was undisputedly the greatest journalist of his time. No one in all American journalism holds a candle to him when the extent and continuity of his influence is considered. For 50 years his editorials were read each day by people all over America, and he was a force and personality in English-speaking lands beyond the seas. That a writer in a newspaper in a relatively small inland town could achieve such worldwide fame and respect testifies to the brilliance and charm of his editorials.

Henry Watterson lived a long life. He was born in Washington in 1840. He showed rare talent as a child pianist until one of his eyes failed him. Later he became a page-boy in Congress, but got into the newspaper game in time to report Lincoln's inauguration. During the Civil War he was a soldier of the Confederacy and editor of the Journal of the Sourthern Cause— THE REBEL. After the war he came to Louisville, helped to consolidate The Courier and The Journal, and began his real career in journalism, which in a few years brought him to the top of his profession.

It is not known what Henry Watterson's salary was as editor of the Courier Journal, but it is said that he "just took what he needed." However, in appreciation of his services publisher Haldemann gave him a 25% interest in the company; according to one contemporary the immediate occasion for this gift was a severe sick spell which "Marse Henry" suffered. Fearing he would not recover, and feeling for his widow, Haldeman transferred one-fourth of the stock to him. But Watterson recovered—a bit richer for the experience!

HENRY WATTERSON, 1840-1921

Later in his career, when syndicated columnists became the vogue, he had opportunities to make a fortune, but he stuck by Walter Haldeman and The Courier-Journal even tho he was only a minority stockholder. It is said that William Randolph Hearst offered him the job which Arthur Brisbane later got (at $365,000 a year!); but "Marse Henry" didn't like the set-up and turned it down. Money was definitely a secondary consideration with the man who sparked World War I with the slogan—"To Hell with the Hohenzollerns and the Hapsburgs!"

Henry Watterson, the most famous Kentuckian of his time, died in retirement in Jacksonville, Florida, in 1921 at the age of 81. A perpetual memorial to him is his fine, large personal library which he left to the Louisville Free Public Library, and is available to the public.

FATHER AND SON—
both great newspapermen

Judge Robert Worth Bingham (right) bought control of *The Courier-Journal* and *The Louisville Times* from the Haldemans and Henry Watterson, August 6, 1918. On July 31, 1919 he acquired the remaining shares and became sole owner of these historic and valuable properties.

In 1912 these newspapers had moved from Fourth and Liberty to the large stone building at Third and Liberty which from 1858 to 1892 had served as the Federal Building of Louisville (right, center). Judge Bingham made extensive improvements, installing the latest presses and equipment—and the prestige and circulation of these newspapers continued to grow. The Judge brought to the newspaper field the highest ideals of public service and a broad, constructive conception of the functions and responsibilities of a modern newspaper.

At his passing, his son Barry Bingham became the head of these two great newspapers and soon demonstrated that even tho young, he had the vision and capacity to carry on in the great tradition. With the enthusiasm, courage, and confidence of youth he visualized a still greater operation. On September 20, 1948, he realized his ambition when The Courier-Journal, The Louisville Times, and WHAS moved into their handsome, modern, multi-million-dollar plant at Sixth and Broadway (see right, below).

BARRY BINGHAM

166

THE FLOODS OF 1883-84

Residents of "the Point" fleeing for safety.

Broadway looking east from Shelby Street.

Many frame houses floated down the river.

The L & N Yards at Tenth and Broadway.

Another view of desolation in East End.

37th & Rudd Avenue—in Portland.

THERE were severe floods in both 1883 and 1884—but the latter was a record breaker exceeded only by the 1937 flood. The Ohio River at Louisville crested at 47 feet in 1884—eleven feet below the 1937 crest. The severity and extent of the flood are indicated in the pictures above. All except the first print (which is a newspaper artist's drawing) are reprints of actual photographs. Charles D. Jacobs, mayor of Louisville at that time, did a grand job in organizing relief, and firms and private citizens contributed generously of time and money. Congress voted $500,000 for flood sufferers.

Fashionable Fourth Avenue

This is the block between Chestnut and Broadway looking south, as it looked in the eighties. Henry Watterson lived in the house with the small porch. Entire block was residential.

Chronology Continued—

Girdler Corporation started in Louisville.

1930 Bank failures in Louisville and other cities of the state.

May 1 . . . 150th birthday of Louisville (sesquicentennial).

November 17th . . . Black Monday, Bank of Kentucky closed and its holding company, Banco, failed.

L & N Annex Building completed in spring.

Largest excursion steamer in U.S., the "America"—3,750 passenger capacity—burnt in dry dock in Louisville during winter.

Cornerstone of new Federal Building on Broadway laid.

Worst drought on record.

Lord Derby is guest of honor at Kentucky Derby.

1931 Depression hits Louisville, Kentucky and the nation.

"Junior Liberty Bank" organized with high school students as officers and directors; object: to teach fundamentals and practice of banking.

WLAP broadcasting station established in Louisville—moved to Lexington when WAVE dedicated.

February . . . University of Louisville formally takes over "Simmon's University." Louisville Municipal College for Negroes.

April . . . Brown & Williamson moves offices to Louisville.

1932 February 1 . . . Alex G. Barret Junior High School completed and occupied.

Camp Knox made permanent military post to be known as Fort Knox, and became the national depository for gold bullion.

"Honorable Order of Kentucky Colonels" organized by Gov. Laffoon.

Air Express started out of Louisville.

Present post office building completed.

1933 Bank holidays in U.S. began February 14; Franklin D. Roosevelt's great radio speech ("All we have to fear is fear itself") restored confidence.

January 14 . . . New Federal Building on Broadway dedicated.

Distilleries resumed operations.

March 3 . . . Paderewski played at Memorial Auditorium.

April 8 . . . Kunz opens "Dutchman" on 4th Street.

December 5 . . . Prohibition definitely over.

Army Air Games at Bowman Field.

1934 January . . . Jenny Benedict's famous confectionery on 4th Street closes. (She died in 1928)

Mrs. Berry V. Stoll (Alice Speed), 26, wife of an oil operator, kidnapped October 10; found October 16, near Scottsburg, Indiana. The kidnapper, Thomas H. Robinson, Jr., caught in California May 11, 1936 and on May 13, sentenced to imprisonment for life.

December 30 . . . Radio station WAVE established.

Regular air mail service started here.

1935 Two Mile House at Douglass and Bardstown Road razed.

Continued on page 177

Tornado Views. *Jefferson bet. 11th + 12th st. Dr. Griffith house + St. John's Church* W. STUBER & BRO., Photo's

LOUISVILLE, MARCH 27TH, 1890.

THE CYCLONE OF 1890

ON MARCH 27, 1890, Louisville was visited by the severest storm in its history. Johnston's *Memorial History of Louisville* reports that there were occasional light rains during the day, with some wind, but with no cyclonic symptoms, until shortly after dark. Then there was heavy rain accompanied by high wind which about 8 o'clock swept through the western district of the city with terrific force and destruction.

The course of the tornado was northeasterly, first entering the city at Parkland and passing through it, cutting a swath about six blocks wide, crossing the river to the eastern part of Jeffersonville and then recrossing at the water works, breaking the stand-pipe tower as if it were a match.

The most easterly limit on Main Street was the Louisville Hotel, (6th and Main) the house adjoining it on the west being destroyed with seven lives lost. The total loss of life during the cyclone amounted to *seventy-six persons* killed outright, with *over two hundred* injured, some of whom died later.

The destruction of property consisted, in whole or part, of five churches, one railroad depot (the Union, at Seventh and River) two public halls, three school buildings, thirty-two manufacturing establishments, ten tobacco warehouses and five hundred and thirty-two dwellings! The streets were so obstructed with debris that it was several days before traffic could be resumed on some of them, and excursion trains were run from numerous points in Kentucky and Indiana, which brought thousands to witness the scenes.

The pecuniary loss was estimated at $2,150,000. Aid was tendered from many other cities, but was respectfully declined, and Louisville never showed greater nobility than in the heroism with which her people sprang to the relief of the unfortunate. At a public meeting held at the Board of Trade rooms next morning $25,000 was subscribed on the spot for relief.

The people contributed $115,000 in cash subscriptions, besides food, shelter, and medical attention furnished by the public committee and private individuals. The losses of the poor were made good including the rebuilding of three hundred houses; furniture destroyed was replaced. All this was done without U.S. Government aid, Red Cross or public funds, but simply by personal charity and voluntary contributions by Louisvillians.

The undertaker's wagon lends a gruesome note to this scene of awful destruction.

The Union Depot—Seventh & River

Baxter Square—Jefferson between 11th & 12th

Stand-pipe tower at Water Works destroyed

Editors' Note: We are indebted to Mr. Lin Caufield for this series of actual photographs —presumbly taken on the day after the cyclone by one of Louisville's famed photographers of that era, W. Stuber & Bro. We were unable to secure reprints of the entire series, but judging from the number "28" on one of the prints there must have been at least that many in the original series. No doubt there was a wide demand for these pictures immediately after the disaster, from newspapers all over the country as well as from individuals. It is surprising how difficult it is to find interesting early photographs of Louisville, even of this not-too-distant period.

Louisville Will Never Forget March 27, 1890

CITY'S GREATEST DISASTER IN LIVES LOST AND PROPERTY TOTALLY DESTROYED

Market looking west from 10th Street

9th and Main looking toward River

Tobacco breaks on Main Street

Main Street, looking east from 9th Street

Looking up Main Street from 10th

Falls City Hall, 12th & Market Streets

The Railway Depot at 7th and Water

10th Street looking south toward Market

5 Million Dollar Lottery Scheme Started Library

PUBLIC LIBRARY OF KENTUCKY, LOUISVILLE.
(Where Kaufman's is now located)

Louisville once thought it was going to have one of the great public libraries and museums of the world—comparable with the fabulous British Museum. But the plans went awry, or the promoters "went South"—anyway, the five "benefit concerts" (terminating July 31, 1894) brought in $5,900,000 and the library got only $450,000. (see C.-J. story Jan. 1, 1942). Col. Reuben T. Durrett, venerable founder of The Filson Club, was president of the group of prominent Louisvillians that sponsored the lotteries; Governor Bramlett was a member. Who got the bulk of the money is still a mystery —and a public scandal which apparently was "hushed up" at the time. The drawing for "20,000 cash gifts" is illustrated below.

J. J. Audubon's "Birds of America" in the Bien elephant-folio edition is one of few treasures inherited by Public Library from old library.

THE PUBLIC LIBRARY OF KENTUCKY.

Col. Reuben T. Durrett

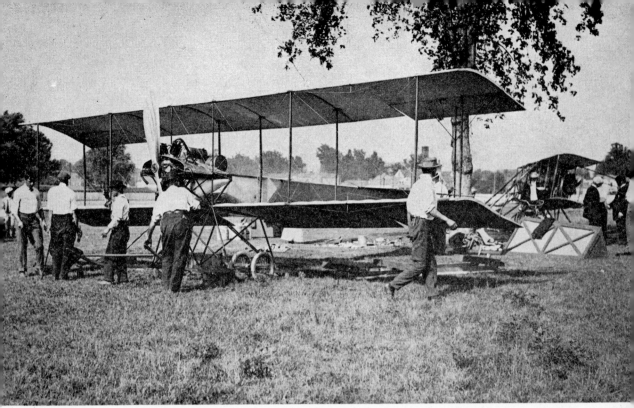

The first aviation meet in Louisville was held at Churchill Downs in 1911. Sponsored by the Elks; J. A. D. McCurdy was the pilot of the above plane; the other plane was unable to get off the ground!

THE HISTORY OF BOWMAN FIELD

LOUISVILLE'S FIRST FLYING FIELD AND AIRPORT

LOUISVILLE'S first introduction to aviation was perhaps when Lincoln Beachey flew at the old fairgrounds. From then until World War I, an airplane in Louisville was a very rare spectacle. During the War, Godman Field was established by the Army at Camp Henry Knox, and Louisville saw more airplanes.

A. H. Bowman, a large trucking operator, became enthusiastically interested in aviation after the war. He bought a plane, a Canadian Jenny, which was flown by the late Robert Gast, a pilot in World War I. After a far-flung search for a suitable field, Mr. Bowman, assisted by Mr. Gast, and Mr. W. S. Park, selected a site on the old Von Zedwitz place on Taylorsville Road for landing purposes.

The first plane landed at "Bowman's Field" in 1919. The first hangar was a wooden shack, later blown down by a windstorm, destroying the plane. The first accident occurred when Bob Gast cracked up trying to miss a thorn tree on the south boundary of the field. (No fatality.)

For several years A. H. Bowman paid rental on the field out of his own pocketbook. As his faith in and enthusiasm for aviation grew, he felt that a municipal flying field would eventually be needed by Louisville. In the meantime the Aero Club of Kentucky helped the cause along: they gave an "air circus" and the public turned out en masse. The flyers electrified the audience by writing H E L L O— U. S. A. in the sky in letters a mile high. The Jefferson County Fiscal Court also supplied some funds for development of the field.

At about this same time in the early 20's, the Army, attempting to stimulate national interest in aviation, was trying to establish "Army Airways." In 1922, through the efforts of Mr. Bowman, Mayor Huston Quin, and others, the Von Sedwitz place was leased by the Army as an intermediate airdrome and placed on the Army Airways. The field was then used as the home of the Army 456th Pursuit Squadron of the Air Corps Reserve, the first Commanding officer being Lieutenant Raymond R. Brown.

Bowman Field about 1933; Administration Building had just been completed; another wing was added late

The field was formally dedicated Saturday, August 25, 1923.

In 1924, passenger service was started by the Yellow Taxi Airline Company. Later passenger and freight service was established between Louisville and Cincinnati. The 540 acre Von Sedwitz estate was purchased by the City of Louisville in 1927 for $750,000 supplied by a bond issue. In 1928, the General Assembly of Kentucky created the Louisville and Jefferson County Air Board, which immediately took over the administration of Bowman Field.

The new Board added lighting equipment, installed obstruction and boundary markers, built an administration building (completed August 1, 1929), leased land to the Curtiss Flying Service for a hangar, and leased land to the War Department. It also erected in the administration building a memorial to Robert Gast, the Louisville resident and veteran of the British Royal Corps, who lost his life in the China Sea while serving as pilot for a subsidiary of Pan-American Airways.

In 1930, a weather station was installed at Bowman Field, and the Air Board constructed six all-metal individual hangars. In 1931, the large dirigible "Akron" passed over Louisville. In 1933, Bowman Field got the highest rating possible from the Department of Commerce. Eastern Airlines inaugurated mail and passenger service from Chicago to Miami through Louisville in 1934.

Bowman Field was a life saver to Louisville during the flood of 1937. The field is high, and planes landed there with supplies when trains were stopped and roads were closed. The administration building was enlarged in 1937.

In the forties it became obvious that Louisville would need a larger airport and longer runways to accommodate the big new 4-motor planes. On November 15, 1947, Standiford Field became the principal airport of Louisville, and overnight, 63% more seating capacity was made available to Louisville air travelers. Now, just a few years later, the problem of still longer runways rises again—to accommodate the new jet planes. Progress marches—rather, *flies* on!

Two of Louisville Aviation's "Greats" are in this picture: A. H. Bowman (center, with derby in hand) for whom Bowman Field was named, and Addison Lee, third from left, for whom Lee Terminal (see below) at Standiford Field is named. Above photo, no doubt taken at Bowman Field, shows Louisville Mayor Huston Quin (1921-25) welcoming a visiting celebrity—who, we do not know—while Mr. Bowman waits for an introduction. She was a "flapper" all right!

Standiford Field and Lee Terminal Building— Louisville's new Airport

RADIO STARTED AT WHAS 32 YEARS AGO

Remember the twin broadcasting towers of WHAS on the old Courier-Journal Building? A far cry from their "Eiffel" tower of today.

SATURDAY, JULY 15, 1922 . . . Two antennae, sixty-foot towers, were raised on the roof of the Courier-Journal building, and practice tests made: phonograph and piano concert. 100 calls reported that it was "loudest, clearest program ever heard".

William Tapp, Upper River Road, using a 25-foot clothesline for antenna, said the program was loud and distinct.

TUESDAY, July 18 . . . 7:20 P.M. Ten minutes to air time. Emmet Graft got the last bug out of the equipment.

JULY 18, 1922, 7:30 PM . . . The red light went on, and Credo Harris announced, in his precise, distinctive voice, "This is WHAS, the radio telephone broadcasting station of The Courier-Journal and the Louisville Times in Louisville, Kentucky." WHAS was born!

Crowds gathered whenever a radio played—in 1922!

Jos. J. Eisenbeis, distinguished tenor, and an employe of Liberty National, has been a feature soloist from the beginning of WHAS.

Youngsters all over America were building radio sets at school and home. A new industry came into being.

Oldsters found an entirely new world of entertainment and recreation in the new invention.

Chronology Continued—

February 11 . . . Great auto show at Armory—over 100 models on display.

March 10 . . . Courier-Journal & Times appeared in clearer, larger new type.

March 24 . . . St. Xavier's Catholic Church interscholastic basketball champions of U.S.

March 28 . . . W. Scowden Kohnhorst, 55, vice president Liberty National Bank and Trust Company, president of Louisville Auto Club, dies of heart attack in bank lobby.

April 27 . . . Wire photo service installed by Courier-Journal & Louisville Times.

May 15 . . . Fire at St. Joseph Orphans' Home —208 children led to safety.

November 5 . . . "Happy" Chandler defeats Swope for Governor.

1936 Although our city is no longer noted for or dependent upon river trade, in this year, 25,000,000 tons were moved worth over $250,000,000. (Total ton miles just short of 3 billion)

January . . . Merle E. Robertson, president of Liberty National begins annual custom of publishing in newspaper—full-page detailed "Report to Stockholders"; perhaps first bank in U.S. to do so.

January 1 . . . Huge ice cakes jam Ohio; worst cold wave in 25 years.

May 6 . . . Seagrams, on 7th Street Road begins; "most complete distillery in the world."

May 21 . . . Police Judge Brachey inaugurates

"9 & 19" to curb drunk driving. (9 days in jail and $19)

June 14 . . . President Roosevelt stops on way to Hodgenville to speak at Lincoln Memorial.

June 22 . . . Work begun on new $1,300,000 overhead L & N structure along Beargrass Creek.

October 30 . . . The Herald Post suspends publication and goes into bankruptcy.

November 17 . . . WGRC established and dedicated.

November 25 . . . First time a one way street proposed for Louisville.

1937 During the fall, on a weekday, in a 12-hour period, 68,831 people pass 4th and Walnut, Louisville's busiest corner.

FLOOD: See detailed story, pp. 179-185.

July 9 . . . Gunmen's war in Jeffersonville brings cleanup of notorious gambling houses. Greentree Manor built.

Only two buildings left standing in Shippingport after the flood—one was the saloon of Jim Porter, "The Giant's Saloon". (Now gone, 1954).

1938 Iroquois Amphitheater built; first performance July 4th.

Double-deck parking structure opens at Main Office of Liberty National—ground level for customers, basement for employees.

New State Board of Health Building 620 S. 3rd,

dedicated to Dr. J. N. McCormack, long head of Board.

Fiscal Court Building built (Court House Annex); replacing Congress Hotel and Home Laundry. Congress Hotel, once famed as the St. Nicholas Hotel, was a center of night life in the 1870's and 1880's.

April . . . Slum clearance and low rent housing—$4,261,000 allotment of federal funds for white and $4,000,000 for colored sections.

July 4 . . . First quiet 4th; fireworks banned by city ordinance.

Joseph D. Scholtz elected Mayor.

December 31 . . . Manual football team, national champions; defeated New Britain, Conn., team.

1939 September 1 . . . Hitler's army attacks Czechoslovakia.

Court House Annex (Fiscal Court Building) completed on site of old Congress Hotel.

1940 United States engineers started surveying Charlestown, east of Jeffersonville (which later became a major war production area, with many thousands of Louisville workers making daily trips to its war plants.)

January 3 . . . Permit given for $200,000 Woolworth Building on Fourth Street.

January 28 . . . Citizens walk across frozen Ohio.

February 3 . . . Reynolds Metals buys old Ford Plant on Third Street.

February 22 . . . National Carbide Co. of New York announces plan to construct $1,000,000 plant on Bell's Lane (opens November 3).

April 1 . . . DuPont announces large new plant.

June 10 . . . Liberty National opens office in Starks Building.

June 15 . . . Radio Station WINN established.

July 15 . . . Fort Knox becomes Headquarters for mechanized forces.

November 19 . . . Navy selects Louisville as site for $4,500,000 Naval Ordnance Plant, to assemble gun mountings.

(In Europe: Dunkerque abandoned June 4 by British).

Louisville won national recognition for excellence of Public Health work.

1941 April 30 . . . Curtiss-Wright announces plans to build new plant at cost of $12,000,000.

December 7 . . . ATTACK ON PEARL HARBOR.

December 8 . . . U.S.A. declares war on Japan.

December 11 . . . U.S.A. declares war on Germany and her Allies.

Many essential war industries located in the State. Louisville and surrounding territory become hub of industrial and military activity.

Land for Standiford Field on Crittenden Drive was acquired.

1942 April 9 . . . After resisting siege for three months Bataan fell.

May 6 . . . Gen. Wainwright surrenders Corrigidor and all of Philippines; McArthur escapes to Australia to take over command of remainder of forces in the East.

Oct. 9 . . . Razing of old Post Office at Fourth and Chestnut Streets started.

Wilson W. Wyatt elected Mayor (served 1942-46) on the Democratic ticket.

Check Master pay-as-you-go checking account service is inaugurated by Liberty National; first of this type offered Louisville public.

Alice Hegan Rice, author of "Mrs. Wiggs of the Cabbage Patch", died in Louisville.

1943 A War Year. With great influx of war workers Louisville over-crowded in every respect; hospitals, public buildings, housing, and schools inadequate. Rationing of all essentials of life—gasoline, rubber, meat, sugar, etc.

April 5 . . . Bowman Field, headquarters for 28th Air Base and 16th Bomber Squadron, became home of the first glider pilot combat training unit in U.S.

September . . . Estimated 15,500 war workers in Louisville.

December 28 . . . Government seized control of railroads.

Louisville Area Development Association (L.A.D.A.) was organized to study Louisville needs and to plan solutions to the many community problems, under the direction of K. P. Vinsel.

Eisenhower named Supreme Commander of the Allied grand assault on Hitler's Europe. Population up from 319,000 in 1941, to nearly 500,000 in 1943, during war.

The Howard Shipyards at Jeffersonville largest producers of L.S.T. boats in the country.

DuPont Smokeless Powder Plant and Hoosier Ordinance Powder Plant at Charlestown employing thousands of Louisville people.

Louisville called "Synthetic Rubber Capital of America" and one of outstanding chemical and plastic centers.

Huge plants on Bell's Lane convert tremendous quantities of alcohol, made by Louisville's great distilleries, into neoprene, butadiene and other synthetic rubber substances.

Among new industries now operating here are: DuPont, B. F. Goodrich, Carbide and Carbon Chemical Co., Westinghouse (Naval Gun Plant).

Local companies in war production: Reynolds, B. F. Avery, Mengel's, Tube Turns, Cochran

Continued on page 186

THE FLOOD OF 1937

LOUISVILLE as a riverfront city, had always been used to minor spring floods, and even major floods now and then such as the one of 1883 when the Ohio rose to the then all-time high mark of 46.7 feet. But Louisville in its entire history had seen nothing to compare with the disaster caused when the muddy Ohio, surging and rolling, left its banks in January, 1937, to reach a crest of 57.1 feet on January 27, engulfing most of the city and causing millions of dollars of property damage and untold suffering and hardship to thousands of Louisville citizens.

The flood started as a result of torrential rains both up the river and locally. The rains con-

tinued almost unabated, with considerable snow and sleet, from about January 9th until January 26th. At first nobody payed much attention to the abnormally heavy rainfall. But as the heavens continued to send water down in torrents, and as the Ohio inched upward, it became clear by January 22 that this was no ordinary flood, and the city as a unit geared to fight a disaster of major proportions.

On January 23, with the rain still falling and the previous high water mark already passed, the city was severed in half by Beargrass Creek, cutting off the Highlands and Crescent Hill from other areas of the city. This posed serious problems of how to transport the marooned

Thousands marooned—Boats to the rescue

"Send a boat"—Radio was a Godsend

Nice rowing at Fourth and Broadway

Looking down Broadway from Barret

people of the West End to higher, safer locations.

Then, as if by magic, churches, families, charitable organizations and everybody who could lend a hand turned to the task. Clothing, food, supplies of every kind were collected. Public buildings such as the Jefferson County Armory and City Hall which were among the few remaining on dry ground, became gathering points for West End refugees. Motor transports of every kind were pressed into service to remove the unfortunates of the western part of Louisville to higher and safer quarters.

By January 24 the backwaters were beginning to back up through the sewer systems and it was obvious then that more than two-thirds of the metropolis would be under water within a few days. By Sunday night, January 24, the main business district of downtown Louisville was an island. Every hotel and large building was crowded with refugees.

Rain and ever more rain. All street lights were turned off to conserve electric power. Food was becoming scarce. All supplies such as lamps and candles were gone from merchants' shelves. Louisville was a flooded city, and the rain still fell in bucketsfull. At 11:39 P.M. Sunday, January 24, the Waterside Plant of the Louisville Gas and Electric Company was flooded out of operation, and the last remaining light instantly went out. Louisville was dark, isolated, a picture of utter desolation.

People huddled together in darkness in hundreds of refugee "collection points" wondering what the next days would bring.

Until all electricity was cut off, Louisville's radio stations did yeoman service by devoting their entire capacities to broadcasting and relaying calls for help. Through this medium, boats were dispatched to marooned refugees. But with no electricity this medium seemed out. However, under the personal direction of Mr. Barry Bingham, owner of the Courier-Journal and the Louisville Times and WHAS, arrangements were made with station WSM in Nashville, Tennessee, to take calls by telephone and in turn broadcast them to distressed Louisville citizens, many of whom could receive the calls and news on battery sets. This almost miraculous combination of telephone and radio over a distance of 200 miles was of tremendous help

Mayor Miller inspects visiting police

Hydro plant under—Lights out!

Refugees everywhere—this was the Madrid

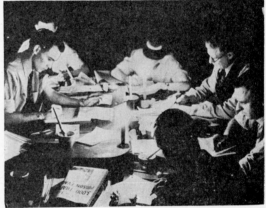

Publishing papers by candle light!

Keeping in contact with the outside world

Baxter Ave. whiskey-barrel pontoon bridge

One day the stores weren't crowded

Coast Guard delivering milk by boat

Churchill Downs—sloppy track

These are the elevated tracks!

The WHAS Crew never stopped

and saved hundreds of families from additional suffering.

One of the most serious handicaps was the shortage of water caused when the Louisville Water Company's pumping stations went out of operation. Thousands caught water which constantly poured from the heavens. Others melted snow for water with which to make coffee. Water for ordinary sanitation purposes was nonexistent.

In its hour of need, Louisville called for help to its neighboring cities across the land. And the response was instantaneous and heartwarming. Cots, blankets, food, medicines and other supplies were flown in, sent by boat, rail, truck, from many areas. President Roosevelt assured Mayor Neville Miller that the resources of the nation would be applied to relieve Louisville's greatest disaster.

The river was still rising on Tuesday, January 26th, and rain, although somewhat lessened, was still falling. A herculean task was to get people from the flooded West End area to collection points at 10th Street Station and the K and I Railroad in order to transfer them to safe areas. Until the water got too high, trucks aided in this task; but as the thoroughfares became rolling torrents of rushing water, only boats could handle the job, which somewhat slowed down the task. Every one who had a boat or who could man one plied the streets as though they were canals, which they actually were. Often without bad weather clothing, these boat operators exposed themselves in rain, sleet, snow, without sleep and rest, to

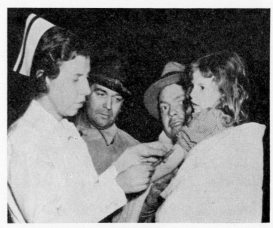

Thousands of children were inoculated

make trip after trip to the marooned areas on errands of relief.

At the peak of the flood, Broadway was a sizeable river, reaching almost 100 feet up beyond Barret Avenue. The current right down the middle of Broadway was so strong that only the strongest motor boats could navigate it. Boats regularly navigated within the ground floor of the Brown Hotel at Fourth and Broadway.

By the 26th or 27th even parts of distant South Louisville were flooded. Rumors were rampant, although usually groundless. Reports of disease epidemics were spread. Gasoline was issued or sold only to cars and trucks in emergency relief work. The remaining water in the reservoirs was rationed by being turned on only twice a day for short periods. The Army elements and the more than 200 out-of-city policemen who assisted Louisville policemen in patrolling the darkened city had orders to "shoot looters on sight".

The first major fire of the disaster was on Tuesday the 26th when the Louisville Paint and Varnish Company suffered a half-million dollar conflagration in its plant at 14th and Maple. On Tuesday a whisky-barrel pontoon bridge was completed from Johnson and Jefferson to Barret Avenue, thus easing the problem of getting refugees to the Crescent Hill Area. The bridge, an amazing feat of impromptu engineering, was constantly patrolled by National Guardsmen, who kept the crossers at ten-foot intervals. On Wednesday, January 27, 273 policemen from Philadelphia, Pittsburgh, Boston and Chicago were flown in to

Fish out of water—No one claimed it

Temporary Quarters for West-Enders

Old Man River Pretty Strong

The Arrow marks the spot

THE GRAVE THAT WASN'T NEEDED!

Few people saw this grave, and perhaps this picture has never been published before, but this large public grave was actually dug in Cave Hill Cemetery in anticipation of an epidemic of disease or mass deaths from drownings and other causes. Fortunately none of these things developed tho they often do in public disasters of this kind. The death rate remained about normal.

assist. Elements of the 11th Infantry Division were encamped at Bowman Field, and for all practical purposes Louisville was under martial law.

The rain now stopped and the water began to recede by inches. Louisville breathed again. Some electricity was piped in from Dix River Dam. A Mayor's committee began inspecting buildings for flood damage. On Friday, January 28, the water had receded enough to be measured at 56.1 feet, a drop of 1 foot. The following Sunday, water was rationed three times daily instead of two, and some businesses were permitted to resume. Louisvillians realized that the flood was spent and that a tremendous rehabilitation job lay ahead.

At 10 P.M. Monday, January 29th, the river had dropped to 51.5 feet, and the streets of Louisville began to reappear littered with mud, muck, and debris of every conceivable kind.

The first week of February was mainly one of Clean up and Wash up for Louisville, and the task was accomplished by the wholehearted cooperation of everybody.

The excitement which always accompanies a great disaster carried people through the terrifying days of the flood, but the task of rehabilitation was the real test of the strength and character of the people. The magnitude of the loss sustained by so many thousands can never be truly understood. Homes that took years to develop, ruined overnight; the accumulations of a life-time, the complete furnishings of hundreds of beautiful homes, libraries, heirlooms, antiques, works of art, pianos, pets—all wiped out by "Old Man River"—it was hard to take, but the people in the low sections of Louisville took it, and the story of their bravery and fortitude is one of the most inspiring chapters in the history of Louisville.

The fact that mayor Neville Miller only 3 months after the Flood, dressed in Royal Court attire, was crowning a King and Queen of Derby Festival Week proves pretty convincingly that Louisville made rapid recovery from the aftermath of the Flood.

THE FLOOD WALL NOW PROTECTS LOUISVILLE FROM DISASTROUS FLOODS—SEE NEXT PAGE

FLOOD PROTECTION PROJECT
LOUISVILLE, KY.

LEGEND

■ PUMPING PLANT
━┿━ EARTH LEVEE
━━ CONCRETE WALL
LIMITS OF 1937 H.W.
LIMITS OF 1945 H.W.
PONDING AREA
CITY LIMITS

72 - SLUICE GATES
10 - SERVICE GATES
12 - RAILROAD CLOSURES
44 - STREET & ROAD CLOSURES
19 - RAMPS TO BE SAND BAGGED

SCALE IN FEET
1,000   0   1,000   2,000   3,000   5,000

CORPS OF ENGINEERS   U.S. ARMY
LOUISVILLE DISTRICT   JUNE 1950

Foil, Porcelain Metals, Wood-Mosaic, and scores of others.

Wartime wages and inflation indicated in rise of Louisville bank deposits from $160,000,000 in 1938 to $368,000,000 on January 1, 1943.

1944 June 6 . . . Tremendous Allied force under Eisenhower invaded Europe thru Normandy beachheads.

President Franklin D. Roosevelt elected for fourth term.

General MacArthur returned victoriously to Philippines; he had said: "I will return."

Gen. Patton led Third Army across France into Paris.

Wendell L. Willkie, Republican candidate for President, died.

1945 February . . . Committee for Kentucky incorporated as educational organization.

April 12 . . . President Roosevelt dies of a cerebral hemorrhage. Vice President Harry S. Truman takes the oath of office as President.

April 28 . . . Mussolini shot and killed.

April 30 . . . Hitler committed suicide.

"Epidemic of remodeling" of Louisville Stores.

May 7 . . . "V.-E." Day; unconditional surrender of Germany; fighting in Europe stops.

August 16 . . . Atom bomb dropped on Hiroshima.

September 2 . . . "V.-J." Day, Japan surrenders and World War II is over.

Armistice Day celebrated wildly in Louisville and all over the free world.

December 23 . . . General Patton died as result of automobile accident in Europe.

1946 Kentucky State Chamber of Commerce established.

December . . . Wilson W. Wyatt, former Mayor of Louisville is appointed National Housing Administrator by President Truman to help solve critical housing shortage.

At the November election Leland Taylor elected Democratic Mayor of Louisville.

One-way streets, and "no parking" established on many downtown streets.

America's biggest (steel) strike; longest major auto strike (General Motors); worst maritime strikes, greatest disruption of coal mining.

Louisville Sewer Board undertakes long-range reconstruction program.

Louisville Railway Company strike occurred in March; lasted for week; some violence.

December . . . Neil Dalton resigned as National Deputy Housing Expediter.

December 30 . . . R. C. Ballard Thruston died, 88 years old; Louisville historian, active in Filson Club.

Wilber C. Fisher elected a commissioner of the Sinking Fund.

In Kentucky $18,185,800 spent on 192 road projects.

Many restrictions on building removed.

Subdivisions laid out and lots offered for sale— (first activity since before War.)

1947 April 7 . . . Henry Ford dies at age of 84.

October 10 . . . Louisville Better Business Bureau incorporated; Leo. A. Meagher, managing director.

Work begun on Louisville's flood wall—a major project to be 18½ miles long.

Commercial airlines transferred operations from Bowman Field to new Standiford Field.

Two old Louisville traditions died—packet-freight service on the Ohio and Al Kolb's beer & oyster bar at 323 W. Liberty, oldest in city.

Prices and womens skirts went up.

"Flying saucers" first reported.

1948 January 30 . . . Mahatma Gandhi murdered at New Delhi at age of 79.

New State Fairgrounds chartered—"Kentucky Exposition Center".

February . . . University of Louisville celebrated 150th birthday.

February 16 . . . Mayor Leland Taylor died.

August 16 . . . Babe Ruth died at age of 53.

Contract let for first leg of Inner Belt Highway Courier-Journal and Times and WHAS— moved into new home at 525 West Broadway.

Thanksgiving Day . . . First TV program on WAVE-TV, the Male-Manual football game, is sponsored by Liberty National Bank.

First man interviewed on TV in Louisville is Merle E. Robertson.

Crowd of 35,000 jammed downtown streets and Armory to see and hear President Truman.

1949 October 5 . . . Official flag adopted by city of Louisville; a circle of stars and three large fleurs-de-lis.

October . . . Matt J. Winn, "Mr. Kentucky Derby" died at 84; had seen all 75 Derbies.

Public enemy #1 Earl Bircham was captured in Louisville after killing one policeman and wounding another; sentenced to death.

Mike Ryba of Scranton succeeded Fred Walters as Manager of Louisville Colonels.

Ponder won "Diamond Jubilee" Derby.

Dr. Murray Kinsman named dean of University of Louisville Medical School.

Charles P. Farnsley inaugurated Mayor of Louisville.

Vice-President Alben Barkley marries Mrs. Carleton Hadley.

Merle E. Robertson elected a commissioner of the Sinking Fund.

Continued on page 195

LOUISVILLE, THEN & NOW

A PORTFOLIO OF CONTRASTING PHOTOGRAPHS WHICH TELLS
THE STORY OF CHANGING DOWNTOWN LOUISVILLE
BETTER PERHAPS THAN MANY WORDS

Solger's at Fourth & Broadway was Louisville's Finest Confectionery—east of here were some of Louisville's finest homes. Look at this block today—thanks to the vision of J. Graham Brown.

Trees and the spires of the Southern Baptist Theological Seminary gave a certain charm to Fifth & Broadway 40 years ago. But streamlined progress is taking over now.

(Below) Whot hoppened? Nobody at Fourth & Broadway but a traffic cop? How things have changed! Then "Hawaiian Gardens" Dance Hall; soon city's tallest building will be on this site.

"ON THE

THROUGH

Elks home and the Pendennis Club were on Walnut between 3rd & 4th—Starks Building not yet. (Below) Walnut St. before Starks Building Annex was started. Historic Macauley's was still there.

Market Street west of Second, in "horse and buggy days." Levy Bros. still dominates the scene. Two doors east of Levy Bros. is the old German Insurance Bank building (see early view, page 197).

(Below) Broadway then was street of imposing homes & beautiful churches. At Third, looking east.

Rare composite photograph of the Liederkranz Singing Society of 1865, the leading musical organization of its day. Young man holding banner is Joe Fischer, later president of German Insurance Bank.

Robert Whitney, conductor of The Louisville Orchestra, is leading musical figure of today; was instrumental in getting $400,000 Rockefeller Foundation grant for Louisville Philharmonic Society.

Jenny Lind, "the Swedish Nightingale," created a greater sensation than all the crooners of today combined—when she gave a concert here in 1850. Tickets sold as high as $175. No wonder—P. T. Barnum managed her!

1950 January 1 . . . Following long tradition of New Year's Day meetings established by Board of Trade, the newly organized Chamber of Commerce meets at the Brown Hotel; the overflow audience is addressed by its new president Thomas A. Ballantine.

Dr. Elmer Henderson became head of the World Medical Association; chief spokesman against socialized medicine.

John Sherman Cooper named special aide to Secretary of State Dean Acheson.

October 1 . . . Thomas Graham re-elected president of the Sinking Fund; Merle E. Robertson elected vice-president; Lee P. Miller elected a commissioner.

October 24 . . . Mayor Charles Farnsley appoints Merle E. Robertson and George W. Norton, Jr., as co-chairmen of a Citizens Committee to help win support for four bond issues totaling $13,500,000: $5,000,000 for street and traffic improvement; $4,000,000 for expressway rights of way; $2,850,000 for grade crossing elimination; $1,500,000 for recreation facilities.

November 4 . . . Thomas A. Ballantine received the Award for Distinguished Leadership offered jointly by the Advertising Club of Louisville and the Louisville Better Business Bureau.

November 7 . . . (Election Day) Final returns showed the four City of Louisville bond issues carried almost 3 to 1.

1951 January 1 . . . Merle E. Robertson installed as President of the Chamber of Commerce.

Wilson Wyatt chosen chairman of Board of Trustees of University of Louisville, succeeding Eli Brown III.

Atomic energy plant begins construction at Paducah, McCracken County.

New industries and expansions by old ones started or planned since 1950 create greatest boom in Louisville's history.

1952 January 1 . . . Hanford Smith elected President Chamber of Commerce.

Louisville voters approved bond issues for General Hospital, University of Louisville, and new Police Department Headquarters.

Wilson Wyatt manages Adlai Stevenson's campaign for Presidency.

Roy Owsley resigns as city consultant to take muncipal job in Portland, Me.

Owsley Brown dies; well known distillery executive.

Male High School, after long bitter controversy, renamed Louisville Male and Girls' High School.

James B. Hill, former President of L & N Railroad dies.

July . . . Dr. Elmer Henderson dies.

Rubbertown factories finance own survey of West-End dust problem.

August 1 . . . John B. Taylor nominated for Mayor on Republican ticket.

August 4 . . . The Jefferson County Medical Society hired its first executive secretary, Jean Clos.

August 4 . . . Gustave Breaux, civic and church leader dies.

August 7 . . . Two Kentucky soldiers, six from Indiana returned by North Korean Reds.

August 8 . . . Rope catches man falling off WAVE-TV tower. Buster Bohannan—rope tangled around leg.

August 11 . . . Wage increases of $100 a year given to 2,580 City School teachers and members of administrative and supervisory staffs.

August 12 . . . Polio researcher, Dr. Alex J. Steigman announced discovery of a new type of polio virus—4th type, hitherto unknown.

August 16 . . . Edwin Ideler, concertmaster of the Louisville Orchestra and U. of L. Professor dies.

August 21 . . . Rush hour stopping banned on the main streets to and from downtown.

August 28 . . . Heigold House, which stood for 90 years at 264 Marion, until dump encroached, moved to Thruston Park as a memorial of the times and as an architectural curiosity.

September 2 . . . Wilber C. Fisher appointed to direct city G.O.P. campaign.

September 8 . . . Chief Justice Fred Vinson, distinguished jurist from Louisa, Ky., died in Washington.

International Harvester plant paralyzed by strike lasting 88 days.

Polio scare cuts State Fair attendance to 304,537.

October 17 . . . Liberty National Bank opens large Broadway Midtown Office, on Broadway between Fifth and Armory Place. Consumer Credit Department moves to this office.

Samuel Cardinal Stritch of Chicago breaks ground for Bellarmine College administration building.

Fire at old Douglas Park race course destroys 68 thorobreds worth $250,000.

Radio Station WKLO gets TV permit.

Ground broken for new Jewish hospital.

Eisenhower named Thurston B. Morton Assistant Secretary of State.

J. Graham Brown announces he will go ahead with plans for 19-story addition to Martin Brown Building.

J. C. Penney's Fourth Street Store opened in May.

Louisville gets $12,000,000 in Defense contracts.

P. G. A. tournament held at Big Springs; George Happell, chairman.

200th birthday of George Rogers Clark celebrated.

1953 January 20 . . . Eisenhower became first Republican President since 1933.

Elizabeth II crowned Queen of England.

March 5 . . . Stalin died.

March 17 . . . Atomic tests in Nevada.

April . . . The Louisville Philharmonic Society announces a $400,000 grant from the Rockefeller Foundation of New York—for 4-year mammoth musical project.

May 27 . . . Louisville's "Founding Festival", celebrates 175th birthday of the city; re-enacts landing of George Rogers Clark.

June 17 . . . New Port-of-Louisville Terminal incorporated and dedicated.

Work begins to eliminate bottle-neck underpass at Brook and Eastern Parkway.

University of Louisville buys Parkway Field.

Louisville has largest industrial private wire telegraph network in South at Reynolds Metals Co.

Stratton & Terstegge occupies new $1,000,000 warehouse.

July 31 . . . Senator Robt. A. Taft, strong contender for Republican nomination for president, died.

September 12 . . . "Wing Commander" won world's 5 gaited championship at Kentucky State Fair—for the sixth year in succession.

September 28 . . . Worst airplane disaster in Louisville history occurs when chartered plane with 38 soldiers aboard crashed in trying to land at Standiford Field; 22 soldiers killed.

September set new record for dryness.

October 5 . . . Water main burst on Lexington Road; estimated 15,000,000 gallons of water cascaded into Beargrass Creek, tearing up street and damaging homes in vicinity.

October 10 . . . City to paint shopping centers in four areas blue, yellow, green, and orange, part of a new psychological city-planning project.

October 11 . . . Ten thousand take part in a "living rosary" ceremony at Parkway Field, honoring the Virgin Mary.

October 15 . . . City of St. Matthews annexes business area.

October 20 . . . Million-dollar fire destroys a plant of General Box Company's Embry Division.

October 27 . . . First rain in 36 days; previous "dry" record 33 days in 1924.

November 2 . . . Bruce Dudley named executive director of the Independent College Foundation.

November 4 . . . Andrew Broaddus, Democratic candidate, elected Mayor of Louisville by 11,525 majority. George S. Wetherby elected County Judge by plurality of 10,955 votes.

November 6 . . . Banker Frank Dugan, vice president of First National Bank dies.

November 10 . . . Campbell-Summerhayes lumber warehouse destroyed by fire; loss estimated $75,000 to $100,000.

November 11 . . . St. Mary Magdalene Church damaged by fire.

November 19 . . . $50,000 fire at Louisville Tin & Stove Co.; "fire bugs" suspected.

November 22 . . . Rejoicing throughout Kentucky when U. of K. football team defeats Tennessee—first time in 18 years.

November 24 . . . Wm. C. Gatchel, of the well known photographic firm, killed when his private plane crashed in hills north of New Albany.

November 29 . . . 427 dogs vaccinated against rabies at Jeffersontown. Recent deaths of children from dog bites causes public out-cry that all dogs be vaccinated.

December 23 . . . Ex-Mayor Farnsley appointed counsel for U. of L.

December 29 . . . U. of L. purchases Parkway Field for $250,000 from Boston Red Sox.

END OF CHRONOLOGY

Editor's Note: We are sorry that space did not permit the inclusion of an Appendix, in which we had planned to reproduce some historical documents including the Act Establishing the Town of Louisville.

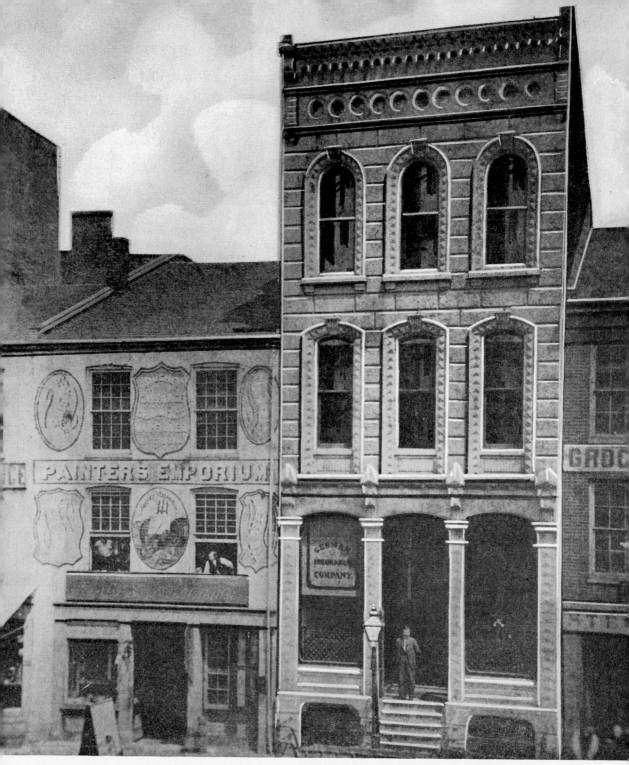

The earliest known picture of the German Insurance Bank and Company, reproduced and enlarged from an old stereopticon slide made in the 70's. This was the *third* office of the institution, the first being at Fourth and Market, the second on Third between Main and Market. The above building still stands at 231 West Market. The man on steps is Cashier "Uncle Joe" Fischer. The man at window next door is Carl Brenner, famous landscape painter.

THE STORY OF LOUISVILLE'S
OLDEST FINANCIAL INSTITUTION

(No picture is known of Jacob Laval, first president)

JOHN H. ROPKE
second president of the Company

JOHN H. ROPKE, the second president of The German Insurance Company, came of a substantial German family. He was born February 10, 1815, in Menslage-Osnabruck, a small village in Germany, and came to America, like so many other Germans of that period, because he saw greater opportunities here for his growing family. When he came to Louisville he had three boys, but in the course of years his family grew to ten.

It is said that, being of a provident and conservative nature, Ropke made sure before coming to America that his family would have provisions for a full year of living without worry. This "nest egg" gave him an opportunity to study business conditions and plan a career without the necessity of taking the first job or offer that presented itself. Apparently he thought well of the new German Insurance Company, for he bought a substantial interest in it, as is attested by the fact that on January 7, 1862, he was elected president. Apparently he wished to keep this position only until the directors could find a man to devote most of his time to the development of the institution, and he was president for only a short time. He died in 1872.

THE HISTORY OF THE INSTITUTION

LIKE the Chemical Bank of New York, which was organized to operate a chemical business; and the Bank of the Manhattan Company, which was established to finance a water system; Liberty National Bank and Trust Company had its origin in an insurance organization, the German Insurance Company.

By an Act of the General Assembly of Kentucky, approved March 9, 1854, The German Insurance Company was incorporated. While the chief business of the corporation so created and organized was that of insurance, its original charter of 1854 vested powers and authority "at any time to invest and reinvest any part of their capital stock, moneys, funds, or other property in any stock or funded debt created, or hereafter created in any State in the United States, or in the stocks of any bank, and the same to sell and transfer at pleasure, or they may *loan* the same or any part thereof to individual or corporate bodies, on real or personal security, on such terms and conditions as

may be required by the said directors not in violation of law."

By amendment to the original charter, Act of Kentucky General Assembly, approved March 2, 1860, the German Insurance Company was given power and authority to employ its moneys "in the purchase or discount of foreign or domestic bills or exchange and promissory notes", etc.

The incorporators were Robert Ernst, Landin Eisenman, Philipp Tomppert, G. Phillip Doern, Lewis Rehm, Gustavius Hein, Jacob Laval, John Durkee, Conrad Schroeder, Elias Hall, John J. Felker, Samuel W. Stone, Herman Justi, A. C. Morse, Frederick Schmidt, and Orville Turman.

Most of these men were substantial merchants of the city, the majority being of German origin or descent: perhaps some of them had come over recently from Germany, for there was a great immigration of Germans to this country

PHILIPP TOMPPERT

The first agent appointed by the German Insurance Company (at a salary of $25.00 per month) later (1865) became Mayor of the City of Louisville!

MAYOR OF LOUISVILLE—1865-1867-1868

in the 1850's, because of conditions in the old country. A good many had settled in Louisville and Cincinnati, coming up the river from New Orleans, the port of entry. That there was a large settlement of Germans here at one time is proved by the fact that there were at least three Louisville newspapers successfully published in the German language. German at that time and at least up into the 80's was taught in the public grade schools of Louisville. In spite of the above facts the first president of the German Insurance Company was apparently French—Jacob Laval (possibly of the French Colony that settled in Shippingport and Portland); and the third, Franz Reidhar, was Swiss. We regret that there is little information, and no portrait available of Mr. Laval who has the distinction of being the first of the nine men who have guided the destiny of Louisville's oldest financial institution since its inception. An early directory indicates Laval was a partner in the firm of Schrodt and Laval—"a distiller of alcohol and pure spirits and dealer in foreign and domestic liquors." His place of business was "Second, below Galt

House", and his residence "N. side Broadway between First and Brook."

The first meeting of stockholders of the German Insurance Company was held at Union Hall; the commissioners were George P. Doern, Conrad Schroeder, G. C. Stein, and Jacob Laval; Carl Buetgenbach was secretary. The first directors of the company were Laval, L. Eisenman, a grocer; E. Sauermann, a hat and cap merchant; Jacob Schmitt, a hardware dealer; Franz Reidhar, a clothing merchant.

At the subsequent meeting of the board of directors Mr. Laval was elected president (no salary mentioned) and Carl Buetgenbach was elected secretary at a salary of $1200 per annum. The office of the president may have been purely honorary—at least it was not a full-time job during this period of organization.

For a number of years following the granting of the charter, the economy of the country was unsettled, there were many bank and commercial failures, and certainly conditions were not propitious for the establishment of new businesses. The fact that the German Insurance Company was able to sell its stock and get into operation under these adverse circumstances, proves the character of its founders and the esteem in which they were held in the community.

The first agent employed by the company, at a salary of $25.00 per month, was Philipp Tomppert, a young man who later (1865) became Mayor of the City of Louisville—and the records show that he was also Mayor in 1867 and 1868 (see portrait). During the first few years the Company had only five directors.

The first dividend of 10% was declared by the board of directors on December 31, 1859. The minutes of this meeting state "that the Secretary produced the books, statements, sketches of accounts, bills discounted and belonging to the Company, cash on hand by the Bank book, etc. All were examined by the board and found correct, and they thereupon declared a dividend of 10% on the Capital Stock on Five Dollars per share, to be credited upon the stock notes of the respective stockholders; said fact to be published through the *Anzeiger*." The directors also stipulated that a statement of the business done during the year ending December 31, 1859 be published.

At the annual meeting of the stockholders, held January 2, 1860, the number of directors was increased from five to seven. New members elected were George Nurnberger, Louis Krieger and John H. Ropke.

The fact that the Company was performing banking functions is indicated in many places in the minutes of the board. For instance on January 3, 1860, it was "further resolved to draw one-half of the loan to John Smidt & Co., of Five Thousand Dollars at 30 days notice, for the use of the Company to discount notes", etc. The Loan Committees for the year were also appointed at this meeting, the committee for each month consisting of two directors and the president, alternating through the list of directors.

The first mention of a division of responsibility of the banking and insurance divisions of the company was in the minutes of the July 15th meeting, 1860, at which time "Mr. Julius Dorn was engaged as *Teller* for the Banking Department of the Company, with a salary of $500.00 per annum."

At a meeting of the directors on September 4, 1861, Mr. Ropke and Mr. Reidhar were appointed as a committee to purchase a burglar-proof safe. At this meeting the secretary was authorized to engage Mr. Edward Ehrman, as assistant clerk.

On January 7, 1862 John H. Ropke succeeded Jacob Laval as president of the Company—at a salary of $1200 per annum! This sounds like peanuts now—but remember, a sumptuous Christmas feast at the Galt House in those days cost only 50 cents. (See chronology: December 25, 1854). The secretary's salary was $1,000; the clerk's $300.

Mr. Franz Reidhar was elected president of the company on July 9th, 1862—at the same salary Ropke received—$100 a month. Edward Ehrman was promoted to Teller and his annual salary increased to $450.

The advertising budget of the Company is discussed in the minutes of January 1st, 1863. It was resolved that the bills of the Anzeiger for $98.00 and the Volksblatt (another German language newspaper) for $20.50 be paid: and it was decided to put a "business card" in the Volksblatt and the Anzeiger for the coming year, the former to cost $30.00, the latter $10.00. Unless this was an error on the part of the secretary, this was an even bigger bargain than the 50¢ Christmas dinner!

The first notice in the minutes of the presence in the organization of a young fellow named Joe Fischer—later to become one of the *great* presidents of the bank—was on February 3, 1863, when Mr. Reidhar announced to his board that Ed Ehrmann and Joseph Fischer had asked for an increase in salary—"whereupon it was resolved that E. Ehrman is to receive $500 per annum plus $150 *if he guarantees the Company against counterfeit or worthless money:* and that Joseph Fischer is to receive $500 per annum." Ehrman accepted the proposition—and, needless to say, Joe Fischer did too. At the annual meeting of directors held January 1st, 1864, a dividend of 20% on the capital stock was declared—which shows that the company was now getting into its stride. Maybe the prosperity of the Company is also reflected in this item—the President's salary was also raised at this meeting—to $1800 per annum. On July 11, 1864, it is recorded that J. H. Ropke has resigned as a director prior to the start of a trip to Europe, which indicates the time element as well as the potential danger involved in such a trip at that time. A man would wind up his affairs, not knowing if he would ever get back; today he steps in a plane and is back before anyone has missed him.

Continued on page 202

FRANZ REIDHAR President, 1863-1889

MR.REIDHAR was the first active, full-time president of both bank and company for 27 in which today's Liberty National Bank and Trust Company had its origin. Actually the first president was Jacob Laval; the second, John H. Ropke; but they served short terms during the period of organization. The Company was chartered March 9, 1854, and had banking privileges and functions from the beginning. Separate corporations were established in 1872; but Mr. Reidhar continued as president of the German Insurance Company, years until his death at the age of 82.

Franz Reidhar was born in the Canton Zug, Switzerland, November 25, 1807. His parents died when he was a small child, and his boyhood was one of indigence and toil. He learned the trade of cabinet-maker and joiner, and was a journeyman for a year when he enlisted in the French army. After serving in some of the wars of the time, he returned to his trade, worked at it for several years, and came to this country in 1834. He landed in New Orleans and came up the Mississippi and Ohio Rivers on a boat in which cholera raged among the emigrant passengers. Landing at Portland, the young man first found work in helping to right a wrecked steamboat, for which he received seventy-five cents a day. He was then employed in making repairs on the interior woodwork of the boat.

After working at his trade in fitting up a store, he was employed as a clerk in the store. Later he established a bakery and confectionery in

Continued on page 205

This is the first advertisement of the Company we have been able to locate. It appeared in the 1859 Louisville Directory and Business Advertiser. It clearly gives the location of the Company at that time as Fourth and Market. Unfortunately no cut or photograph of the building survives.

History of Bank continued

Conditions must have been getting better all the time at this period, (or Joe Fischer kept needling the directors) because on January 3rd. 1865 the board decided that "Mr. Joseph Fischer, the teller, shall have a salary of $1800 for the next 12 months." Joe was now making as much as his boss, the President! On this date the name of Adolph Reutlinger, deputy clerk, is first mentioned. He also got an increase in salary—to $900. per annum. Reutlinger was the grandfather of the late Adolph Reutlinger, former president of the Liberty Fire Insurance Company, and the great-grandfather of Kenneth Reutlinger, present head of the Liberty Insurance Agency, which also had its origin in the German Insurance Company.

At this time the bank—for it seemed to be more bank than insurance company—had two discount days in the week, Tuesday and Friday. The President, it is pointed out in the minutes, "has no power or right to discount or buy a note, without the consent of the Board, and such notes are only to be taken on the above-named discount days."

But here's a surprising item: "The Teller has a right to let parties overdraw without the consent of the President (!)." But read on for the explanation—"Resolved, that the Teller must give *unlimited security* for the faithful performance of his duties . . . The Teller is to be responsible for losses in his department". So—the Company couldn't lose—but who supplied the unlimited security? It was before the day of

the large Surety Company—so no doubt some substantial friends or relatives stood as security for the Teller (always spelled with a capital T in the minutes.) On the human side it is interesting to note that the board (March 7, 1865—right before the end of the Civil War) gave "$50 to a fund for the relief of soldiers's wives and the poor of the city". It is also noted when Phil. Tomppert resigned as an agent of the Company (April 3, 1865) no doubt to get his campaign started for Mayor of Louisville.

As stated elsewhere in this volume, Louisville seemed to profit by the Civil War. This is borne out in the case of the Company by the fact that a 40% stock dividend was declared on December 30, 1865—and there was no shortage of cash, as it was stipulated that "if any of the Stockholders prefers cash to the said stock, the Cashier shall pay said stockholder his dividends at par value."

On January 1st, 1866, Joseph J. Fischer was elected secretary of the Company, and Adolph Reutlinger became Teller at a salary of $1500; both had to give security to the amount of $5,000 "and be responsible for mistakes, losses and counterfeits." On April 3rd 1866, it was agreed that on discount days, Tuesdays and Fridays, "all directors shall convene at the office and attend to the discounting of notes at nine o'clock A.M."

Well, the institution continued to grow and prosper, paying good dividends, raising salaries gradually. The original office was at the north-
Continued on page 204

JOSEPH J. FISCHER, President 1889-1896

JOSEPH J. "UNCLE JOE" FISCHER was one of the most widely known and most popular bank officers in Louisville for the quarter century from 1872 until his death in 1896. His great business capacity, his tact, and his uniform courtesy have been commented upon by many older customers of the bank who still remember him.

Mr. Fischer was born in Bieberich, Nassau, Germany, December 5, 1842. In 1854 (the very year the bank started as the German Insurance Company) he came to America with his parents, who shortly afterward made Louisville their home. Joe Fischer was a pupil of the public grade schools here; and was then apprenticed as a printer in the office of the Anzeiger, the leading German language newspaper of Louis-

ville. He left the printing-office to learn book-keeping in a business college.

In 1862, he went into the office of the German Insurance Company as messenger, and later became bookkeeper. His promotion was rapid, for in less than five years he was made secretary of the company. When the bank and the insurance company were made separate institutions in 1872, he became the first cashier of the bank. He held this position for 17 years, and as President Reidhar grew older, took on more and more responsibility. In 1889 Franz Reidhar died at the venerable age of 82, and "Joe" Fischer was made president.

The bank enjoyed a period of splendid growth and development under his administration. It outgrew its original limitations of catering

Continued on page 213

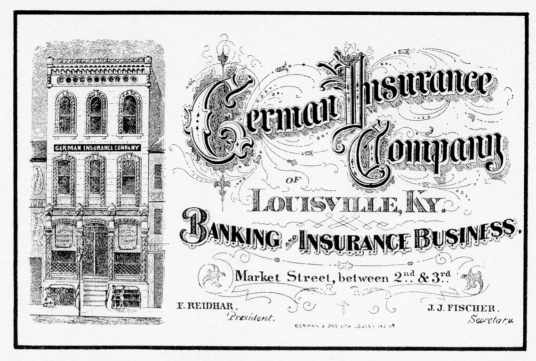

The original of this early advertisement, which appeared as a full page in the Louisville City Guide of 1869, is an elegant steel engraving. It indicates that even at this early date the Banking Division was more important than the Insurance Department.

History of Bank continued

east corner of Fourth and Market; but apparently in the early 60's the company moved to Third between Main and Market—the records do not say when. However by 1868 the business had obviously outgrown its quarters, and the banking operation had become increasingly important.

September 7, 1868 was an eventful day for the Company for on that day the Board of directors decided to employ the city's best architect to design a large new building "for our Banking and Insurance business". The president was authorized to purchase a house and lot on the north side of Market Street, between Second and Third, for $8,025.00.

Architect C. L. Mergeld, who also designed Louisville's present City Hall, came forth with plans for a very substantial 3-story brick building with stone front. In due course of time the contracts were awarded as follows: Stone work went to Schuler and McDonald for the sum of $2,650.00; the iron work was awarded to Y. W. Merz for the sum of $3,195.00; John Hehl took the carpenter and brick work for $8,725.00; the contract for the water and gas fixtures went to Ramsey and Jaeger for $1035.00. Architect Mergell was to receive

"5% of the entire cost ($23,630) of the Bank Building." The final total cost was $24,811.50. That all these gentlemen did a good job is obvious—for the building served its purpose well until it was again outgrown and a much larger structure built in 1887. Actually it has served several other businesses since and is still standing in good condition and in daily use. The building inspector says it ought to last another hundred years!

The first floor of the building has been brought down to street level (see cut of original building) but some of the features of the original building are still intact, such as the old double-door battle-ship plate type vault in the basement, the decorative cornice on the main floor, and the handsome walnut staircase between the second and third floors.

Despite the cost of a new building, in which the Banking and Insurance Departments were planned as separate operations, the Company on December 29, 1868, managed to declare another substantial dividend—this time $10 per share. On July 3rd, 1869, a semi-annual cash dividend of 14% was declared, and it was further resolved that the capital stock be increased to half a million dollars . . . "present

Continued on page 207

Franz Reidhar, continued

Jeffersonville, and was successful in this venture. The following year he embarked in the clothing business in Louisville, and afterward established branch houses in Portland and Henderson, Kentucky. He sold the Louisville store, and in 1856 and 1861 withdrew from the other stores and bought substantial holdings in the newly formed German Insurance Company. In 1863 he was elected President of the Company, and in 1872, President of the Bank. His wife was Jarme Claude Millet, a woman of French descent, and they had five children.

Besides being a successful, self-made business man and banker, Franz Reidhar, despite little formal education, was a gentleman of culture and refinement. He lived graciously in a fine house with a beautiful garden, located on Broadway where the Brown Coffee Shop and Theater now stand. According to a living descendant he bought this property for a few thousand dollars and later sold it for some $300,000—which indicated good business foresight (or good luck) and is also indicative of the growth of Louisville and the increase in real estate values in one man's life time.

Franz Reidhar died a wealthy man, admired and respected, and his life proved once again that the America of free enterprise was indeed a land of opportunity, even for an immigrant orphan boy.

ONLY HALF OF THE BUILDING WAS FINISHED ☞ **in 1887, but it included the clock tower, on corner, since become a famous landmark. Note black clock-dial**

Below: Adv. of about 1900; note banking room.

CAPITAL, - - - - - - - - $249,500.00
SURPLUS, - : - - - - - - $375,000.00

OFFICERS

W. H. EDINGER
President
HENRY C. WALBECK
Cashier
EDMUND RAPP
Ass't Cashier
CHAS. C. VOGT
Vice President

We solicit the accounts of Corporations, Firms, and Individuals.

DIRECTORS

CHARLES WINKLER
THEO. AHRENS
HENRY KRAFT
CHAS. C. VOGT
GEORGE KOPMEIER
A. N. STRUCK
W. H. EDINGER

WILLIAM H. EDINGER
President 1896-1910

WILLIAM HENRY EDINGER was born in Marietta, Ohio, October 18, 1843, but was brought to Louisville by his parents when he was an infant. As a boy he worked on the farm of his brother-in-law, Frederick Baringer— land which is now part of Cherokee Park. One of his duties was that of "market boy" at the old market house which was built in the middle of Market Street and ran from Third to Fourth Street. It is said his pay at the beginning was three dollars a month. On January 1, 1864, Edinger became a "route boy" for the Louisville Anzeiger, then an influential newspaper printed in the German language. His higher earnings enabled him to attend Boyd's Commercial School, where he finished the bookkeeping course in three months, and then entered the wholesale grocery firm of Billing and Dreisbach, a company which he later came to own, renamed W. H. Edinger & Bro.

While in the grocery business he became a director in the German Insurance Bank and later became active in its management. In 1896, following the death of the president, Mr. Joseph J. Fischer, Mr. Edinger was chosen as the head of the bank, and as was customary, also became president of the affiliated institution, the German Insurance Company. Mr. Edinger was identified with several other commercial enterprises in addition to his banking business. At the time of his death he was a director of eight companies, including the Louisville Lighting Company and Peter & Melcher Steam Stone Works. The latter firm constructed many important Louisville buildings including the Galt House and the present City Hall.

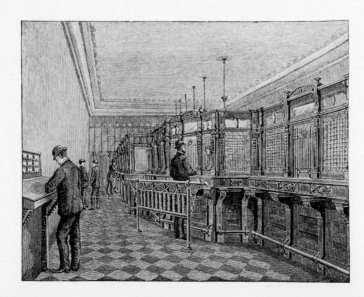

50 or 60 years ago this was the "last word" in banking room fixtures. Note footrail.

stockholders are alone entitled to an additional number of shares, equal to what they had previously held." This strengthening of the capital structure of the Bank and Company laid a firm foundation for greater growth.

New State laws in January of 1872 made it mandatory to separate the banking from the insurance operation, and the Company applied to the Legislature to procure a new banking charter. At a called meeting February 14, 1872, the attorneys for the company, Messrs. Barr, Goodloe, and Humphries, were instructed "to draw up a new Charter for our new Banking Institution, also amendments to the Charter of our Insurance Company, having in view to separate one from the other."

Then on May 25, 1872, at a called meeting of the directors it was resolved that Three Hundred Thousand Dollars be withdrawn from the assets of the Company for the formation of the German Insurance Bank.

The new planning of the building for the operation of the two now separate and distinct institutions was given due consideration by the directors. At this same most important meeting it was also resolved "that we deposit all our surplus funds in the German Insurance Bank, provided said Bank agrees to pay 5% on said deposits."

Franz Reidhar was elected president and Jos. J. Fischer cashier of the German Insurance Bank; and these men also continued respectively as President and Secretary of the German Insurance Company. The directors remained the same for both institutions.

The last pages of this first Minute-Book of Louisville's oldest financial institution, tells of the death of John H. Ropke, second president and for many years an active director. As a sign of respect the bank closed at 2 P.M. on the day of the funeral, August 30, 1872, and all of the employees attended the funeral. As was the custom in those days "the usual signs of mourning were displayed in the banking house for the next thirty days in honor of the deceased."

In about 15 years the bank and company had outgrown the home at 231 West Market which they thought would be adequate for generations. So they bought a large lot near Second and Market and began to plan a new, much bigger and more impressive building, with a tall clock tower. Completed in 1887, this 3-story stone structure, with several major enlargements and remodelings since (and with floor space more than tripled) is still serving as the Main Office of Liberty National Bank and Trust Company. While certainly not the most handsome bank building in town, it is one of the most unusual and distinctive. Its clock tower, which has faithfully rung out the hours of every day since 1887, and provided remarkably correct time through the years, is one of Louisville's famous landmarks. With the building of the George Rogers Clark bridge it became a still more important part of Louisville's skyline as seen from the Ohio. The scores of thousand of people approaching Louisville daily from the Indiana side, can check their watches by "the Big Clock". As "identification advertising" it would be hard to beat.

So, Franz Reidhar did a good job for the bank —and for himself—for he died a rich man. His home was located on the ground where part of the Brown Hotel now stands, and when his son sold it some 30 years ago, he is reputed to have received something over $300,000 for the property.

Reidhar had an able assistant in his cashier, Joseph J. Fischer, who is still remembered with affection by some of the older customers of the bank. "Uncle Joe", as he was known, is given credit for a great deal of the progress made by the bank during the last quarter of the 19th century. He was a man of dignity combined with personal charm. He always wore a tall silk hat but he was never "high hat". He was perhaps the first Liberty executive to realize the importance of "personal service" in building a bank.

In that day most loans were made on character rather than on financial statements. Each transaction was a personal one between him and the customer. It is said that when he shook hands on a loan and looked the man straight in the eye and said, "I expect you to pay this on such and such a date", the borrower seldom failed to perform. Uncle Joe liked to help business men who deserved help. He had a large wooden block on his tall desk—where he *stood,* not sat—and he personally cancelled every note when it was paid by hitting it with a heavy cancelling hammer—the sound of which would reverberate through-out the banking room.

It was a good sound to his ears and not a bad idea to let the other customers know that loans were being paid off regularly. It may have been a little embarrassing to the borrower who was standing there waiting for his cancelled note.

Continued on page 214

HENRY C. WALBECK was a native Louisvillian, born August 17, 1848, on Main Street near Second, just one block from the bank of which he eventually became president. He was the son of Peter Van Walbeck, a native of Amsterdam, Holland, who came to Louisville in 1840, and established the first furniture factory in Louisville. Henry C. Walbeck the family apparently dropped the Van) was educated in the Louisville public schools, Boyd's Commercial School, and Meyer's Commercial School.

He started work at 13 as a clerk in the U. S. Quartermaster's Department, then located in Louisville. He later worked for Brenner, Socksteder and Bates, "dealers in artists' paints and materials", a firm located on Market Street, next door to the German Insurance Company. The head of this firm was Carl Brenner, Louisville's most famous landscape painter.

Henry Walbeck entered the banking field as a bookkeeper in the German Security Bank, Preston & Market; later he became a teller in the German Bank at Fifth and Market; and rose to the position of cashier. On January 1, 1896, he was elected cashier of the German Insurance Bank. He held this position until the death of W. H. Edinger in August, 1910, when he succeeded him as president of the Bank and of the German Insurance Co.

HENRY C. WALBECK
President 1910-1919

Mr. Walbeck's daughter Eveline had the distinction of designing the "log cabin" as the emblem of the Republican Party. When Mr. Winkler became president of the bank in 1919, Mr. Walbeck became chairman of the board. He retired some years later.

In an address delivered at the unveiling of a "waving" electric American Flag in 1917, Col. Colson, of the First Kentucky Regiment, praised the bank for its record of leadership in selling World War I Liberty Bonds.

208

A. P. WINKLER
President 1919-1926

ANDREW P. WINKLER was born in 1860 in Louisville. He attended the old Floyd and Chestnut Streets public school, but quit after completing the sixth grade to work for his father; he continued studying at night, and to a great extent was self-educated. He was the seventh son of ten children. The seven boys were all in the wholesale grocery business with their father, Philip Winkler, who had established the company in 1842. Philip Winkler was one of the founders and on the original Board of Directors of the German Insurance Bank, and served on that board until his death.

A. P. Winkler was made a director while president of the wholesale grocery firm of P. Winkler's Sons, Floyd and Market; and several years later was elected vice president of the bank.

After two years as vice president he succeeded Henry Walbeck as president, Mr. Walbeck retiring because of ill health. It was during A. P.'s term as president that the Second and Market bank was modernized and the present safety vault installed. During modernization, the bank operated in temporary quarters in the present Vaughn Building at Third and Main.

Also during his presidency the name of the bank was changed to the *Liberty* Insurance Bank and the first branch bank was opened. In 1926, Mr. Winkler was elected Chairman of the Board and served in that capacity until his death in 1931.

Opening Day of the Remodelled Main Office. Thousands signed the register that day.

JOHN E. HUHN
President, 1926-1933

JOHN E. HUHN was born May 8, 1880. He attended grade school, and began to work his way through Male High, then located at 9th and Chestnut. To save the 5 cents car-fare, Johnnie walked to school every day from his home at 22nd and Walnut. He worked after school and Saturdays delivering groceries. He liked his job because he drove a horse and wagon—and made 50 cents!

Knowing of Johnnie's industry and ambition, an officer of the German Insurance Bank offered him a job in the bank. He was just 15, had two years more to complete high school, but he was flattered to get a chance to work in a bank! He consulted his teachers, Professors Snively and Maxwell. Maxwell said "No"; Snively said, "Yes, since you have no opportunity to go to college anyway." Johnnie took Snively's advice. He started as a runner in 1895.

By hard work and constant application, supplemented by home reading and study, he advanced steadily. He saw that for a bank to grow it had to serve individuals as well as business firms. While a teller he advocated the establishment of a savings department, and the accepting of individual savings accounts, even in small amounts. Huhn got his first big break when the bank opened a savings department in 1913 and appointed him manager. His aggressive promotion and development of savings impressed the directors. He rose rapidly to assistant cashier and vice-president. He continued to enlarge the service facilities of the bank; added a trust department; established neighborhood branches; and promoted business and civic projects through aggressive advertising and lobby exhibits. In December, 1926, John Huhn realized his life's ambition when he was elected president of the bank.

Liberty operated in this building at Third and Main while its bank was being remodeled.

Liberty inaugurated "School Savings," operated by teachers and students, to encourage thrift.

THE JUNIOR LIBERTY BANK was primarily educational. It was set up to give high school students an opportunity to learn about the practical operation of a bank. Lectures on all phases of banking theory and practice were given for the students by officers of the bank. A "Junior" bank was actually organized. Directors and officers were elected as in the senior bank; under the supervision of a senior officer. The Junior Bank was open only on Saturdays when the children were not at school. Several of these "junior bankers" became regular employees of the bank upon graduation. With advanced methods of teaching, this type of vocational training is now available in the schools.

BELOW is a group of flower lovers at one of the many flower shows which were held monthly in the bank lobby during the flower season. The moving spirit in these exhibitions was Miss Emilie Yunker, supervisor of horticulture in the public schools, shown on extreme right. Picture was taken about 1919.

LIBERTY NATIONAL was the first bank in Louisville to receive a deposit by airplane, and thus to inaugurate a speedier handling of deposits and collection items for correspondent banks. The photograph in lower right shows some of the bank staff on the roof of the main office, having just witnessed the receipt of the package from an out-of-town bank, dropped by plane. This type of delivery from a low-flying plane would be unthinkable today—but aviation was in its infancy and practically unrestricted in 1920.

The Children's "Junior Liberty Bank"

Flag Day Unveiling of Betsy Ross Portrait

December 1, 1933, Merle E. Robertson became president of the bank at age of 33, one of the youngest bank presidents in the nation. Director and Chairman of the Executive Committee F. Jos. Herrmann is standing beside him. Others, left to right, are: Ashby Millican, Innes W. Dobbins, Jr., Edward F. Kohnhorst, Rodgers Wyckoff, Elizabeth Gray, and Fred Strobel.

Main Office, showing Annex, which more than doubled working area of bank.

North side of Broadway between Fifth and Center in 1898. Note first type electric car and old Post Office tower.

Section of same block—1953. This is Liberty's new Broadway Midtown Office. There's still a tower in the picture—this time the television tower of WHAS-TV.

Joseph J. Fischer, continued

mainly to the Germans in Louisville, and gained the respect of all the people. It became a bank appealing not only to the smaller merchants, but because of its conservative management and sound policies, began to attract big business. It also welcomed the banking business of individuals and encouraged thrift through the issuance of interest-bearing certificates of deposit.

"Joe" Fischer was a man of magnetic personality with a host of friends. He possessed a lot of dignity, dressed conservatively, and always wore a high silk hat, but he knew his customers intimately and always evinced a friendly interest in their problems. In that day, when the number of customers of a bank was comparatively small, it was possible for the cashier or president of a bank personally to know most of his depositors and borrowers. In making loans it is said that Joe Fischer relied more on character than on a man's financial statement, and he obviously had an uncanny knowledge of human nature, for he made very few bad loans.

J. J. Fischer, as he signed his name, was interested in other things besides business and banking. His greatest hobby and recreation was music, and his business judgment and aggressiveness combined with his knowledge and love of music to make him a moving spirit in the musical activities of his day. His special interest was the Liederkranz Singing Society of which he was president for many years.

When "Uncle Joe" died of pneumonia at the age of only 54, there was widespread sorrow in the city, and it is said that he was honored with the longest funeral procession ever seen in Louisville up to that time! Perhaps that was the way that people of the not-always-gay nineties showed their final respect and affection.

Joe Fischer, active in musical circles, was president of the Louisville Liederkranze Singing Society, which had local societies in most of the big cities of the country. They sponsored a large part of the outstanding musical events of Louisville in the decades between 1850 and the beginning of World War I.—bringing operas, "Saengerfests", celebrated artists, and symphony orchestras to the city. Joe Fischer, the most colorful Louisville banker of his time, died December 23, 1896, loved and respected by all; which is doubly proved by the fact that he had the "longest funeral procession ever seen in Louisville."

Fischer was followed successively by W. H. Edinger, Henry C. Walbeck and A. P. Winkler, and the institution continued to prosper. During the administration of Mr. Walbeck, a savings department was instituted for the first time (1913). Before that time the only form of savings available at most commercial banks was the certificate of deposit. With the establishment of a savings department under the management of John E. Huhn, the bank started a new era of growth. Aggressive advertising began about this time, with small newspaper ads, gradually increasing in size, and with other media such as street car cards, direct mail, and outdoor advertising being added from time to time. To this day Liberty National has the largest total savings deposits of any financial institution in Kentucky.

During World War I the name of the bank was changed from German to *Liberty* Insurance

"The Spirit of 1918"

The time has passed when "America" will be known as a nation composed of all nationalities. We are "Americans" to the core, and "Being American" embodies more than ever before. Many lives have been sacrificed to uphold our principles and we must at all costs be victorious in this mighty struggle to make the world safe for these principles.

Banks, Insurance Companies and Merchants in every section of our Great Country, who many years back incorporated themselves under names such as Scandinavian, Hibernian, Italian and German, have seen fit to change these titles and henceforth be known by names which in no way intimate reverence of Foreign Countries.

So, in the "Spirit of 1918," these Institutions of Public Service, being "American" in every sense of the word, have also changed their names and in the future the.

German Insurance Bank
Louisville, Ky., will be known as the
Liberty Insurance Bank
LOUISVILLE, KY.

German Security Bank
Louisville, Ky.. will be known as the
Security Bank
LOUISVILLE, KY.

German Insurance Company
Louisville, Ky., will be known as the
Liberty Fire Insurance Co.
LOUISVILLE, KY.

German-American Bank and Trust Co.
New Albany, Ind.. will be known as the
American Bank and Trust Co.
NEW ALBANY, IND.

Joint announcement (1918) by four financial institutions of change of name (greatly reduced)

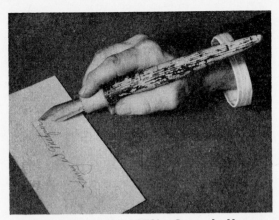

A bookkeeper of the 1870's, Oscar A. Metzner, had "writer's cramp" so Pres. Franz Reidhar gave him this over-sized pen, now owned by his grandson, Henry W. Metzner.

Bank. At that time a large advertisement headed "The Spirit of 1918" was published in the newspapers, signed jointly by four institutions. All announced that the word "German" was being dropped from their corporate name. (See reproduction on opposite page.)

Liberty Bank took a very active part in the Liberty Loan drives and was cited for outstanding service to the government in World War I; just as in World War II it was again a leader in the sale of War Bonds.

In 1919 the bank building was completely remodeled in its interior, becoming the most modern banking room of the twenties in Louisville. A magnificent safety vault was installed, which was one of the largest and finest in the country at that time. Many new services and departments were added during the next decade. John E. Huhn became president in 1926. A system of branch banks was inaugurated; a personal loan department was established; then a trust department and a real estate loan department.

With the establishment of the Trust Department the name of the bank was changed to Liberty Bank and Trust Company. The scope and activity of the bank continued to increase. Special appeals were made for the business of individuals; many types of lobby displays were instituted, including monthly flower shows during the flower season; commercial, educational and industrial exhibits of various kinds. A school savings division, and later a "Junior" Liberty Bank were inaugurated to encourage thrift among children, and a better understanding of banking principles and practices.

The Depression and the bank "holiday" brought to an abrupt ending many of these promotions—here, as in banks throughout the nation. The failure of Kentucky's largest bank, The Bank of Kentucky, and several other Louisville banks created the most serious financial and economic situation Louisville had ever known. Louisville suffered the first big bank failure in the country, but many followed in almost every city, until the "bank-holiday" and the re-establishment of confidence with the organization of the Federal Deposit Insurance Corporation, which now insures deposits up to $10,000 for every bank customer.

The new times called for a different type of leadership, and a young New York banker who had distinguished himself as a brilliant credit manager, was called to the presidency of Liberty Bank and Trust Company. Merle E. Robertson became president in December 1933, at the age of only 33. Although seemingly young for this eminent position, he had "proved his metal" as an outstanding credit executive of two great banks of the east—the Chemical Bank of New York and the National Shawmut Bank of Boston.

George C. Weldon was chairman of the board of directors that elected Mr. Robertson to the position of chief executive of the bank; F. Joseph Herrmann was chairman of the executive committee. Both men were of great assistance to the new president in the arduous tasks

Continued on page 220

The late George C. Weldon

The "National Poster girl of 1947" is here presenting a certificate of appreciation to Merle E. Robertson for his five years work as Treasurer and executive committee member of the Kentucky Chapter of the National Foundation for Infantile Paralysis. Little Nancy Drury, of Louisville, had her picture on the posters all over the nation during the 1947 campaign.

THE SPOTLIGHT, as stated above, is Liberty National's Employees' Magazine —a 5½″ x 8½″ profusely illustrated, slick-paper monthly—written, planned and edited by the employees themselves, with a little help and supervision from the officers. Vincent Welch is present editor, and the comments from the readers (which includes all the stockholders of the bank) indicates he is doing a good job. The bank has had a monthly house-organ for over 30 years, but Spotlight in the new format was the first to win an award of merit as one of the outstanding Commercial publications in the State.

Below: This is B-I-E Day (Business-Industry-Education) sponsored by the Chamber of Commerce and Louisville business houses. John W. Kigel, vice-president of Liberty National is conducting a party of visiting school teachers and others through the transit department of the bank, explaining the operation of some of the wonderful new machines that facilitate today's tremendous volume of banking transactions.

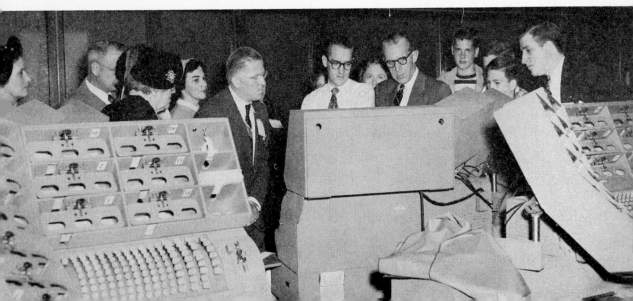

NEW TREND
in bank design shown in latest Liberty offices

COMMERCIAL and industrial design, to a more marked degree than residential design, is becoming more functional.

Banks generally have avoided the extremes in modernism and the best bank architecture of today is perhaps a simplified traditional, sometimes called "modern-classic", such as in Liberty's new Broadway Midtown office where traditional stone, marble, and paneling are used, but in a contemporary manner.

An exception to this style is the extremely functional 26th and Broadway Branch where an oversized vitreous brick was used for both inside and outside walls.

Larger parking areas and the so-called "Drive-In" windows are features of modern bank planning.

Broadway Midtown—spacious and warmly dignified

26th & Broadway Branch is "Functional Modern"

Shelby Branch "Drive-in" Window

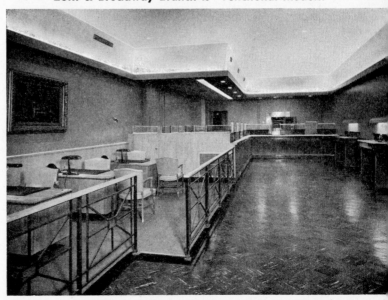

Fifth Street Office—Compact, Modern, Efficient

President Robertson congratulates the three officers that have served the bank longest. Left to right: R. M. Fible, Vice-President, 50 years; Edw. F. Kohnhorst, Vice-President, 61 years; Robert G. Bickel, Assistant Cashier, 51 years. These three men were eligible for retirement at the close of 1953, but, at the bank's request, will remain on the staff until the close of the 100th anniversary year.

In addition to retirement at 65, Liberty National offers its employees free health and life insurance on the group plan; very favorable working conditions; vacations with pay; bonuses based on salary, service, and effort; and many minor amenities that make life more pleasant—such as free turkeys at Thanksgiving and Christmas, an annual Christmas party, planned summer outings, sports activities, an employees magazine, etc.

There has always been an active participation in sports and friendly competition among employees. Liberty has had many outstanding basketball, soft-ball and bowling teams. During the summer there are several horseshoe tournaments at the president's summer cottage at Belknap Beach.

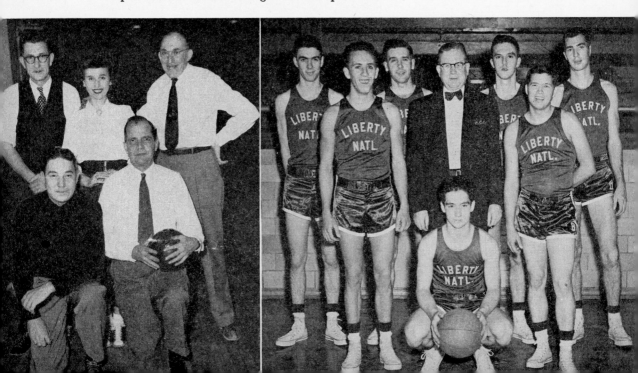

CHRISTMAS PARTIES
for employees and their children are a tradition at Liberty National

A CHRISTMAS party in the lobby for the small children of all employees—with ice cream and cake, Christmas tree, Santa Claus, gifts, and all the trimmings—is an annual event.

A big Christmas party for all employees at which there is generally a distribution of bonus checks, has been held every Christmas for nearly half a century. At right is pictured the modest party held in the basement of the Main Office in December 1919, shortly after the building was remodeled.

To the right is a flash taken at the 1953 Liberty Christmas party at the Pendennis Club, which was attended by 280 employees.

◀ Extreme left: Liberty National's Bowling team, 1953. Front row, Irvin Friess, Henry V. Sanders; back row, Wm. F. Kern, Jr., Vonretta Sweat, Theodore Knackwafel.

◀ Left: Liberty's 1953 Basketball team, Goebel Caton, manager (center, standing).

confronting him during this period of national depression and financial distress.

Under M.E.R.'s sound, conservative, and adroit management Liberty Bank passed safely through the shoals that were besieging all banks at that period. Revitalized, it entered an era of new growth and development which has been by far the greatest in its history. The prestige of Louisville's oldest financial institution was fully restored—and much *enhanced* when Liberty became a National bank in 1935. Now, 19 years later, Mr. Robertson has not only realized his goal of "A Hundred Million Dollar Bank for the 100th Anniversary" (he brought it up from a bank of 15 millions in deposits)—but he has earned the respect of the community, not only as a banker and business leader but as one deeply interested in the civic life of the community.

It is always difficult to understand how extremely busy men—the "top" executives of a city—find time to devote to educational, civic and charitable affairs, and the fact is that it can only be done at great personal sacrifice.

Mr. Robertson has contributed to local government by serving as a Commissioner of the Sinking Fund; he is now vice-president of that important municipal-finance body.

In 1950 he served as co-chairman with George W. Norton of the Citizens Committee supporting the City Bond Issues, which "sold" Louisville on a $13,350,000.00 civic program for major streets and traffic improvements, expressway rights, grade crossing elimination, and recreation facilities. (At the November election the voters approved the bond issues, *three to one*—although similar bond issues had been defeated on numerous occasions before.)

As a member of the Board of Overseers of the University of Louisville and as Treasurer of the Kentucky Independent College Foundation he participates in the field of education.

He was the first president of the Kentucky Heart Association and has been Treasurer of the Kentucky Chapter of the National Foundation for Infantile Paralysis since its inception.

He is Treasurer of the Louisville Safety Council, of the Kentucky Bookmobile Project and of the Kentucky Committee of the Newcomen Society of England.

In his own field of banking, he is a past-president of the Kentucky Bankers Association (1944-45-46), and has been a member of important National Commissions and Committees of the American Bankers Association. He was the second president of the Louisville Chamber of Commerce (1951). He serves on ten boards of directors.

Liberty National, "Louisville's Oldest Financial Institution", enters the second century of its usefulness strong in resources, rich in experience—but President Robertson makes it abundantly clear that it is not resting on its laurels. He has expressed the thought that the first century has been but a period of preparation for the second.

Among far-reaching plans for the future of Liberty National was the purchase several years ago by a bank subsidiary, of a large and valuable income-producing piece of property extending from Jefferson to Liberty, between Fourth and Fifth Streets. This may well be the future location of the Main Office of Liberty National Bank and Trust Company, the bank which has enjoyed a century of natural growth and development and has become a leading bank of the South and Mid-west.

THE FAMOUS CLOCK-TOWER AT NIGHT

CHECKS FOR CHRISTMAS CLUB MEMBERS, 1923

Liberty National annually plays host at a luncheon for all the Kentucky Bankers attending the K.B.A. Convention in Louisville. Above: Crystal Ballroom, Brown Hotel, October 19, 1953.

FAYETTE C. DORSEY

Vice President of Liberty National and for many years in charge of the Department of Banks, was President of the Kentucky Bankers Association 1928-29; active on Agriculture Committee.

S. M. Harris (left) of Mt. Washington, Treasurer of the Kentucky Bankers Association, and Merle E. Robertson (center), President, 1944-45-46, congratulate the incoming President Finley L. Cisco of Hazard.

Below: October, 1949—Vice-President of U. S. Alben W. Barkley, just before addressing the K.B.A. Convention in Louisville. Others—l. to r. Geo. S. Hart, Murray; Merle E. Robertson, toastmaster; and Lieut. Gov. Lawrence Wetherby, now Governor.

221

JUDGE ARTHUR PETER

ASHBY MILLICAN

CYRUS S. RADFORD

PRESENT BOARD OF DIRECTORS

LIBERTY NATIONAL BANK AND TRUST COMPANY

WILTON H. TERSTEGGE

ADOLPH N. GOSSMANN

MERLE E. ROBERTSON

W. C. FISHER

F. W. CURRAN

TINE W. DAVIS

J. A. DISHMAN

INNES W. DOBBINS, JR.

JUDGE JOHN MARSHALL

R. NORVELLE WATHEN

JAMES T. DUFFY
(Died January 14, 1955)

Deposits, Dec. 31, 1901 . . . . $4,393,042.33
Deposits, Mar. 9, 1954 . . . $105,947,493.29

The growth of this bank as well as the growth of Louisville is reflected in these two condensed financial statements—one showing the size and condition of the bank near the beginning of the 20th Century; the other on the day of its 100th anniversary.

German Insurance Bank
Condensed Statement as of December 31, 1901

ASSETS

Notes and Bills Discounted		$ 2,839,475.64
Banking-house and Other Real Estate		64,500.00
Bonds and Stocks		780,000.00
Cash Items:		
Due by Banks and Bankers	$ 249,721.43	
Eastern Exchange	680,326.45	
Cash on Hand	398,034.08	1,328,081.96
Total		$ 5,012,057.60

LIABILITIES

Capital Stock	$ 249,500.00
Surplus Fund	300,000.00
Profit and Loss	24,657.62
Fund to Pay Taxes	5,292.12
Dividends	12,852.50
Due to Banks and Bankers	26,713.03
Deposits	4,393,042.33
Total	$ 5,012,057.60

Liberty National Bank and Trust Company
Condensed Statement as of March 9, 1954—the 100th Anniversary

RESOURCES

Cash and Due from Banks	$ 29,464,310.46
U.S. Government Obligations	42,096,648.90
Governmental Institution Obligations	1,403,221.32
Municipal Obligations	2,304,632.24
Federal Reserve Bank Stock	126,000.00
Other Investment Securities	273,660.20
Loans and Discounts	36,667,241.49
Bank Buildings, Safety Vaults and Equipment	545,712.75
Interest Receivable	406,355.13
Other Assets and Letters of Credit	306,211.63
Total	$113,593,994.12

LIABILITIES

Demand Deposits	$70,597,414.53	
Time Deposits	22,294,779.69	
(Does not include Reciprocal Inter-Bank Deposits of $1,917,574.05)	$92,892,194.22	
U.S. Government and Other Public Funds	13,055,299.07	
Total Deposits		$105,947,493.29
Interest Collected, but not earned		708,129.75
Other Liabilities and Letters of Credit		755,055.06
Reserve for Income Taxes		480,747.02
Dividend Payable May 1st, 1954		42,000.00
Capital Stock	$ 2,100,000.00	
Surplus and Undivided Profits	2,560,569.00	
Reserves for Contingencies	1,000,000.00	
		$ 5,660,569.00
Total		$113,593,994.12

LOUISVILLE
TOMORROW

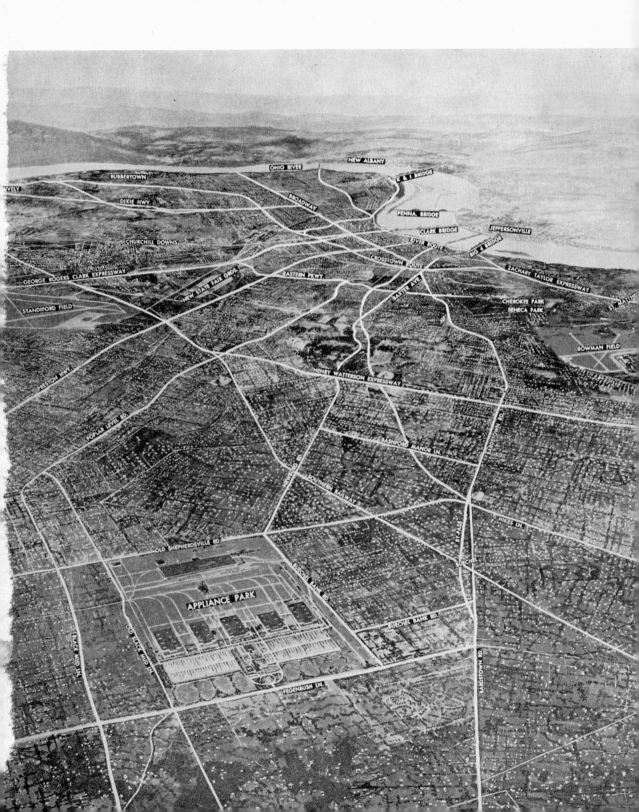

The proposed North-South Expressway is drawn in on this aerial view of downtown Louisville. On the left is a close-up of the newly conceived approach to the George Rogers Clark Bridge at Second and Main Streets. If budgets permit work should start soon.

THE MAP OF LOUISVILLE OF TOMORROW shown on the previous page is reprinted through the courtesy of The Courier Journal, and appeared originally in a special edition welcoming General Electric's Appliance Park to Louisville. Incorporated in this projection are the expressways that are planned or in process of construction, and other major improvements—with a visualization of Louisville 10 years from now.

New Section of "Inner Belt" near Dixie Highwa

BEGINNING OF A $90,000,000 POWER PROJECT

THIS is the Cane Run Power Plant, of Louisville Gas & Electric Company, the first unit in a 6-unit major project, which will be built over a period of 10 years at an estimated total cost of 90 million dollars. The first unit will be completed by late summer, 1954; the second unit will be ready in 1956. Together these two 100,000 kilowatt plants will generate 1 billion 400 million kilowatts per year.

An electric power company must be able to anticipate the needs of industry, business and individual consumers. It must always have a *surplus* of power—and since it takes years and many millions of dollars to build a power plant it requires the highest type of judgment coupled with intelligent planning.

The Louisville Gas and Electric Company, as a result of a continuing study anticipates that the electric power needs of metropolitan Louisville will "double" in the next ten years. It now has three generating plants in operation: the Waterside plant in downtown Louisville; the Hydro-Electric plant near the falls; and Paddy's Run, on the river west of the city. The latter is a 315,000 kilowatt plant built in 1942 at a cost of 40 million dollars. Both Cane Run and Paddy's Run are coal-burning plants and are situated well above the 1937 floodstage.

The Louisville Gas & Electric Company uses more than a million tons of coal a year, as well as a tremendous amount of "summer surplus" gas to create electric power.

1950 AND 1951

Thomas A. Ballantine, President of Yellow Cab, popular civic and business leader (the "James Guthrie" of present day Louisville and "Man of the Year" in 1950) was chosen to be the first president of the newly organized Louisville Chamber of Commerce. The second president was Merle E. Robertson. The genial gentleman between the two presidents is J. Marcus Greer head of the Retail Merchants' Division of the Chamber.

First Five

New Year's Day, 1951—Thos. A. Ballantine (right) first president of C. C. receives silver bowl from incoming president, Merle E. Robertson.

Louisville's growth shown at a glance: the first city directory (1832) and the latest (1953)

1952

Hanford Smith

1953

Wathen R. Knebelkamp

1954

Archie P. Cochran

Presidents, Chamber of Commerce

The State Fair Grounds of tomorrow—bet. Preston Highway & Crittenden Drive.   Tremendous plans are laid.

The "Inner Belt" Highway will circle Louisville; above, crossing Southern Parkway.

City, County, State Plan for the Future

Mayor Andrew Broaddus with two Louisville spokesmen, Lisle Baker, Jr., vice president and general manager of The Courier Journal and The Louisville Times (left) and K. P. Vinsel, executive vice-president of the Louisville Chamber of Commerce (4th from left) confer with State highway authorities in Frankfort—State highway commissioner W. P. Curlin (seated) and Mack Galbreath, federal road engineer for Kentucky—on rights of way and other matters in the road-building program of City and State.

City and Jefferson County officials are working on a comprehensive new urban planning study and survey—including a master-plan for zoning, major streets, parks, public transportation, waterfront development, etc.

Louisville's new Police Building (below) will be the finest in the United States.

STARKS BLDG.

ARMORY

M.E. TAYLOR BLDG.

K.Y. HOME LIFE BLDG.

COURT HOUSE

The arrow points to a large income-producing property running from Jefferson to Liberty, between Fourth and Fifth Streets. This will be the future site of the Main Office of Liberty National Bank and Trust Company. It now belongs to a subsidiary of the bank.

OFFICERS OF LIBERTY NATIONAL BANK AND TRUST COMPANY

at the Close of the First Century – March 9, 1954

MERLE E. ROBERTSON, *President and Chairman of the Board*

ASHBY MILLICAN, *First Vice President*

W. C. FISHER, *Vice President and Cashier*

Vice Presidents
I. W. DOBBINS, JR.
F. C. DORSEY
R. M. FIBLE
JOHN F. GRAHAM
LAWRENCE IRWIN
COLEMAN L. ISAACS
JOHN W. KIGEL
EDW. F. KOHNHORST
WM. J. RAEUCHLE

ANDREW B. ROSE
HENRY V. SANDERS
RALPH G. STROTHER
RODGERS L. WYCKOFF

Assistant Vice Presidents
DAN J. CRONEN
EDW. M. EISENBEIS
A. H. FRENKE
ASA W. FULLER

RUSSELL D. HAUSS
WALTER E. SCHOTT

Assistant Cashiers
JOHN M. ABBOTT
R. G. BICKEL
GOEBEL W. CATON
OSCAR H. DOLSON
JOHN E. ECKERT
M. S. FERREE

ALPHONSE J. GOSS
GILBERT E. HAUCK
C. L. HELCK
F. L. JOHNSON
EDWARD R. KAISER
J. R. KREBS
MARVIN C. LAUFER
EDWARD F. RILEY
VINCENT WELCH
LESLIE L. YOUNG

CHAS. M. GIPPERICH, *Trust Officer*

C. A. RUEFF AND H. M. HIGGINS *Assistant Trust Officers*

VIRGIL N. REILING, *Auditor*

ALFRED F. KLUSMAN, *Ass't Auditor*

INDEX OF ILLUSTRATIONS

INDEX OF IMPORTANT STORIES, PERSONS, AND EVENTS

ACKNOWLEDGEMENTS

We wish to thank all who have helped us in the preparation of this volume—those who have supplied old photographs and other illustrations; those who have given us permission to photograph or reproduce interesting historical material; and those who have aided us in research. We particularly want to thank the staffs of The Filson Club, The Kentucky Room and Reference Room of The Louisville Free Public Library and the Library of The Courier-Journal and The Louisville Times. We are indebted to the following individuals: Miss Ludie J. Kinkead, Mrs. Dorothy Thomas Cullen, Miss Evelyn R. Dale, Miss Mary Verhoeff, Mr. Richard H. Hill, Miss Ellen T. Harding, Mrs. Cornelia Boone, Mr. Martin L. Schmidt, Mr. Don D. John, Mr. F. C. Dorsey, Col. Lucien Beckner, Mr. A. H. Tarvin, Mr. and Mrs. Edward C. Shrader, Jr., Mr. Billy Davis and his staff, Caufield and Shook, my wife, and many others. We regret that much of the material gathered had to be condensed or selected; at least a hundred more excellent photographs and engravings might have been included had space permitted. After all, a complete history of Louisville would fill many volumes; this book gives only the historical *highlights.*

R. C. R.

AND NOW WE HAIL OUR

SECOND CENTURY

FOR WHICH WE HAVE PREPARED

THESE HUNDRED YEARS!